The Ethics of Information
Technology and Business

Foundations of Business Ethics

Series editors: W. Michael Hoffman and Robert E. Frederick

Written by an assembly of the most distinguished figures in business ethics, the Foundations of Business Ethics series aims to explain and assess the fundamental issues that motivate interest in each of the main subjects of contemporary research. In addition to a general introduction to business ethics, individual volumes cover key ethical issues in management, marketing, finance, accounting, and computing. The volumes, which are complementary yet complete in themselves, allow instructors maximum flexibility in the design and presentation of course materials without sacrificing either depth of coverage or the discipline-based focus of many business courses. The volumes can be used separately or in combination with anthologies and case studies, depending on the needs and interests of the instructors and students.

Series List:

The Ethics of Information Technology and Business

Richard T. De George

Blackwell
Publishing

© 2003 by Richard T. De George

350 Main Street, Malden, MA 02148-5018, USA
108 Cowley Road, Oxford OX4 1JF, UK
550 Swanston Street, Carlton South, Melbourne, Victoria 3053, Australia
Kurfürstendamm 57, 10707 Berlin, Germany

First published 2003 by Blackwell Publishing Ltd

Library of Congress Cataloging-in-Publication Data

De George, Richard T.
 The ethics of information technology and business / Richard T. De
George.
  p. cm. — (Foundations of business ethics ; 3)
Includes bibliographical references and index.
 ISBN 0-631-21424-0 (hardcover) — ISBN 0-631-21425-9 (pbk.)
 1. Business ethics. 2. Information technology—Moral and ethical
aspects. I. Title. II. Series.
 HF5387.D383 2003
 174′.4—dc21

                                              2002005756

A catalogue record for this book is available from the British Library.

Typeset in 10.5/12.5 Plantin
by SetSystems Ltd, Saffron Walden, Essex
Printed in United Kingdom
by MPG Books, Bodmin, Cornwall

For further information on
Blackwell Publishing, visit our website:
http://www.blackwellpublishing.com

Contents

Preface

By the mid-1990s business ethics was firmly established and widely accepted. Many businesses, especially the large corporations, had adopted some sort of code or value statement outlining proper behavior, the commitment of the company to ethical practices, and often a statement of morally praiseworthy aspirations or ideals. Many also had an ethics and a social responsibility component in their employee training programs. The importance of business ethics was stated by public figures from President Clinton to Secretary General of the United Nations, Kofi Annan. Business schools routinely had courses in business ethics, articles appeared in a variety of journals, both specialized and general. Academic research in the area was recognized as legitimate and conferences on business ethics issues had become commonplace.

By this time the major issues of the area encompassed by business ethics had been unearthed, discussed, and analyzed. Many of those were issues concerning the treatment of employees and of customers, truth in advertising, product safety, environmental protection, emerging global issues (such as the role of business in global warming), and international issues (such as bribery and child labor). Business, however, is a moving target. And at the same time that what are now considered standard issues in business ethics were acknowledged and to some extent resolved, business was evolving from the Industrial Age into the Information Age, and the United States was moving from an economy based on production to a service and information-based economy.

Ethical issues in business have a way of emerging only slowly and of being recognized even more slowly. Of course, the basic ethical norms prohibiting murder, stealing, lying, and so on, always apply. But issues about the ethics of new practices typically come into focus only after the practice has been in place for some time and the harm that the practice causes slowly becomes clear. This has been happening as business has changed in the recent period.

Computers have come to play a larger and larger role in business. The Internet is widely used in business as well as in homes, and business interests loom large in its development. Other technological advances from global positioning technology to cell phones to ever newly developed electronic marvels have been subtly changing the way business is done. In the process the new scenarios create new ethical challenges, which, as in the past, have first to be uncovered and then discussed and analyzed in an attempt to limit the harm done or threatened by them. Sometimes simply uncovering an ethical issue is sufficient to resolve it, for it will not be practiced in the light of day and it survives only when covert. Some unethical practices can be policed by those in the industry itself; others require legislation or social policy.

For a number of years there has been a debate among some academics about whether there is a field called "computer ethics" comparable to the fields of business ethics and medical ethics. Whether or not there is such a field, many of the issues that arise from the use of computers and from information technology more generally, have a connection in one way or another with business. There is clearly a computer industry, involving not only the creation of hardware but also of software. Computers are widely used in business, and although we would not talk about "typewriter ethics" simply because typewriters were (and still are) used in business, the use of computers in business has been sufficiently wide ranging to spawn a host of problems with an ethical dimension.

This book focuses on the ethical issues raised in businesses by computers and information technology. It looks both at the ethical issues for those in the computer and information technology industries and at the ethical issues raised by the use of computers and information technology for businesses in other industries. Many of the issues are still emerging, are not clear, and are the focus of debate about whether they are ethical issues and how they should be handled. Often, as with a newly emerging social innovation, the ethical issues have been ignored or submerged, not consciously or deliberately, but simply because the focus has been on development. In fact the development has been so rapid that society as a whole has not had the time to digest its ethical implications.

This fact has made this book difficult to write. On the one hand new issues are constantly emerging, so that any book of this type is necessarily incomplete and to some extent behind the newest issues before it emerges in print. On the other hand, some issues that are pressing at a given time are quickly left behind and become unimportant as technology develops and the issue is no longer center stage. A clear instance of this is what is known as the Y2K problem, or the worry about what would happen at the change of the millennium, since most programs were written using only the last two digits in specifying a year, and assumed "19" preceded those digits. Businesses and governments were forced to spend billions of dollars worldwide correcting computer code and ensuring that their programs and that airplanes and elevators would work properly with the change of centuries. As it turned out, business and government did act in time and January 1, 2000, arrived with no major disruptions anywhere in the world. There are lessons to be learned from that experience, but the Y2K problem is no longer a problem in the sense that it was prior to that January 1.

In writing this book I have developed in various ways four major interrelated themes. The first is what I have called the "Myth of Amoral Computing and Information Technology." This refers to the widespread phenomenon that the ethical dimension of computer and information technology development and use have been largely ignored both by those in the industry and by the general public. The second is the danger posed by the "Lure of the Technological Imperative," or the tendency to pursue technological development to the extent possible with little thought to the social implications and repercussions of such development. The third is the "Danger of the Hidden Substructure," which is in part a result of the fact that so much computer and information technological development and use take place behind the public scene and are not transparent to users or those affected by it, thus precluding public debate about the ethical impact of such development and use. The fourth theme is the "Acceptance of Technological Inertia" or the widespread failure to appreciate the fact that although computers and information technology have developed in certain ways, from an ethical point of view these are not necessarily the best ways they could have developed. Where this is the case, they can and should be changed. Computers and information technology should help and serve people and society. Where they do not, they should not be passively accepted. The four themes are sometimes stated explicitly, sometimes lurk in the background, where the attentive reader will see them. They are themes that I hope others will agree with and develop further. For this book has often done no more than raise them for discussion, and there is a great deal more to be done. In this way I consider this book a beginning, rather than the last word on any of the topics with which it deals.

Readers of this book may sometimes be frustrated, as I have been, by citations and notes to websites that no longer exist or no longer contain the information they contained when I used them. This, unfortunately, is one of the problems with electronic sources that is yet to be faced, much less resolved. Yet much information, both current and older, is so readily accessible on the Web, and is so often only accessible there, that reliance on it has become standard.

My special thanks go to my wife, who has endured my complaints and frustrations as my computer crashed or problems that were central faded to be replaced by others which had to be researched anew. I have tried out some of my ideas on students in my class on Moral Issues in Computer Technology, and I have learned a great deal from them about their perception of the issues. To them and unnamed others who have listened to my papers and presentations on ethical issues in information technology go my thanks.

Richard T. De George

chapter one

Ethics and the
Information Revolution

One second after midnight January 1, 2000, marked a banner moment encapsulating the promise and problems of the new millennium, the age of the information revolution. At that moment all the computers of the world either recorded the date as 2000, 1900, or as some default date. If the computer registered 1900 or some default date in any of its operations, depending on its function, the results would range from the humorous or trivial to the serious. Many people had avoided flying the night of December 31, 1999, in order not to be caught in case of a disaster. The Chinese government had ordered airline executives to be aloft at midnight to guarantee that the proper computer corrections had been made and to offset the fears of the general population. Despite many worries and predictions, planes did not fall from the sky and most electrical grids operated. Potential disasters were averted. Yet the beginning of the new millennium was inextricably linked in the minds of many throughout the world with the realization of their dependence on the computer, on computer-embedded chips, and on the new technology that had emerged and had already taken society captive.

The Y2K problem, as it was called, is in some ways a uniquely computer problem. It has significant implications for business and for society as a whole, and is symptomatic of the extent to which the information society has integrated computers into everyday life and the extent to which we depend on computers.[1] Most often everyday use takes place without the typical person realizing the extent of the dependence, the consequences of such dependence, and the degree to which human beings have abdicated responsibility for what they do or for what happens to them as a result of such abdication. The Y2K problem thus provides a microcosm of a variety of ethical issues both individual and collective or societal.

The Y2K problem arose because in the early days of computers computer memory was so limited and precious that programmers sought every way possible to conserve it. One obvious way was to represent the year by only the last two digits rather than all four. Those who considered the problem at all back in the early days of programming may have felt that the problem, if there was one, could be easily fixed by a small patch at a later time when more memory became available. The problem became more and more serious as different programmers wrote different instructions to handle dates in the programs they developed. In addition they used early programming languages, such as COBOL, which were later superseded. Newer versions of a program were not completely rewritten. Rather they were added to, and new programs incorporated old routines or whole programs. By the 1990s many programs used by large businesses (as well as by government) included millions of lines of code, written over many years. No one knew exactly what was contained in all the lines or how dates and commands relating to them had been incorporated. Therefore no simple patch or program could be used to fix the situation. Because of different programming instructions and languages, not all the bugs or incompatibilities in large programs could be foreseen. Solving the problem, it was estimated in 1996, would cost an estimated US$600 billion worldwide.[2] Although the actual figure turned out to be considerably less, government and business in the United States alone spent approximately $34 billion to correct the problem.

Who was responsible for the costs, worry, and aggravation coming from this seemingly simple error? Surely the year 2000 did not come upon us unannounced.

Shareholders might hold company managers responsible for not preventing the inordinate costs of fixing a foreseeable difficulty. Managers might in turn hold the firm or person from whom the company bought the computer responsible. A software company could attempt to switch the blame onto the individual programmers who many years ago first introduced the problem in order to save memory space. They are like terrorists who set bombs to go off some period of time after they have left the scene. But surely the early programmers did not maliciously decide to use two digits instead of four. At the time and given the constraints under which they worked, this was a justifiable solution – or so they might well claim.

What the Y2K problems demonstrate very clearly is the subtle and not so subtle ways in which computers influence our lives, our dependence upon them, and the complicated issues they can raise concerning responsibility and the liabilities and obligations of business.

▲ THE INFORMATION REVOLUTION ▲

The Industrial Age has given way to the Information Age. Business is in the midst of adjusting to the information revolution. As it does, it faces new challenges, many of which have an ethical dimension and ethical implications. Information technology has changed and will increasingly change the way business is done. A business office without a computer has become almost a contradiction in terms. The days of the manual or of the electric typewriter are over. Retyping a page for two inverted letters, or retyping many pages for a missed line on the first page is grossly inefficient compared with entering the correction on the computer and printing out the new page or pages. That simple increase in efficiency is nothing compared to the time and effort saved with database manipulation, spreadsheets, and the host of programs available to secretaries and office workers today. Whether computers have increased overall productivity commensurate with their cost is still debated. But they have certainly increased efficiency in many areas.

The information revolution is not just one thing but it encompasses a great many different innovations. Essential to all of them is some aspect of what is generally termed "information," which is often used in a very broad and not very precise way. The information revolution includes, for instance, what is sometimes called the knowledge revolution.

The knowledge revolution refers to the exponential growth in knowledge in the past several decades. Our knowledge in the sciences is increasing at a rate far greater than at any time in the past. It increases so fast that no one can keep up with all the changes in any field, much less in all fields. The result is increasing specialization. Not only is the store of knowledge increasing, but it is increasingly being put to practical use. Inventions proliferate, as do startup companies anxious to bring them to market.

This is one aspect of knowledge. But knowledge is used in many ways, and businesses have found that although knowledge is power, knowledge is only productive if it is used. There is a tension in business between managers and senior executives wishing to keep much knowledge of the company and of its operations and functioning to themselves as a source of power and the need to share it and make it available to more and more employees so they can perform their functions better.

A third aspect of knowledge is the increase in knowledge that even entry-level members of the workforce need to perform their jobs. More education and training are needed not only to work on the new computers and manage the new programs, but also to learn how to learn in order to keep up with the rapid pace of change. If once a high-school education was sufficient for most jobs, that is no longer the case. The jobs requiring little or no knowledge have more and more been outsourced to developing countries where the cost of labor is comparatively cheap. This in turn raises problems about developing countries and possible exploitation.

What we refer to as knowledge is generally true or correct statements about the world. We sometimes use the term "information" in a similar way. Information is less global than knowledge, and is often discrete and disjointed. Bits of information go to make up the larger picture that we consider knowledge. Information may be trivial or important, useful or useless. Information overload consists in such a large amount of information that the user is unable to sort out the useful from the useless, the trivial from the important simply because of the sheer volume. Information overload is obvious to anyone who has sought information on the Internet and received several thousand hits when searching for a particular bit of information. Researchers encounter a similar problem when looking for information on a topic and being presented with thousands of articles and books somehow related to the topic with no indication of which are the best sources for which purposes. Information, like knowledge, is usually presumed to be true, although people do speak of false information and false knowledge, when it would be more accurate to speak of false beliefs.

"Data" is another term that is often used interchangeably with information. But while information usually refers to facts, or statements about the way the world is, data do not necessarily refer to facts. Data may represent information but they may also represent misinformation, they may be inaccurate, unreliable, and false. A problem with data is that, although they may be false or meaningless, once entered into computers they operate as if they represent information and are treated as if they do.

Information and data raise problems of their own for business and for those affected by business. Since the data often represent information about individuals, they are most useful if true. If inaccurate or false, they can affect individuals adversely, for instance, with respect to their credit ratings.

▲ THE MYTH OF AMORAL COMPUTING ▲ AND INFORMATION TECHNOLOGY

The ubiquitousness of computers, highlighted by the Y2K problem, is one indication of the fact that developed societies have moved into a post-industrial age, frequently called the Information Age. Although this is widely acknowledged and often repeated, exactly what that means is vague. In part it means that what American society does primarily is not engage in the manufacture of products, even though it still does this, but that it engages in the generation, manipulation, and transfer of information. More people are engaged in this process than in the making of goods. Advances depend on knowledge and its application. The new breakthroughs are in computer technology, in biotechnology, and in information systems. Knowledge is readily at hand through the resources of the Internet. Anyone who wishes can develop a Web page. Computers can process information at incredible speeds and problems that took months to do by hand or calculator can now be done in minutes. We can test new designs by computer without having to actually build them; through techniques of virtual reality we can design and furnish our homes and walk through them before we begin construction. We can communicate with people anywhere in the world almost instantaneously through e-mail and the Internet. Governments are no longer able to block news of what happens in their countries through iron or bamboo or any other kind of curtain.

All of these changes have occurred with remarkable speed. They have in fact occurred with such speed that society has not had time to fully adjust to the changes, to experience and weigh the consequences, to pick and choose what is and what is not worth developing and what should be aborted before it develops further. Technology has developed faster than our evaluation of it, and the values society developed over centuries to cope with life in an agricultural and then in an industrial era are still the values that society holds and by which it lives. Businesses have sprung up to develop and exploit whatever is technologically possible before society has determined the overall social impact of such developments. The result has been the development of what I shall call the Myth of Amoral Computing and Information Technology, or MACIT.

The myth, like all myths, partially reveals and partially hides reality. We are all familiar with the excuse, made so often to customers by business representatives, "It's the computer's fault" or "computer error," as if the computer, and not some human being, were at fault or had made an error. The phrases are ways in which people and businesses say that they are not responsible for whatever it is that has happened and adversely affected someone else. The myth is expressed in language in which computers are the culprits, and of course, since computers are not moral beings, they can bear no moral responsibility. Hence, when the computer is down, that is no one's fault. When programs malfunction or software has bugs, that is no one's fault. In general anything that has to do with computers and information technology has a life of its own and is not susceptible to moral evaluation or blame or censure.

The truth is that often the operator or person at the terminal is not at fault and is struggling with something over which they have no control. What is covered up is the fact that somewhere in the process some human being is at fault or made an error. The implication that is often drawn is that since the mistake is the computer's, and the computer is not a moral being, there is no moral blame to be assigned, and no one to be held responsible or accountable. While it is true that the computer is not a moral being, it is not true that no one is or should be held morally responsible and accountable.

The Myth of Amoral Computing and Information Technology takes many forms. It does not hold that computing is immoral. Rather in holding that it is amoral MACIT says that it is improper, a conceptual mistake, to apply moral language and terms to computers and what they do. This much is correct. But what is false is that it is improper or a conceptual mistake to apply moral language and terms to what human beings do with computers, how they design, develop and apply them, how they manipulate and use information. Companies and schools order computers for all their employees or students, and anyone who is not computer literate will be left behind in the Information Age. This is not questioned, but is taken for granted. There is no debate about whether the members of society wish such a society and no discussion of how to guide the development of the society along these lines. What technology can do and can be developed will be done and developed. The MACIT implicitly sanctions this. According to the myth, these are not issues that have moral import or deserve moral scrutiny. Reality and progress march on, and attempting to stand in the way, slow the march, or evaluate them critically is to misconstrue the future. The result is resigned acceptance of what is developed and how.

The development of the Internet is a case in point. It has grown exponentially over a very short period of time. It crosses geographical borders with ease. It has many centers, its electronic packets pass over many different routes on their way from A to B. There is little regulation. It is perhaps the first instance of functional anarchy on a large scale. Its development has far outstripped societal debate about whether such a phenomenon is good or bad for all societies, and attempts at partial control by individual governments have quickly taught us that individual governmental control is at best difficult and often ineffective. The information revolution is descending upon societies that have not gone through the industrial revolution. And the MACIT accompanies each incursion into different societies.

The fact that the MACIT is a myth is not appreciated, not only by many ordinary people and most businesses, but also by many computer professionals, who see their task as technical, as pushing technology forward, as increasing speed and memory and computing capability, applying it wherever those who want it indicate and finding uses and applications others have not previously entertained. Computer professionals and computer-related businesses are often driven by fierce competition to get the next innovation first, to develop the new product or program before someone else does. For the pervading belief is that if it is possible someone will do it, and the first one to do it often captures the prize, whatever that is – riches, market share, fame. The result is that many do not take full responsibility for what they do or develop, they release products before they are adequately debugged and tested, and in other ways fail to consider the effects on people, which is at the heart of ethical thinking. The MACIT covers over their need to do so.

Another facet of the MACIT is that legislation has stepped in prior to ethical discussion, rather than as usual, following it. The typical pattern is for an action to be determined to be unethical or immoral, to harm people or society, and then to be legally controlled. But a result of the MACIT has been to preempt ethical discourse in this realm, and vested interests have prevailed in influencing legislation. The rules that we have and the laws that we have in this realm with respect to property and privacy, for instance, are most often not the result of widespread social discussion but are rather the result of lobbying, limited legislative hearings, and passage of bills dealing with issues that many of the legislators voting on them do not really understand.

Only slowly is the MACIT being uncovered and exposed for what it is – a partial story. Only slowly is society coming to grips with the changes that it is involved in. Only slowly are the members of society feeling the impacts of the information revolution sufficiently to begin attempting to evaluate it. A difficulty is that the revolution is a moving target, and even as society focuses on one part or issue, it tends to develop and evolve before closure is possible, and before all the facts can be properly evaluated, defensible conclusions drawn, and moral judgments rendered.

The reasons for the pervasiveness of the myth can be found to a large extent in the role of computer and information technology in society and to the nature of computers and information technology themselves. We can capture some of these in a variety of syndromes.

The ignorance syndrome

We have already noted how to most ordinary computer users, the computer is more or less a black box. They know how to use it and how to run various applications. But actual programming and fixing code is beyond their capabilities. To a large extent they are ignorant of the complexities and so rely on the experts. This in turn both helps relieve them of any feeling of responsibility when something goes wrong, and by extension, often leads to a feeling that things going wrong are normal and part of the price one pays for the new technology, and so not anything for which one holds others morally responsible.

The complexity syndrome

We have come to understand and accept that some programs are incompatible with other programs. Hence when something goes wrong, the ordinary computer user may not know whom to hold at fault or where to attribute blame. No one is responsible for making sure that operating systems and applications and a wide variety of applications are all compatible. If something goes wrong it is not unusual for each component maker to deny responsibility and to place the cause of the failure on some other component. The user has no way of knowing who is correct – or if there is any sense in which it is proper to ask who is correct.

The virtual reality syndrome

This is perhaps the most pervasive reason for the myth. What is done on the computer that interactively affects others – e.g., communicating by e-mail, entering another's computer, carrying on activities on the Internet – are all done in what is sometimes called cyberspace. There is no face-to-face meeting or confrontation, no physical trespass in the ordinary sense (since there is no real space involved). If one looks at a colleague's e-mail or computer files by entering his or her password, it is done from the privacy of one's room or office. This provides a psychic distance that seems to relieve one of responsibility or the feeling that one is really doing anything wrong. There is no physical harm done, to a large extent no tracks are left, no one is physically hurt. Ethics applies to the real world. Cyberspace is not the real world. And the notion of a cyber ethics appropriate to cyberspace has not yet become part of the general public's consciousness – nor of the consciousness of many in the computer and information technology field. That cyberspace is really part of the world in which we live and that what goes on there impacts real people and so is governed by the same ethical rules as all other areas of human activity is for the most part ignored or covered over.

This is the context in which business in the United States and in most of the industrially developed parts of the world finds itself. Business is an integral part of society and is neither in a privileged nor in an inferior position *vis-à-vis* the rest of society. Since the 1960s American business has been called upon more and more to hold itself morally or ethically accountable for what it does and for how it treats its workers, customers, suppliers, the environment, the communities in which it is located, and society at large. What can be called the Myth of Amoral Business, or the view that business is not appropriately held morally accountable for what it does, has largely been dispelled. But that part of it which overlaps with the MACIT remains.

▲ THE MYTH OF AMORAL COMPUTING ▲
AND INFORMATION TECHNOLOGY
AND THE Y2K PROBLEM

The Y2K problem provides an interesting mirror on the Myth of Amoral Computing and Information Technology. Although fixing the problem cost over $34 billion in the United States, there was no public discussion of moral responsibility, much less of any moral accountability or blame. Any moral judgment seems to have been irrelevant, and so, apparently, no one was to blame and no one was to be held accountable. The problem just "happened," like a force of nature which causes harm but for which no person is responsible.

One aspect of the application of the myth was to call the problem the "Y2K bug." A "bug" in a computer program is usually some defect in the program that is unknown to those writing the program and that appears only in use. Calling "Y2K" a bug, therefore, implies that programmers did not know that the year 2000 was coming and that assuming "19" before a date field of the remaining two places would cause problems starting with the year 2000. Of course they knew this. As we have seen most of the early computer programmers made a conscious decision to use only two places in order to save expensive memory – which they succeeded in doing.

Those who made and printed paper forms did not consider this a problem and reasonably assumed that people could properly inter-pret "'99" as the year 1999 and "'00" as the year 2000. It is likely, because it was so general a practice, that early programmers, who were interested in saving space, did not think of possible problems the convention might cause some thirty years later.

This is an explanation of why the convention in writing computer code developed and was followed. It says in effect that programmers were just like other people in using the convention and that they did not consider consequences thirty or more years away. Nor could they foresee the exponential growth of computer use. They in all likelihood did not imagine that the programs they wrote would be used and built on indefinitely and that they were writing in a sense for centuries.

There is no one we can point to who made the decision for a two-place year field, no one we can identify who started the convention. It is difficult morally to fault any individual in those days for not seeing ahead. Yet we can legitimately raise the question: should computer programmers have seen ahead? If the answer is no, then are we faced with a situation in which technology simply develops with no one being responsible for being conscious or aware of its implications, with no one taking responsibility for it, and with no one being accountable for how it develops and for the harm that it does? If so, this is a greater problem than the Y2K problem.

Somewhere along the line, as programmers built on previous programs and as they incorporated subroutines from other programs into their own, they must have realized that they were no longer sure of what a particular program contained or did not contain. It functioned as desired, but it was no longer the product of someone or some group that had mastery of the whole. Early programmers typically documented their programs. But documentation was often lost or ignored.

By the time some programmer or some manager discovered that they were no longer sure what their programs contained or how they were structured, the problem was that there might have been millions of lines of a program, and the cost of redoing it all from scratch would be enormous. At which point we begin to hold people responsible for what is in their programs and for what they sell or use is not entirely clear.

Moral responsibility requires causal responsibility or connection with the events in question, knowledge of what one is doing, and consent to doing it. Moral responsibility can be mitigated or lessened if any of the three conditions are not satisfied. The conditions which mitigate responsibility are known as excusing conditions, and they may excuse one from responsibility to a greater or lesser extent.

Surely all programmers in the 1950s, 1960s, and 1970s knew that the year 2000 was coming and that assuming the first two digits of the date as "19" would be valid only up through the year 1999. Bob Bemer, who worked for IBM, foresaw the problem in the 1970s, and suggested that the year field be four digits rather than two.[3] Obviously he was ignored.

Early programmers cannot claim ignorance of the fact that the year 2000 was coming as an excusing condition. Nor does the fact that people customarily wrote dates using the last two digits of the year provide an excuse. Yet I have suggested that because of the expense of computer memory in those decades, and the fact that the early programmers could not foresee the development of cheap memory or the fact that their programs would be built upon instead of being replaced, might provide some excuse and so some – or perhaps even complete – mitigation of moral blame.

If programmers in those decades could not foresee problems with the year 2000, programmers in the early 1990s were certainly close enough to consider what would happen with the close of the old century. Clearly someone at some point not only recognized the problem but started to do something about it. Those closest to the problem had the responsibility to foresee difficulties and to report that something had to be done. Since any firm that had been in business for more than a decade and used mainframe computers had the problem, all the companies should have been informed of it. It was then the responsibility of those with the authority to do something about the problem to take the appropriate action.

The likely scenario suggested by the Myth of Amoral Computing and Information Technology is that the general managers, who were not computer programmers and may have been barely computer literate, probably did not appreciate the enormity of the problem. That Information Technology and computer people could not get the attention of management long before the approach of the year 2000 to fix a problem the technicians knew existed and would have to be faced sooner or later is a sad reflection on business managers. Undoubtedly, many did not understand the problem or its scope, and many who did were unwilling to spend the millions of dollars it would take to fix their systems before they had to, even though the delay added to the cost. In some instances managers saw that this was a problem that could be passed on to their successors, and that they would not be held responsible for not having acted in a timely fashion. They could avoid taking the financial hit during their tenure, leaving their replacement to come up with the needed money and to suffer any negative repercussions. The tendency to avoid taking responsibility for timely action seems to have been rampant.

Information Systems (IS) and Information Technology (IT) offices are not typically center stage at corporate headquarters, and the typical manager is not a computer techie. If presented early by their Information Systems people with the very large projected cost of correcting it, the general managers perhaps understandably did not immediately authorize the expenditure of millions of dollars for what seemed at the time a far off problem. Most firms had what plausibly appeared at the time as more immediate problems with which to deal. Understanding this reaction, however, is not the same as exonerating from moral responsibility those who had it, or for their delaying fixing it sooner rather than later, and thus at lesser rather than greater expense to the firm.

The delayed response to the Y2K problem indicates that management for the most part still tends to think of Information Systems and Information Technology as something that remains a service function of the corporation, off in a back set of rooms, instead of being prominently in the center of the corporation. The disconnection between corporate leaders and their technical divisions is the clearest indication that firms have not moved consciously into the Information Age. They are backing into it or being pulled by a technology they do not completely understand, even as they become more and more dependent on it. Yet if we are truly in a developing Information Age, then IS and IT need to be at the center of things, and management has to both understand it and take responsibility for it.

It is generally accepted that those who produce harm are responsible for the harm they cause. Corporations that harm their customers are morally and usually legally responsible for making good on the harm caused. We can trace the causal link back, as lawyers are wont to do. In the case of the user of a product that contains a program that causes the product not to operate as normally expected, the customer has recourse to the supplier of the product. If the product contained a program that is defective in some way, the producer may be the developer of the product or may simply have purchased or licensed the product or had it developed by a subcontractor. Responsibility for the program devolves then on the producer of the program. Programmers who work for an employer are responsible to the employer, but the employer owns their products as "work for hire" and so is responsible for the use to which it is put. Ethically each company bears responsibility for its products and for the harm it does by failures due to its products.

We can generalize beyond the Y2K problem. Those who produce or incorporate programs into products are responsible for those products and programs, just as they are responsible for other products or goods they sell. Yet there is a tendency which we have noted in the Myth of Amoral Computing and Information Technology for companies to disown responsibility for computer malfunctions or breakdowns, and for commercial software producers to issue disclaimers with their products claiming that by opening the product the user relieves them of all responsibility. That this has been accepted without much complaint by the general public is at best puzzling. One result has been for software producers to release their products before they are ready. Savvy software users know better than to purchase the first version of any new software product. Users have learned that instead of the extensive testing that should be done before a product is released, producers release a product which they know still has defects, and which they correct as the defects are reported to them. The general public thus provides some of the testing the producer should have done. Yet the buyer is not informed of this service to the producer, or paid for it if he or she reports a difficulty; nor does the product cost less because it has not been completely debugged when marketed. All of this is contrary to the general policy with respect to other products.

What has happened in these cases as with most other ethical issues related to computers is that the ethical dimension has been pre-empted by the legal dimension, and the laws have tended to reflect the business interests of the providers of computer programs and services.

Even in the 1990s, instead of changing all the old two-digit fields to four digits, many companies and programmers decided to stick with a two-digit field and rely on some fix such as to treat "00" as greater than "99" in fields dealing with years, or treating all dates lower than some number, e.g., "20" as being in the twenty-first century instead of the twentieth, a solution that will be good only until the year 2020 approaches. For some companies this is ethically responsible. For others it is not, and those responsible are simply shifting the problem forward, when it will be harder to fix.

There was no excuse in the late 1990s for programmers writing new programs to use two digits rather than four for years in new programs; yet many did, using some algorithm or other to keep the two centuries straight and assuming that there will never be a need for more than two centuries and that their programs will not be in use by the time the algorithm no longer works because of the next century. A lesson to be learned from the Y2K problem is that no one presently knows how long programs that are being written today will be embedded in programs used many years into the future, and that programmers have the moral responsibility to avoid problems that can be avoided, even if the problems are foreseeable only for the distant future.

The Y2K problem points to a larger and potentially more significant problem. With the thirty to forty year experience we have with computers and computer programs thus far, the Y2K problem demonstrates the extent to which society, government, and businesses, as well as individual users, are losing control over the programs that we use and have come to rely upon.

The Y2K problem arose in many cases because of early programming, which was often idiosyncratic in labeling and documentation. There were few imposed and widely recognized standards, since the standards had yet to be developed. Most of the programming was done in COBOL, which was widely taught in colleges, but which has long since been replaced by more advanced programming languages. Hence to correct the Y2K problem, step one was to find people who knew COBOL and could go back and read the old lines of instruction. The number of people proficient in COBOL was comparatively small, and a large number of those who worked on the problems were people who had retired and had been lured out of retirement by the high pay people with such knowledge commanded.

It does not take much imagination to see what would happen if a similar problem arose twenty years from now. The number of people skilled in COBOL would by then have shrunk to a very small number. Eventually the language will be unknown by any but perhaps historians of computer languages. By continuing to rely on old programs instead of rewriting them, as many companies did in correcting their Y2K problems, society as a whole could run the risk of eventually using and relying on programs that no one can fix, and that no one can even examine knowledgeably. Computers will be black boxes with output that one takes on faith without any experts to guarantee that what goes on within them is reliable. Nor is the problem only with COBOL. The life-span of computer languages is already incredibly brief. As programmers continuously incorporate older programming code into new programs or as they build on existing programs, it is not hard to foresee that society in general as well as governments, individual firms, and organizations will be relying on embedded code that no one can any longer read.

Because programs now often involve millions of lines of code, it is not possible for any single individual to write or rewrite it all. Nor would that be of particular use, since that person would then be the only one with command of the whole.

With loss of control there is a tendency to disclaim responsibility. If unforeseen and untoward events occur, they are blamed on the computer, which is to say that no blame is assigned or assumed.

Unforeseen computer events become unforeseeable computer events, which take on the status of acts of God. Only in this case God is the computer. Acts of God are events that typically are excluded from insurance policies, although one can insure against certain specific damages, such as that caused by flood or earthquake. Insurance companies might similarly start issuing computer damage insurance, or alternatively they might start excluding such harm from their umbrella or specific policies. This scenario accepts the current trend towards lack of control and lack of responsibility and accountability as inevitable. Such an attitude reinforces the cause and provides no incentive to find a way to reverse or push back or stop the loss of control. If no one is responsible for doing anything along these lines, no one will do anything to change present procedures or attitudes.

Since the new millennium arrived with no computer-related disaster, many adopted the attitude that Y2K had not been a problem after all, and that companies and governments and individuals had been subjected to some sort of scam or scare without foundation. In fact, however, it is only because those responsible did finally take corrective action at great cost that disaster was averted. The many law suits that had been feared did not materialize, and hence many felt that there was no need to look into the issue of responsibility or to worry about changing procedures that help people avoid accountability. The lack of disaster in turn reinforced the Myth of Amoral Computing and Information Technology. Yet the myth is not a solution but the heart of the problem, and Y2K illustrated its depth and pervasiveness.

▲ INFORMATION, ETHICS, AND LAW ▲

The Myth of Amoral Computing and Information Technology comes in many varieties. One is to equate whatever is required of anyone in computing or information systems with what is required by law. If it is legal, it is permissible. If it is illegal, it is not permissible. The view is a simple one, but it fails to capture the reality of the relation between law and ethics.

To begin with, the criminal law in general tends to make illegal what is unethical. In the obvious cases of murder, stealing, perjury, and the like, what is made criminal is what is unethical. The force of law is brought to reinforce the moral sanctions society already imposes for these actions. In the case of computer-related activities, part of the task before passing legislation is coming to a prior conclusion about the morality of new practices as they arise. Good legal practice allows people freedom of activity to the broadest extent possible compatible with a similar freedom for all. It does not criminalize activity unless it is harmful in some way, and so unless it is unethical. The decision of whether it is harmful and the extent thereof, and so whether it is unethical, is not decided by looking at law, but rather law looks at ethics. Because of this there is generally a lag of law behind ethics. Slavery was unethical before it was made illegal, as were discrimination and sexual harassment and other actions that in more recent times have been made illegal. We can and do consider actions or practices unethical before they are made illegal, and so should expect this to be the pattern with respect to computers and information technology. Spreading computer viruses that destroy the recipient's files or in other ways harm the recipient's files or computer was unethical before it was made illegal.

A second reason we should not equate law with ethics is that we can evaluate any law from an ethical point of view, asking, is it in fact a just or good law? Some laws, such as the apartheid laws in South Africa that enforced segregation and discrimination against black people in that country, are unethical. In such cases, they should be repealed. If law and ethics were identical, there would be no way to raise the issue of whether the law was ethically defensible, which is clearly not the case. Hence just because something is either permitted or prohibited by law with respect to computers does not necessitate the conclusion that it is a just law, although the presumption is generally in favor of that assumption.

Third, not everything that is unethical can or should be made illegal. Not everything that is unethical can be made illegal because the sphere of ethics is very broad and allows of degrees. Not every lie is illegal, even though lying in general is unethical. The law singles out certain categories with respect to truth telling, and, for instance, prohibits perjury, and false advertising, but not instances of one individual's lying to another on private matters. It would be impossible to police a law that prohibited all lying, and one result would be to inculcate disrespect for the law. This leads to the reasons why not all unethical activity, even if it could be made illegal, should be made illegal. The cost of enforcing the law might be more than the good obtained by having the law; the harm done by the unethical practice might be negligible; the practice might not be widespread enough to make illegal; the wording of the law might not be able to capture the wrong without also outlawing permissible behavior, and so on. The difficulty of drafting legislation that keeps pornography out of the view of children on the Internet while at the same time not violating the rights of adults to freedom of speech and of access to what they wish to view is an instance of this. Until proper language can be drafted, no legislation is appropriate. Yet the pandering of pornography to minors is arguably unethical.

Although the relation of ethics and law puts the priority on ethics before law, there is a relation in the other direction. Although some actions in themselves, such as murder, are morally wrong, most actions are morally neutral. Yet some of them become actions that we are to avoid simply because they are made illegal. Whether one drives on the right hand side of the road or on the left hand side is in itself a matter of moral indifference. Nonetheless, it is clear that if people are to get anywhere quickly and efficiently, there should be some agreement on which side of the road to drive on. Otherwise people will continually be in each other's way, and traffic will get nowhere. Since the side of the road on which people drive is in itself not an ethical matter, there is no ethically correct side on which to drive. But once a country decides that all traffic will drive on the left, for instance, then not to drive on the left is to endanger both oneself and others, as well as to undermine efficiency. Hence, once a country legislates that traffic is to move on the left, it becomes ethically required that one drive on the left. In this case it is ethically required not only because not to do so threatens harm but also because it is required by law. Once a law is passed, therefore, an action that was previously permitted may now be legally prohibited, and hence at least indirectly unethical. In general there is an ethical obligation to obey just laws. Just laws are laws that do not require that one do anything that is unethical, and that are in general passed in the appropriate way and passed for the common good. The presumption generally is that laws are to be obeyed. In a defensible legal system laws are passed for the common good, and to go against the common good by breaking the law is in general prima facie wrong. Thus, in a system of law that is generally ethically defensible, not only do laws carry with them legal obligations, but one also has the moral or ethical obligation to obey them. Civil disobedience, which consists in breaking a just law to protest an unjust one, might be justified, but the onus is on those who would break the law, and the permissible means for expressing civil disobedience have to be met.

This is significant with respect to information technology because much of what is right or wrong in this area is not right or wrong in itself but has become right or wrong because of the legislation that has been passed. Computer programs, for instance, might be considered proprietary or they might be considered in the public domain. If there were no legislation governing computer programs, they might be considered either. There is no ethical presumption in favor of one or the other, just as there is no ethical presumption in favor of driving on the right or on the left. But once legislation states that the presumption is in favor of ownership, and that unless put into the public domain programs are proprietary, then there is an ethical requirement not to copy such protected work unless authorized to do so. Someone may claim that the law should be otherwise. But that claim does not in itself change the law. Since it is not clearly unethical to allow protection to programs, copying them without authorization becomes unethical because illegal. If the law is changed, then it would not be unethical to copy them, because doing so is not unethical in itself.

Since this is the case, and since in the United States – much less in the world – there are many different juridical jurisdictions, what is illegal in one state or country may be legal in another. Hence, it is arguably the case that at least in some instances, what is ethical because legally permitted in one jurisdiction may be unethical because illegal in another. Uniformity in computer-related legislation is an ideal that requires coordination and reciprocity that has not yet emerged.

The relation between law and morality with respect to computers and information technology presently is in a state of evolution and flux. Whether the common good is better served by extending laws governing property to include software and websites, or whether it would be better to draft specific legislation governing these, for instance, is an open issue. The issue should not be decided simply by vested interests influencing legislation in one direction or another. Ethics has an important role to play in the discussions and in a just or fair outcome. The Myth of Amoral Computing and Information Technology hides rather than reveals this fact, and by equating obligation with law inhibits discussion and appropriate ethical consideration of emerging practices, possibilities, and alternatives.

Although a great deal of what is ethical or not in the area of information technology is dependent on the applicable laws, company policy is also often a determining factor. What a company allows or does not allow is in numerous cases up to the company and not to be decided in advance by ethical considerations. But once it has decided, for instance, that its employees may not use the Internet for personal purposes, then it is unethical for employees to do so.

Ethical discussion of information technology thus operates on at least three levels. One is the level of what is right or wrong in itself, such as stealing. Whatever ethical basis we use to justify those norms – be they religious, philosophical, or personal – they are almost universally accepted and applied. A second level is what is wrong because of existing legislation. Prior to legislation different people may argue that the law should be one way or another. And they may each give ethical as well as other kinds of reasons in defense of their claims. But unless the action legislated is wrong in itself, the legislative decision has ethical implications. The third level is the level of the firm or company that owns the information technology in question. It is circumscribed by both ethics and the law. Nonetheless that leaves a great deal of leeway about what it permits or does not permit its employees to do. If it decides on a policy, and that policy is not unethical, then employees are bound by it and the requirements are not only corporate requirements but become ethical requirements.

To the extent that this is an accurate description, if one company decides on one policy, and another company on another policy, each governs its own domain. If one country decides on one policy and another country decides on a different, and perhaps the opposite policy, then there is no difficulty as long as one stays within either country. When in Britain drive on the left; when in the United States drive on the right. But the matter is not so easy when information technology crosses borders. What is unethical in itself – stealing – is wrong in all countries. But what constitutes stealing is dependent in part on how a society defines property. Hence there are many issues of information technology on the international level that are not easily resolved and that involve different laws and different expectations, customs, presumptions, and the like in different countries. In these instances neither side can claim to have the only correct position, because each position is ethically permissible, even if they clash because they are incompatible when considered together. Such situations require negotiation. In such instances, since there is no ethically correct position, but since one position is required, there must be a decision made. Once the decision is made, then it becomes binding, just as decisions made into law or decisions made by corporate executives become binding.

What is just, and so what is ethical in such situations, is what all the parties importantly affected by the policy agree to as just, whatever notion of justice they use or whatever ethical position they embrace. If the United States has certain laws or policies or views concerning intellectual property and China has different laws or policies or views that conflict with those of the US, which laws ought to prevail? Within each country when dealing with their own contributions, people are governed by the local laws and customs. But if the Chinese want to use US-developed products without respecting US copyright or patent protection of intellectual property, there will be difficulty. What from the US perspective is seen as theft or piracy might be seen from the Chinese perspective as fair use. In such instances what is fair or just cannot be decided unilaterally, since the two sides disagree and each believes its position justified. If there is to be interaction, and if one side is not simply to impose its position on the other by force, then there must be negotiation. This will involve both parties giving up something to which it thinks it has a right. But giving up something in order to obtain a desired overall agreement of greater value or interest is ethically permitted and violates no ethical norm. One may not compromise on what is ethically forbidden. But one can give up some of what one feels one is entitled to, and that is what takes place in negotiation. If the result is a policy that all importantly affected parties, armed with adequate information and free from force, agree is just, then the agreement is just. It might later be rethought or reconsidered and reasons might become apparent as to why, from some perspective, the policy is not just. In that case it will need renegotiation. But there is no overarching notion of justice to which any have access and to which all must submit.

Nonetheless, what society has learned in other aspects of business is that the market is not always self-correcting and that law is sometimes necessary to overcome market failures. We have also learned that to get uniformity of compliance to what is right, we often cannot rely simply on self-compliance and self-policing by business. This is becoming clear in many aspects of information technology – including privacy, as we shall see in detail in a later chapter. At the same time, however, we have also learned that laws can in some instances impede progress. In the field of computers and information technology some fear, with good reason, poorly crafted laws that outlaw techniques and approaches to computing that may be potentially fruitful as well as posing dangers. To block both in an attempt to prevent the latter is counterproductive from society's point of view. Walking the narrow line between underlegislating and overlegislating can sometimes be achieved by prohibiting anything that yields socially harmful results rather than by making illegal specific technical computer activities and types of programs. Legislation against computer viruses is a case in point. The aim of law should be to prevent harm to people's computers, data, and programs, not to outlaw certain ways of writing programs or outlawing attachments to e-mail or self-propagating or self-destructing programs of all kinds.

▲ VIRTUES AND ETHICS IN THE ▲ INFORMATION AGE

The basic norms of morality of course apply to all areas and all aspects of the lives of all of us. We should not murder, or steal, or in general harm others. But the information revolution brings to the fore certain values that are central to its success, and these values take on special significance. When the industrial revolution took place, people moved from the countryside to the cities to work in factories. The basic norms of morality did not change, but industry demanded certain values, and certain virtues, that farming did not. Farmers judge time by the sun and by the seasons. Industry judges time by the minute. With the industrial revolution punctuality became not only a value but a virtue that employers sought in their employees and that families started inculcating in their children. The clock took on an importance it formerly did not have. Similarly, with the introduction of the assembly line, new values were introduced. One person could not perform his or her designated task until several people up the line had performed theirs. Interdependence became a fact of production, and there was a need for each to perform his or her task correctly. Tolerance for error diminished as more and more accuracy became necessary for producing machines and for what the machines produced. Efficiency in turn became a value. The efficient person came to be in demand, and efficiency became a virtue.

Those traits that are necessary for a certain task become values if one seeks to accomplish that task. We want surgeons to have steady hands and bankers to be honest.

Once information comes center stage it too carries with it certain values. We noted that for information to be useful it must be true and accurate; otherwise what passes as information is disruptive and counterproductive. Thus, although truth telling – as opposed to lying – is a traditional virtue, it takes on added importance in the area of information technology. Unless we can all reasonably assume that most of the information people supply is truthfully supplied, the information revolution will grind to a halt. The cost of checking all our information is prohibitive, as well as often being well beyond the capabilities of any of us. Lying is so serious an infraction of the basic norm of information technology that it ought to be treated harshly. Although paradoxically the possibility of misrepresentation becomes easier because of the anonymity of sources of information such as the World Wide Web, the need for truthfulness is greater than ever. How that need is to be communicated and the virtue developed and inculcated are but two of the problems connected with the information revolution. We have all heard the adage "garbage in, garbage out." Computers can process data at blinding speed. But unless the data represents reality, the decisions based on them will not achieve the ends desired. Unless managers can rely on getting truthful reports from those below them, their decisions will be distorted accordingly, and if this were to happen at each level of the reporting process, those at the top will act in ignorance. This observation is not new, but its import is magnified in an age that relies on information.

Truthfulness is only one of the values necessary for the success of the information revolution. A lie consists in one party making a statement that he or she believes is false with the intent of deceiving someone else. This locates the evil in the intent of the speaker, who wishes to deceive. Yet misinformation that one repeats, believing it to be true, is not a lie but may be just as harmful if acted upon by the hearer. Hence joined to truthfulness, accuracy and the correctness of the statements made are equally essential. Accuracy and correctness thus become values, and those involved in handling information need to develop the habits or cultivate the virtues of accuracy and of seeking to state and spread only that which is true or correct. The rapid dissemination characteristic of the information revolution means that misinformation can be spread as quickly as accurate information.

One of the results of the easy availability of information is information overload. This consists in having accessible so much information that one either does not know how to separate out the useful from the less useful or the not-at-all useful, or that it takes longer to separate out the useful information than one has time to do so. Thus expertise in filtering information becomes important. Sharing information is useful, but sharing so much information that those who receive it cannot digest it or use it fruitfully is clearly counterproductive. If we follow Aristotle's model of the virtue being the mean between extremes, the virtue in this case falls between the extremes of overinforming and underinforming those with whom we work and deal.

Closely related to all of these considerations is trust. Trust has two pertinent dimensions. On the one hand, the person has to develop the virtue of trustfulness. This requires opening up oneself to receiving and accepting information. The other is the dimension of being trustworthy. This requires that one supply true and accurate information. The viability of the Information Age requires the general and widespread development and inculcation of these two aspects of the virtue of trust. Trust is easily broken when one is deceived or otherwise penalized for having trusted the untrustworthy. On the other hand, refusal to trust anyone and to attempt to do without trust is to undermine the benefits of transactions or make transaction costs prohibitively expensive. Business has always required and been built on trust. Once again, the Information Age magnifies the importance of a traditional virtue.

Information has traditionally yielded power to those who had it as opposed to those who did not. In business information is often closely guarded from competitors. Similarly executives wielded power in many instances by not sharing the information they had. They sometimes forced those who needed it to request it, and the possessor decided whether or not to share it. This sometimes led to the false belief that those in positions of power knew more than those below them and had answers to questions to which lower-level employees did not have access. The senior people were credited with a broader view that explained corporate inefficiencies or anomalies or apparent unethical behavior. Of course this was not necessarily the case. But controlling access to information is one classic way to control power. Although this remains true in the age of information technology, the information revolution carries with it the realization that only by sharing information is it useful. Hence there is a built-in value to sharing information rather than hoarding it. One of the salient aspects of information is that it can be shared without being lost. It is a kind of wealth that can be shared to the benefit of all its recipients. This is true not only with respect to corporate knowledge, but worldwide with respect to those nations that are information rich and able to advance knowledge and those that are relatively information poor, but could make advances in many areas if they and their people had ready access to appropriate information and knowledge. The virtue of generosity is one dimension of the willingness to share information; the virtue of commonality, or giving up individual control and power, for the greater benefit of one's corporation or of the common good on a national or international level, is another dimension. We have no word to describe this precise virtue, but it will be an important virtue if the Information Age is to realize its promise.

At the same time, the Information Age has made information a valuable commodity. Sometimes it is appropriate to guard it and there is a temptation to seek information to which one has no right, such as personal information for marketing purposes. The ease of duplication also carries with it the temptation to duplicate that to which one has no right. Respect for confidentiality on the one hand, and for property rights on the other, are virtues that also need cultivation and inculcation. The line between what is public and what is private is blurring in many areas and in many ways, and the appropriate virtues in some cases have yet to emerge.

As we view different problems connected with business and the use of information technology, the values necessary to the successful use of such technology can serve as excellent guides to what is ethical and what is not in this area.

In approaching ethical issues in computer technology we shall use the basic moral norms common to most societies and generally held in the developed nations; we shall use the values and norms that underpin either business or information technology; and we shall argue by analogy from accepted ethical or unethical practices in one area to new or newly emerging practices in the field of information technology. We of course do not want to reinvent the wheel. We have developed notions of privacy, for instance, with respect to mail. Can we argue by analogy from that with respect to e-mail? We should not simply ignore our accepted practices and should attempt to make our judgments about new practices cohere with the judgments we already make about common practices in daily life and business. Yet we must remain open to the possibility that analogies do not hold and that several different analogies might be applied to a case or situation or practice and that the different analogies will lead to different judgments about the rightness or wrongness of the action in question. In arriving at a final determination of the ethics of particular actions or classes of actions, we should be open to pertinent considerations of a variety of kinds.

The Myth of Amoral Business has given way and led to the development in the 1970s of a field that is commonly called business ethics. The name is modeled after the name medical (or biomedical) ethics, a field that had developed ten years earlier. Medical ethics deals with issues related to medicine and its practice – to doctor–patient confidentiality, to patients' rights, such as the right to informed consent before submitting to a medical procedure, and to other issues that have to do with the doctor–patient relationship. But what spurred the development of a specialized field was the development of new technologies, such as heart transplants and *in vitro* fertilization, towards which society had no developed moral intuitions. Similarly what spurred the development of business ethics was the development of the chemical industry and business's ability to seriously and adversely affect the environment and the health and lives of millions of people, as well as the growth of internationalization and new ways of doing business for which, once again, society had developed no moral intuitions. In the absence of developed intuitions, the morality of practices, actions, and technologies had to be evaluated using the best techniques of moral analysis and argumentation that the members of society had. By analogy, some have claimed that the new developments in computing and information technology demand a new field, computer ethics, in which these developments, in the absence of adequate moral intuitions, can be discussed and defensible moral judgments made.

Whether there is a field properly called computer ethics is debated. And there is no consensus on, even if the field exists, exactly what it consists of. For some it is restricted to issues that concern computer professionals, others see it broadly as encompassing the social impact of computers on society and the formulation and justification of policies controlling that use, others consider it confined specifically to issues raised by computer technology, and there are other views as well. We need not solve this issue of definition here. For our purposes we shall be interested in the moral or ethical issues raised by computers and information technology in business, including their impact on society, of which business is a part. Some, perhaps many of the issues might well be considered issues in business ethics. But there is no need to draw a sharp distinction between business ethics and computer ethics. Rather than being constrained by definitions we shall be guided by issues, problems, and the implication of technological development. Whatever name is given to the subfield of study, all the various specialized ethics are subordinate to general ethics. We are not faced with two different ethics – a general ethics by which we live our ordinary lives and a computer ethics or a business ethics by which we live our business or professional lives. We are not allowed to do in business or in technological development anything that we are not allowed to do in other realms. If lying, stealing, cheating, harming people are wrong in general, they are also wrong in business and in developing and applying technology. One of the advances made by those in medical ethics has been to make this claim clear. Doctors may not lie to patients any more than they may lie to others. Patients do not give up their human rights when they enter hospitals, any more than they give them up when they enter other environments. Workers remain human beings even when hired to do specific jobs. Lawyers are not permitted to do for their clients what it would be immoral or unethical for their clients to do for themselves. To call specialized discussion of ethical issues in certain domains biomedical or business or legal or computer ethics does not imply and should not be understood as providing license to act in ways that are otherwise unethical.

The ethical issues in business of the Industrial Age are those with which we are familiar, and track what can be called the logic of the Industrial Age. The development of the Information Age came about without conscious direction. It resulted as technology developed and came along as a handmaiden. One consequence is that society is following the technological imperative – what can be developed, is being developed and implemented. Because the transition to the Information Age is in the process of taking place and the ethical issues have not clearly jelled, there are few solutions. For they would be solutions in search of a problem. The task is to at least keep up with the developments and identify problems and potential problems before they cause great harm and before they become embedded ways of doing business, such that they are difficult to change.

There are two approaches to uncovering ethical issues. One is empirical or experiential and the other is logical or conceptual. In the first, we typically wait for problems to arise, practices to develop, and harm to be done. This gives rise to an ethical analysis, to judgments about the morality of the action or practices, and sometimes, if the harm is serious, to legislation. This method is essentially reactive, and it is the dominant approach we find in business ethics as well as in most other areas of life considered from a moral point of view.

The second is logical or conceptual. There are three typical ways it can be used. The first is to search for the logical presuppositions – in this case – the logically necessary values that underpin the practice or system. The second is to analyze the structure or organization and identify the crisis points at which problems are likely to occur so they can be anticipated. The third is to ask how values can be built into structures as they arise and develop.

Society in general could wait for ethical problems and injustices of the Information Age to arise, and do our analysis after the fact. Far preferable is to anticipate harm and injustice and prevent them from appearing, forming structures and developing practices that are ethically justifiable, rather than having to undo and attempt to reform structures and practices that are unfair, socially disruptive, and harmful to some of the parties. We of course cannot anticipate all the ethical issues that will arise, and experience and the empirical approach are also necessary. But the logical or conceptual route can take us farther than we might expect, and now is the time to start this analysis as we enter the Information Age. We do not need a new ethics, but we have to apply and possibly revise our ethical concepts and norms to fit the new environment. We need an imaginative analysis of the potential harms to people.

We can start by a simple analysis of information. A second step is to superimpose the analysis of information upon the analysis of industrialization to see how it changes production, exchange, advertising, conditions of employment, ownership rights, and so on. Each of these is transformed in the Information Age and the transformation requires new thinking about its effect on people.

Questions that immediately arise are: information of what or of whom and for what or for whom? Information about the world or scientific information is one kind of information; information about societies or social information is another kind; information about people and corporations is another kind. Important to all of them in an Information Age is ownership, and together with ownership is power. Information about individuals clearly raises the issue of privacy, and information about corporations leads to the comparable problems associated with trade secrecy and espionage. The issues of ownership are much more complicated than ownership with respect to industry. We have already seen how such an approach can yield some plausible appropriate virtues. As we shall see, we can similarly tease out applicable action guidelines and rules.

▲ RESPONSIBILITY AND ACCOUNTABILITY ▲

The responsibility of business with respect to computers varies depending on the business and the computer use. Nonetheless, businesses and the people who run them are ultimately responsible for anything that computers do or fail to do. Computers are not the kind of entity that can be responsible. Strictly speaking there is no such thing as a computer error. Computers may be down or non-functioning. People using computers may generate faulty reports, or documents, or records. The result may be an erroneous billing, or payment, or credit history. None of this is the fault of the computer but of the people who made the computer or the program that it is running or those who enter the data that it is manipulating. Who is liable may be difficult to determine, and a computer operator who wishes to claim that he or she is not at fault may blame the computer. At best this is a shorthanded way of saying that that individual feels no blame and accepts no responsibility for whatever happened or failed to happen.

Computers in some ways make it easier and in other ways make it more difficult to hold people and businesses responsible and accountable.

We briefly touched on moral responsibility with respect to the Y2K problem. We can, however, more fully develop the notion. To be morally responsible three conditions must be fulfilled. First there must be a causal connection between the agent in question and the result for which the person is held responsible. This is causal responsibility. If I accidentally break a lamp, I am causally responsible for it. The line of causal responsibility may be a long one. If I give an order to a subordinate, who in turn gives it to another subordinate and so on until finally the action is performed, the person performing the action and those who transmitted it are all part of the causal chain which originated with me. An object might also be the cause, and we might say the object was causally responsible for certain consequences. The volcano was responsible for destroying the village. The runaway car was responsible for killing the child. An error in the computer program was responsible for the mistaken bill. In the case of the volcano, we do not look for a person as the cause of the volcano's eruption. In the case of the runaway car and of the computer error, we might well look for a person as the cause. Who left the car in neutral without pulling the brake; who wrote the program with the error? Causal responsibility, however, is not enough for moral responsibility. Objects might be causally responsible for certain consequences, but they cannot be morally responsible because they are not moral actors. In addition to causal responsibility, the assigning of moral responsibility requires that the actor or agent perform the action knowingly and that the actor or agent perform the action willingly, where this means without force or coercion. Given these requirements, human beings can be and are held morally responsible for their actions. Corporations are also held morally responsible for their actions. Different people explain the corporation's responsibility in different ways. If one conceives the corporation as an entity that acts, then its actions can be morally evaluated. Corporations only act though the people who run them and work for them. Whether we construe talk about corporations as a shorthand way of talking about the people, individually and collectively, who make happen whatever it is that corporations do, or whether we construe the corporation as an entity that in its own right can be held morally responsible, in ordinary everyday speech people do make moral judgments about corporations and hold them morally responsible, whether or not that also means holding specific individuals within the corporation morally responsible. We need not resolve that issue here.

For our purposes two consequences follow. The first is that computers and information systems cannot be held morally responsible, even though we speak of them as causal agents and hence often view them as causally responsible for certain results. Those who build, program, run, own, and/or manage the computers or information systems are the only ones who can be held morally responsible for results. The second consequence is that corporations and the people in them can be held morally responsible for the consequences of actions of the corporation, whether done by computers or information systems or in any other way. How responsibility is distributed within the corporation for failures of harm caused is a separate issue. Sometimes it is worth pursuing this question, sometimes not.

Moral responsibility, like legal responsibility, can be diminished or one can be totally relieved of it by what are called excusing conditions. These are conditions that undermine in some way the three necessary conditions of moral responsibility. If one's place in the causal chain is insignificant, or if one can show that one was not in the causal chain at all, then one's responsibility for the outcome in question is either lessened or totally absent. If one can show that one could not know or that reasonable people could not be expected to know something essential in the performing of the action, that also removes or diminishes responsibility. Similarly, if one can show that one was not free – that one was forced by threat or psychological compulsion or some other factor – then one's responsibility is diminished or removed accordingly. In the area of computers and information technology excusing conditions are often given and are sometimes valid.

Closely related to responsibility are the notions of accountability and of liability. Accountability refers to the right people having to ask for an accounting or explanation or justification of those who are responsible either for actions that adversely influence them or for affairs over which they have control when acting for others, for example, as fiduciary agents. Liability refers to the fact that those who are responsible may be held to pay or otherwise make good for any damages their actions cause to others. A legal doctrine called *strict liability* in tort law holds that in certain circumstances excusing conditions do not apply to corporations, and that they are liable for the harm they do whether they intend it or foresee it or not. There is no comparable doctrine with respect to moral responsibility.

These notions apply to persons and corporations both in general and also with respect to computers and information systems. They also come into play in special and sometimes peculiar ways with respect to computers and information systems; and in some cases they are not called into play although there is no obvious reason why they should not be so called. In later chapters we shall deal with cases having to do with responsibility for the reliability of computer programs and information systems, and we shall see some of the difficulties that arise in attempting to assign responsibility in many complex information systems. We shall also deal with the liability or the lack thereof for harm done by the use of computer programs and information systems.

▲ HACKING, VIRUSES, AND WORMS ▲

There is little need to argue at length that the surreptitious intrusion of worms or viruses (which require a host program to which they are attached) into someone else's computer or system is unethical and morally wrong. General consensus has developed on this issue, and the consensus is based on the obvious fact that such programs cause harm to the users or owners of the computer or system that is infiltrated and attacked. The destruction of other people's work, of their files or data, is clearly destruction of property, and as such unethical. But even the intrusion of worms or viruses that do not do such damage and that, for instance, simply post an unexpected message at a certain time, are intrusions. Such intrusions are an invasion of privacy, a violation of property, and often entail the cost of verifying that no damage has been done, no files or data erased or changed – which costs time and often money. The destruction of someone else's property is sufficiently clearly unethical that it needs no long defense here, and the same is true of vandalism performed on the computer or via the computer. Yet the ethics of simple entry, without the intent to damage, has been defended by some in the computer field and deserves at least some discussion.

Surreptitious entry or unauthorized entry into another's computer or into a system is not an uncommon event. The image that often comes to mind is that of a hacker seeking entry into a corporate or government or university mainframe, sometimes simply to see if he or she can find a weakness in the system, and perhaps feel that he or she is better at computing than the experts who devised and tried to protect the system. Yet the instances of that are probably much less frequent than the instances of someone in an office who is curious about what is on the computer of a fellow worker, and who tries to guess that person's password to browse the contents of that computer when the colleague is away. The principle is the same, even though the expertise needed might be very different.

In all instances unauthorized entry violates the property rights of the owner of the computer or the system, often violates a person's privacy, and causes harm by raising uncertainty about whether any changes were made, logic bombs implanted that might explode in the future, or any other tampering that could cause problems.

In discussing these issues arguments are often made from analogy. They are useful to a large extent, but not always decisive, because the analogies do not hold completely. Passwords, for instance, are similar to keys and locks on doors in that they signify that the area is protected, private, and should not be entered by those unauthorized to do so. Locks on doors keep out honest people. They can be drilled, broken and the door destroyed by someone intent on entering. Windows that are locked can be broken. Yet we do not build our houses like steel cells or safes in order to keep out intruders. That would be too expensive, impractical, and not cost effective. Similarly, we do not place insurmountable electronic safeguards on all our computers or systems. Just as banks have steel safes to protect valuable assets, so they use strong protection to safeguard their accounts and their depositors' accounts. Both can be compromised. Yet we do not consider safecrackers and bank robbers heroes when they crack a bank safe or rob a bank, claiming that they have demonstrated the bank is vulnerable and needs to install better protection for what it wants to safeguard. Yet some people consider those who compromise computer networks or systems heroes who have shown that the networks or systems are vulnerable. By analogy, they are not. Although there is a difference between physically breaking into a bank or home and doing so electronically, both are unauthorized entry.

If a company or governmental agency wished to offer a reward to anyone who could crack its computer security system so that it would learn of possible weaknesses in the system, it could surely do so. Those who penetrated the system would deserve the reward. But unless invited to do so, those who try to enter have no right to do so and do not serve a social purpose or benefit the company or agency if they do penetrate. They have not been invited to do so, the entry is unwanted, and the service they supposedly do for the recipient is a service the recipient does not request and does not welcome. Yet some hackers persist in their belief that they are performing a valuable service by breaking into systems and discovering weaknesses, whether or not they report them and indicate how they achieved their feat so that others could not do so as well. The belief is a misplaced one. Often those who manage computers, networks, and systems know that they are vulnerable, just as ordinary people know their houses are vulnerable. But there are valid reasons for not building impregnable structures and there are valid reasons for not using impregnable electronic safeguards. The cost of doing so is one consideration. Another is the fact that any system devised by a human being for protection can probably be compromised by another human. Different levels of security are appropriate for different purposes and information. Local banks are not protected as well as Fort Knox. Office computers are not protected as well as FBI files. But this is simply a function of how much protection is deemed necessary, given the circumstances, money available, ease of use and access against which security must be balanced, and other relevant factors.

Just as everyone knows that a locked door indicates restricted access to those who legitimately have the key, so everyone should know that computers, systems, and networks that are protected by passwords, encryption, codes, or other devices indicate that entry is not permitted except to those authorized to enter.

The differences between physical entry into a physical space and entry into a computer or computer system are psychologically noteworthy. But they do not change the morality of the action. In physical entry one may be caught and there is the possibility of physical confrontation and perhaps violence, either on the part of the intruder or of the owner or occupant or others, including the police. This danger is not present in computer entry, where there is no physical confrontation or possible physical violence. The chance of being caught is often less than in a physical entry, one can withdraw by the press of a key on a keyboard, and one leaves not even a footprint. This may explain in part why some consider electronic entry less bad than physical entry, especially when there is no intent to do damage and where one does no damage, just sees if he or she is clever enough to enter or perhaps, out of curiosity, looks around to see where someone has surfed the Web, or what they have stored in their e-mail, or how far along they are on their report.

The final argument of the hacker is that there are some computer sites – governmental, corporate, perhaps those of banks and financial institutions – about which people in general have an interest in their being secure. If a hacker finds that one of them is not, then the only way that he or she can often get the owners of the system to make the system secure is to demonstrate that it is not so. Actually entering a site is convincing evidence of its vulnerability. Let us grant that not all systems are as secure as they should be. And let us grant that it is appropriate to insist that all such sites be as secure as appropriate. Yet it is unlikely that the only way to effect such security is by breaking into the site, and it is unlikely that this is the actual motive of the hackers who attempt to – and sometimes succeed in – doing so. If it were, then the rules that justify civil disobedience would apply, namely that the person be willing to make the act public, accept public responsibility for it, and be willing to suffer the consequences of his or her action. If the failure threatened public safety or the safety of individuals and those responsible did nothing in response to claimed vulnerabilities, then making that public through the media or reporting it to government would be the more appropriate way of dealing with it and getting a satisfactory resolution, namely correction of the defect.

The MACIT plays a role in at least some people's feeling that such entry is not so bad, and in some people's feeling that it is not bad or unethical at all. But the myth provides no justification, and the arguments given in defense of such action do not serve as justifications.

In the chapters that follow we shall examine in greater detail some of the issues we have touched upon in this chapter, as well as many others. Throughout, unmasking the Myth of Amoral Computing and Information Technology will be an abiding concern.

▲ NOTES ▲

1. For details on the Y2K problem and the way it was treated before the change of the millennium, see "Y2K Resources," from the Oregon State University Extension Service, at http://www.orst.edu/extension/y2k/

2. This was the Gartner Group's widely reported estimate. See, for example, Lee Gomes, "Why Prepping Mainframes for 2000 Is So Tough," *Wall Street Journal*, December 9, 1996, p. B1.

3. Lynda Radosevich, "Millennium Bug Already Taking its Toll," *Info World*, January 12, 1998, vol. 20, 2, p. 19.

chapter two

Marketing, Privacy, and the Protection of Personal Information

INFORMATION PRIVACY AND LOTUS MARKETPLACE: INDIVIDUALS

In April 1990 Lotus Development Corporation announced that it had joined with Equifax Inc., a consumer information company, and that it planned to release a new product called Lotus Marketplace: Households. The Equifax company collects and sells credit and other consumer information, and is one of several such companies that routinely supply information for people who apply for bank loans, credit cards, and mortgages. The company has records on approximately 120 million individuals and households. It routinely sells information about these people to lenders as well as to large corporations interested in marketing a product to a particular segment of the population. Equifax sells appropriately segmented lists of people with characteristics that fit the profiles the marketers desire.

Lotus Marketplace: Households aimed to make this list of 120 million potential customers, previously available only to large corporations, available to small and medium-size businesses. Such businesses, of course, could not use the whole database of 120 million people. Lotus Marketplace: Households would sell a compact disk containing a program and a preselected list of 5,000 names for $695.00. It would charge $400 for each additional 5,000 names. Information on individuals included information based on actual information and inferred information. Sources included information collected from credit card and loan applications and inferred from census data and zip code plus four postal listings, from surveys at 8,500 shopping centers and retailers, and from information provided on product registration cards, from magazine subscriptions, and from a variety of other sources. Included were the individual's name, address, marital status, gender (inferred from the person's first name), average neighborhood incomes, plus demographic and prior-purchasing data. The program developed fifty "psychographic" categories, such as "accumulated wealth" and "mobile home families." The user could choose any of the fifty categories and from the database of names the user had purchased could generate a mailing list of people who fit that category. It would not be possible to input a particular name and retrieve information about that person. Lotus intended to sell the program to small businesses and nonprofit organizations.

It is already possible to get an individual's address and telephone number and to locate the person's residence on a map by using search programs available on the World Wide Web.

An article in the *Wall Street Journal* on November 13, 1990, reported on the product, and shortly thereafter a campaign was mounted via the Internet protesting the planned product. Lotus received more than 30,000 requests from people asking to have their names removed from the list, and a corresponding number of complaints and expressions of fear about how the product might be used. The general claim was that the product constituted an invasion of the privacy of those people whose names were included in the list. The arguments were multiple. First, although it was possible to ask to have one's name removed, most people would not know that their names were included or would not know about the product and so could not ask to have their names removed. Second, even if one asked to have one's name removed after the product was made available, one's name might already have been sold. Third, the company could not adequately control who would have access to the lists. Lotus might intend to sell the product only to legitimate businesses and nonprofit organizations that intended to use it for legitimate purposes, such as mail solicitations for their products. But Lotus could not guarantee how the lists would be used or who might gain access to them, and could not guarantee the lists might not be used to harm those on it in some way. Fourth, there was some fear that once such a product became available, other firms would compete by producing lists with more and more personal information included, and the potential for invasion of privacy and harm would greatly increase.

On January 24, 1991, Lotus announced that it had canceled

Lotus Marketplace: Households because of consumer complaints and the unexpected cost of adequately addressing consumer privacy issues.

Nonetheless, such compilations of and extrapolations from information about individuals is not illegal, they are already purchased by large corporations, and another company might well make such a product available at any time.

The case raises at least two issues. First, did the product pose a potential violation of privacy, and, if so, why? Second, did Lotus Marketplace: Households threaten Americans in some other way? The reaction of 30,000 people out of 120,000,000 may show the fear of some people, or the power of the Internet in generating a protest, or a misperception of what the product could do, or a well-grounded fear of privacy violation.

Since 1990 other similar attempts at compiling and selling information from huge databases on individuals for marketing purposes have generated similar protests, including the celebrated Double-Click case, which we shall examine in another chapter. Although the protests are frequently mounted and reported in terms of violations or potential violations of privacy, there is actually much more involved. As a result of overuse, the concept of privacy is either diminished in importance or it is confusingly expanded to include breaches of confidentiality, failure to secure informed consent, loss of anonymity, and potential or actual harms of various kinds. Part of the overuse and expansion stems from the fact that the concept of privacy is far from clear. It varies from society to society and to some extent from time to time; it is seen as the opposite of publicity, while in fact the two are often intertwined; it is often confused with anonymity; and it has been used in such a way as to justify such disparate issues as the right to abortion on the one hand and the defense of personal information on the other.

As an example of the complexity of the issues, consider the simple case of one's name. Is the fact that I have a certain name a public fact or is it somehow a private one, such that I have ownership rights in it or privacy rights with respect to it? Obviously, we are each named at birth, and that forms part of the public record. Our name is the way in which we are identified for social purposes. Yet not everyone has a right to know our name. If someone approaches us on the street (and so in public) and asks our name, we are under no obligation to provide it. Part of the reason might be that the request is a violation of our privacy; a stronger reason might be that we are under no obligation to answer questions from strangers, or even from friends and acquaintances. If someone asks me the name of someone else whom they point out or identify, I do not necessarily violate that person's privacy by giving the inquirer his or her name. I may have other reasons not to do so, but privacy is not necessarily one of them. If I make a purchase and the clerk asks for my name and address to put on the receipt for the cash I paid, I may refuse to give it. A condition of most purchases is not that I identify myself. I may purchase most items anonymously. The vendor may want my name and address to notify me in case of defects in the item I purchase, or to use for marketing purposes. But I am under no obligation to reveal this, even though my name is not a secret and is public in at least some sense, and even though my address is accessible in the phone book, and to that extent public. Clearly, that my name and address are in some ways publicly available does not mean that I must supply them to anyone who wants them. Nor, on the other hand, does it mean that anyone who accesses them violates my privacy. If I then add additional information about myself that is also in some sense public, does the compilation come to violate my privacy? If so, how? Much of the information compiled for Lotus Marketplace: Households was of this type. Even if the compilation does not violate my privacy, however, it may pose threats to me in other ways. Hence, insisting only on privacy may not accomplish the goal of protection from a variety of harms that people in fact implicitly desire.

▲ THE CONCEPT OF PRIVACY ▲

Privacy, we have already noted, is not a clear notion. There are many versions of what it means, and the claims made with respect to it vary depending on circumstances, purpose, and culture. Although often referred to as a right, it is not always clear what kind of right it is or against whom it is exercised. Sometimes "private" is opposed to "public." There is considerable confusion about what privacy means; and there is also disagreement about its importance. There is a great deal of ambiguity in many of the claims made in the name of privacy and much more is claimed in its name than can be successfully justified. Hence many issues dealing with privacy in the business arena are contentious. In one way or another privacy considerations enter in business relations with employees, customers, potential customers, clients, competitors, government, and the general public. The development of computer technology has made possible the accumulation and correlation of vast amounts of data on each individual, which in turn has affected both the general public's (and business's) view of privacy, and the issues of protection of personal information.

The notion of privacy is to some extent relative to one's culture. What is right or wrong, good or bad, with respect to privacy is hence in part culturally determined, and how privacy claims are interpreted and applied in different societies depends on cultural expectations, history, accepted practices, existing law, and other factors. Different societies have different views about what constitutes privacy, about how important it is, and about how much it needs or deserves protection. Americans often think of themselves as valuing privacy highly, more so than many other societies, because of the American tradition of rugged individualism. Individuals could start afresh and were not bogged down by their class position, and they were not necessarily identified as the son or daughter of so-and-so. Whether they do in fact value it highly has become open to question. Although there is growing concern about privacy among some people in the United States, there are others who seem content to give up or freely give away a good deal of their privacy.[1]

In order to determine with some consistency which practices do and which do not violate privacy, and so to provide a reasonable basis for business practices as well as for possible legislation and social policy, we should get some clear notion of the concept of privacy, an answer to the question of why privacy is important, and a determination as to the status of the claimed right to privacy. A reasonable place to begin might seem to be the law. But, as we shall see, it provides a sometimes confusing and unclear characterization of both the concept of privacy and the justification for the right to privacy.

We can start by noting that the Universal Declaration of Human Rights in Article 12 states "No one shall be subjected to arbitrary interference with his privacy, family, home or correspondence, nor to attacks upon his honour and reputation. Everyone has the right to the protection of the law against such interference or attacks."[2] This is taken as an affirmation of the human right to privacy, as well as of other rights. The right to privacy thus has international standing. But exactly what privacy means here is left undefined, and it is open to interpretation by different legislatures in different societies.

In the US legal tradition the right to privacy is a late comer. The term is not mentioned in the Constitution. In 1890 Samuel D. Warren and Louis D. Brandeis wrote an influential article in the *Harvard Law Review*, "The Right to Privacy."[3] They claim that the right to life was gradually broadened to the right to enjoy life, which they equate with what Judge Cooley called "the right to be let alone." The concern of both the authors and of Judge Cooley was with invasions of privacy by newspapers. "These considerations lead," they say, "to the conclusion that the protection afforded to thoughts, sentiments, and emotions, expressed through the medium of writing or of the arts, so far as it consists in preventing publication, is merely an instance of the more general right of the individual to be let alone" (ibid: 205). This first attempt to define privacy, although couched in terms of being let alone, is concerned almost exclusively with what newspapers may and may not legitimately publish concerning individuals. Although the legal view on this has evolved, this starting point is significant.

The two landmark Supreme Court cases dealing with privacy concern a different aspect or kind of privacy. *Griswold v. Connecticut*,[4] which deals with birth control and doctor–patient relations, argues that "the First Amendment has a penumbra where privacy is protected from governmental intrusion" (ibid: 483) and "The Fourth and Fifth Amendments [provide] . . . protection against all governmental invasions 'of the sanctity of a man's home and the privacies of life'" (ibid: 484). Justice Goldberg, concurring, adds the Ninth (and later the Fourteenth) Amendment as a basis for saying the Connecticut law intrudes upon "the right of marital privacy" (ibid: 486). The Supreme Court did not say anything about the privacy of unmarried persons, and continued to allow states to forbid "extramarital sexuality," among other acts. Justice Black, on the other hand, wrote in his dissenting opinion: "I get nowhere in this case by talk about a constitutional 'right of privacy' as an emanation from one or more constitutional provisions. I like my privacy as well as the next, but I am nevertheless compelled to admit that government has a right to invade it unless prohibited by some specific constitutional provision" (ibid: 509–10); and Justice Stewart in his dissent says, "With all deference, I can find no such general right of privacy in the Bill of Rights, in any other part of the Constitution, or in any case ever decided by this Court" (ibid: 530).

The 1973 decision of *Roe v. Wade*,[5] dealing with abortion, adds a different dimension to the Constitutional protection of privacy.

Pointing to past Court decisions it states: "These decisions make it clear that only personal rights that can be deemed 'fundamental' or 'implicit in the concept of ordered liberty' . . . are included in this guarantee of personal privacy. They also make it clear that the right has some extension to activities relating to marriage . . . ; procreation . . . ; contraception . . . ; family relationships . . . ; and child rearing and education" (ibid: 152–3). This includes "a woman's decision whether or not to terminate her pregnancy" (ibid: 153), which nonetheless "acknowledges that some state regulation in areas protected by that right is appropriate" (ibid: 154). Nonetheless, Justice Rehnquist, dissenting, writes, "I have difficulty in concluding, as the Court does, that the right of 'privacy' is involved in this case . . . Nor is the 'privacy' that the Court finds here even a distant relative of the freedom from searches and seizures protected by the Fourth Amendment to the Constitution . . . If the Court means by the term 'privacy' no more than that the claim of a person to be free from unwanted state regulation of consensual transactions may be a form of 'liberty' protected by the Fourteenth Amendment, there is no doubt that similar claims have been upheld in our earlier decisions on the basis of that liberty" (ibid: 172).

While these decisions establish a constitutional right to privacy, the exact nature of that right beyond the specific issues decided by the cases is far from clear. Based on the Court's decisions, privacy, like most of the rights in the Bill of Rights, is a right against government – in this case government interference of some sort. They cluster around marriage, sex, and abortion, and rule that these areas of life and decisions individuals make and actions they perform in these areas, within certain limits, are protected from interference from the government.

The philosophical literature on privacy exhibits some of the same difficulties reflected in the legal cases. Some of the Supreme Court justices fail to find privacy in the Constitution, but readily grant the other protections contained therein and sometimes feel that these are sufficient to provide the protection the majority seems to desire for the case in question. Likewise, some philosophers, such as Judith Jarvis Thomson,[6] hold that whatever we wish to protect by any claimed right to privacy can be protected by some other right or cluster of rights. Hence, we really gain nothing by referring to the right to privacy. Many others disagree.[7] But there is no consensus on exactly what the right to privacy is, what it protects or prohibits, what its justification is, and so how it supplies a principled basis for legislation or social policy.

That philosophers and other theorists disagree on the specifics of the right reflects what one finds in the popular media, as well as in both state and federal legislation.[8]

Part of the problem is that the term "privacy" is often used to cover too much. It needs to be distinguished from a number of other concepts with which it tends to overlap to some extent: intimacy, anonymity, and confidentiality, among others. Various attempts at defining privacy have been made and found wanting. The claim that it is the right to be let alone is clearly much too broad, for there are many instances in which we are not let alone by others or by government and in which our privacy is not violated. Some try to define privacy in terms of knowledge or information about oneself. W. A. Parent, for example, defends the claim that privacy is the absence of undocumented knowledge about a person,[9] and others similarly try to define privacy in terms of information about oneself.[10] While I shall argue for personal information privacy, it is by no means clear how the above Supreme Court decisions on the right to privacy *vis-à-vis* one's use of contraception or abortion involves information. It is not that one's right is violated if someone or if the government finds out what one does or decides. It is rather that one is free to make these decisions and to act on them without government interference, and that one's privacy is violated by any intrusion on the decision or the act. That this freedom right is said to involve privacy, if it makes sense, is to say more than that privacy consist in some form of knowledge.

Others attempt to define privacy in terms of control, either control of information about oneself or control of access to oneself.[11] Yet control is too strong, either with respect to information about us or access to ourselves, for when we are in public we cannot control what others know, see, or learn about us, nor can we control visual or other kinds of access to ourselves. Nevertheless, people do not thereby violate our privacy.

For purposes of discussing issues of privacy and business it will be helpful to distinguish different kinds or realms of privacy and then see if there is anything they all have in common. I shall distinguish six kinds of privacy. Since the concept itself is not clear, the six kinds are not mutually exclusive and some privacy claims may come under more than one of them. I shall call them space privacy, body/mental privacy, personal information privacy, communication privacy, personal privacy, and cyber privacy.

By *space privacy* I mean those claims that people often make concerning the inviolability or protection of their space from intrusion. It is in this sense that one may make privacy claims with respect to one's desk or drawers or file cabinet or office or room or home. The intrusion may be an individual's opening or tampering with what is within my private space; but it may be a claimed right to freedom from eavesdropping or peeping toms or from observation. If I have my drapes open and you look into my home in passing, it is not clear whether you violate my privacy, even though it is my home. If I pull my drapes and you come up to the window and peek through a small crack not completely covered by the drapes, you clearly intend to intrude upon space that I have intended to protect from observation by others. Yet clearly my claim to privacy is not violated by those within the room. Only those outside the room are excluded. If it is my space, then I may share it with whomever I choose, and they do not violate my claim to privacy by being in the room.

Do I violate my host's privacy by opening up the medicine cabinet in the bathroom when using the toilet? Some would say yes, others no. The medicine cabinet is usually not locked, may be ajar, and the convention is not entirely clear. The guest has been given access to the room. Knowing this, is it up to the host to remove objects that he or she does not want seen? If one looks through the medicine cabinet to discover medicines or similar items that the host has not revealed to the person, then the intent is to go beyond what the host wishes to reveal and so is intended to be a violation of privacy.

The right to space privacy, just as the right to any other variety of privacy, is alienable. Similarly, the right to space privacy, just as the right to any other variety of privacy, is not absolute and may be overridden by other rights and possibly by strong pertinent interests on the part of the state or of an employer *vis-à-vis* an employee, for instance. Whether my computer is like my desk drawer or my file cabinet, whether accessing it and simply looking violates my privacy, and whether that violation is a violation of space privacy, are at this stage open issues.[12]

Body/mental privacy refers to claims made about privacy with respect to one's body and mind. Modesty in our society includes keeping covered our sex organs or "private parts." This is a requirement in most areas of public life. But it is also something that most

Americans consider their right. They cannot be asked or required to expose themselves or parts of their bodies to others. They claim the right to privacy when it comes to bodily functions, as well as such private acts as sexual acts. These are to be done in private, unless all involved agree otherwise. It is not that there is anything wrong or shameful, for instance, in sexual intercourse between a married couple. It is not anything that is to be kept secret. These considerations may apply in some circumstances, but they are by no means necessary for claims of privacy. With respect to body privacy Americans in some situations are different from the Japanese, for instance, for whom public baths with both sexes are normal, unlike the view taken by most Americans. One complaint voiced by some Americans against drug testing is that it violates their privacy because it requires viewing by an inspector as the person gives a urine sample. Similarly, body searches are considered by many demeaning and an invasion of their privacy.

Also included in body/mental privacy is the claimed right to keep one's thoughts and feelings private or secret, unless one chooses to expose them to certain or to all others. Such a notion of privacy comes close to claims of bodily integrity and to respect for one's person. We are importantly what we think and feel and any attempt to invade these areas invades our person. We protect ourselves against such invasions to some extent by the privacy claims we make in these areas. One objection to polygraph or lie detector tests is that the machine monitors one's biochemical reactions and to that extent is an intrusion into the privacy of one's body, although the intent is to determine the truth of one's statements.

Space and body privacy sometimes overlap. On a very crowded subway one's space is extremely limited and bodies are crushed together. Yet even in this situation there is a marked difference between being squeezed between people and rubbing or touching that is not the result of the lack of space. As the subway car becomes less crowded, there is no longer justification for anyone to remain squeezed next to another and one rightly expects to have one's own space, limited though it be and public though it be.

The third kind is *personal information privacy*. This concerns certain information about oneself. The general claim that one has a right to control information about oneself is an overstatement, for what one does in public is public and one cannot claim that information about what one does in public is properly considered private. Much information about oneself is part of the public record.

One's birth is recorded and is part of the public record as are other aspects of one's life – one's marriage, one's ownership of real estate, or one's criminal record. The public nature of such records are necessary to carry on various activities of social and public life. What is reported about one in the newspaper is public and, if it is accurate, one cannot claim control over it or limit access to it. Much other information about ourselves is public in the sense that it is information people have of us who have observed us in public. That information is as much their as it is ours. There is in addition information that we willingly and knowingly reveal about ourselves and make public in one way or another. Nonetheless there are many areas of oneself and of one's life that we can limit access to information about and it is in these areas that claims to information privacy make sense. Under usual circumstances we are not required to reveal more about ourselves than we wish. And we often reveal some things about ourselves with the expectation or the requirement that they will be kept confidential and will not be divulged to others, will not be used for purposes other than the ones we specify, and will not be made public. This is what is usually intended by the right to control information about ourselves. But this is limited to that information that we can legitimately keep secret or not reveal if we do not wish. It cannot cover information that is public or that we make public. How we do and how we should draw the line between public and private is a topic I shall deal with later in this chapter.

Closely related to information privacy is *communication privacy*. As the name implies, this covers claims about the privacy of communication between and among individuals. I may convey my thoughts and my feelings to others, and just as my thoughts and feelings are mine and private, so my communication of them is private. I may reveal them to whom I choose and I may conceal them from whom I choose. I may also communicate information. Communication privacy might cover all the ways in which I communicate, as well as what I communicate. Of course, if I communicate publicly, then I cannot claim any privacy rights. In the United States there are laws that forbid anyone from tampering with, including unauthorized opening of, anyone else's mail, or listening in on their telephone conversations. Yet there are many grey areas here as well. Is my privacy violated if someone overhears my telephone conversation made from a public telephone or if people at the table next to mine in a restaurant overhear my conversation with a friend or business associate? Eavesdropping invades my privacy, just as wiretapping does; overhearing usually does not, even though one can pay more or less attention to what one overhears and the line between eavesdropping and attentively overhearing may not always be sharp. The use of electronic devices to listen to our conversations through walls or great distances is illegal. Yet it is not illegal to overhear a loud conversation; nor is it illegal to capture a radio transmission, even if that transmission is a cell phone conversation carried via radio waves; or to look at e-mail en route through one computer to another that passes through our computer. The issues of what should and should not be legally allowed, what is and is not ethical, in the area of communication via new electronic sources are yet to be adequately addressed.

The fifth kind of privacy, *personal privacy*, refers to the claim that our lives are our own and that we can appropriately compartmentalize our lives with respect to others. What I do at work is in large part public with respect to the firm employing me, but might appropriately be considered private by my employer with respect to its competitors. On the other hand, what I do off the job, if it in no way affects my job performance, I might consider private, in the sense that it need not be made known to my employer, that my employer has no right to know it, and if by chance my employer learns something about my non-job related activities off the job, such information should be considered irrelevant to any decisions made about my advancement within or retention by the company.

I appropriately reveal certain aspects of my life to close friends and do so in the reasonable expectation that they will not divulge revelations made in confidence or experiences shared in private. I reveal more of myself to my family, and spouses typically reveal themselves more to each other than to others. American law recognizes this special and privileged relation insofar as spouses cannot be forced to testify against one another in a court of law, as well as in *Griswold*. I may choose to reveal different facts about myself and show different facets of myself to different people and groups, and choose to keep other facts unrevealed. This is part of what makes possible certain relations with some people and in some settings and which enables us to lead rich and varied lives. As with body privacy, it is not necessary that I have anything to hide or of which I am ashamed, nor is it necessary that I wish to keep certain things about me secret. Rather, certain self-revelations are appropriate to some people and not to others. Those others not only have no right to know or see or participate, but also some relations are best kept relatively impersonal. Personal privacy here overlaps with information privacy, body privacy, and space privacy, but it is not reducible to them. As with the other varieties of privacy, there are more or less clear cases, but also much unclarity as to where to draw the line. Those who admit that one's employer has no right to know many aspects of one's private life off the job may not be entirely sure about what aspects of one's life off the job may affect one's job performance or the reputation of the company for which one works.[13]

The sixth kind of privacy can be called *cyber privacy*. It is similar in some ways to the other kinds of privacy and yet requires a category of it own since it raises special kinds of issues. When we speak of space privacy or body privacy, we refer to physical space. Cyberspace is not physical, and the conventions that divide the public sphere and the private sphere in cyberspace are different from those that divide them in physical space. In most regards the conventions are still being determined. What is public and what is private in cyberspace do not match up well or closely with physical space. When I shop in stores in physical space, what I do is public if they can be viewed by anyone who happens to be in the area. When I shop online from the supposed privacy of my home, my actions are neither private nor public in the usual sense. I am in the privacy of my physical space, but my actions take place in cyberspace, which is neither public nor private space in the ordinary meaning of those terms. What is public and what is private in cyberspace requires not only arguing by analogy, but also realizing that there are real differences that require new analysis and thought and discussion.

What do all of these kinds of privacy have in common? The common feature is a claim that we may choose to reveal or not to reveal certain portions of ourselves, of information about us, of our communications, and of our thoughts. Hence we can define privacy as the state of limited access to certain aspects of ourselves or to areas of our lives that we set and enjoy in order to preserve them from unwanted intrusion. This provides both the necessary and the sufficient conditions for privacy claims. This is the central core of privacy. Unwanted intrusion beyond the limits we set constitutes a violation of our privacy. We set the limits either explicitly, e.g, by posting a "Private" sign on a door, or conventionally, e.g., by drawing the shades in a room.

Privacy applies to persons but the adjective "private" applies also to things, such as private property, a private hospital room, a private house, a private house, a private diary, and so on, to which access by others is limited by the person whose thing it is. What differentiates the different kinds of privacy are the different additional specific claims and protections that each kind requires. Privacy is basic and we ask how much privacy it is reasonable to give up for various reasons.

The right to privacy is the right to set limits on access to ourselves. Intrusions beyond the limits by others or by government have to be justified. The notion of privacy is similar to the notion of property, in which the different kinds of property are marked out by a different bundle of rights, despite a central core of ownership common to them all. What the Supreme Court called "marital privacy" in *Griswold* is a combination of personal, body/mental and space privacy. The penumbra of rights that the justices referred to that emerge from the Bill of Rights includes in its shadow different kinds of privacy rights. The Fourth Amendment's protection from unreasonable search overlaps with the claims of space and body/mental privacy. The right to such privacy might even be used to defend the right to unreasonable search, rather than the other way around. But since the Fourth Amendment refers primarily to search by the government, it does not extend as far as the rights to space and body/mental privacy which extend as well, for instance, to businesses and other people.

Although privacy is a state, it is a relational one. It involves one person (a) setting limits on access by others (b) with respect to some domain (c). Privacy also admits of degrees. One can have more or less privacy, and be more or less secure in one's privacy.

This definition is descriptive, insofar as it claims to capture the way the term is generally used at least in most clear cases. It is initially neutral. However, when one makes a claim to a right to privacy, if justifiable, that claim is prescriptive, since it carves out an area that others are not to violate and imposes on them an obligation not to violate it.

▲ THE JUSTIFICATION OF THE RIGHT ▲ TO PRIVACY

To be an actual rather than a manifesto right a rights-claim must be defensible. A moral right is defended on moral grounds, a legal or civil right is written into law. Each right imposes an obligation on others to act in a certain way, either positively or negatively. How can we defend the claim of a moral right to privacy?

The arguments in support of the right to privacy divide into intrinsic and instrumental, and in both groups there are deontological and consequentialist variations.

The strongest argument holds that privacy is an essential component of respect for persons. To respect a person is to see that person as a center of value in himself, as someone who is to be treated as an end in himself and never as a means only. This Kantian formulation is the starting point. To treat someone as an end is to see them as having the right to hold their own beliefs and opinions and to make their own decisions, for which they are held accountable. What it is to be a person is to develop as an end in oneself. One's thoughts and decisions help make one what one is. Any attempt to manipulate them is an affront both to one's autonomy and is to treat one as a means only. But this means that persons must be accorded the right to determine what they will reveal and what they will not reveal about themselves – about their thoughts, feelings, inner lives – to others. This is what the right to privacy involves. The formulation in terms of body/mental privacy and of communication privacy is easily stated in these terms.

Moreover, since we are social beings and in need of social contact and intimacy,[14] part of our development as persons is tied to our relations to others. What differentiate relationships to a large extent are the ways in which and the extent to which one person reveals or makes himself available to another. The right to develop these relations based on self-revelation to some and not to others is again part of what we wish to achieve by claims to the right to privacy. Some of what we wish is also the freedom to act as we choose so long as it does not harm others, a basic right that goes with our being ends in ourselves and worthy of respect. By recognizing personal privacy we recognize that personal relations are important to an individual's being what he or she is and that persons have a right to limit the extent to which they are available to others – to strangers, to government, to casual acquaintances, on the one hand, and to family members, friends, and associates on the other. Each of the relations is different, and each involves a different degree of access accorded by the person to others. The Supreme Court in referring to marital privacy simply affirmed what is generally acknowledged, namely, that marriage is a special relationship in which the partners reveal and allow access to themselves in ways and to an extent that they do not typically do to others. For that relation to flourish, marital privacy – the way the partners interrelate, share their lives, and work through their problems – is seen as necessary. Without such privacy marriage would simply not be the kind of institution that it has traditionally been recognized as being. A similar sort of claim can be made with respect to the family and to close friends.

Privacy allows one the opportunity to try on different personas, to entertain a variety of hopes and dreams that one may legitimately keep to oneself or that one may share with another or with a small number of others. Privacy allows one the possibility of failing, or practicing, of deciding whom or what one wants to be, without acting that out in public and being held to the public consequences until one chooses to do so. Privacy allows one to escape the constant scrutiny and evaluation by others, to relax and recharge one's energies. All of these are ingredients in treating persons as ends in themselves and are arguably necessary for developing as a complete person.

The peeping tom may do one no harm, yet the one spied upon rightly complains of a violation of privacy. One is being used as a means by the voyeur, and to that extent the person's value and dignity are denied. This is an intrinsic argument for privacy. Though couched in Kantian language, a consequentialist argument can also be given in its defense as intrinsic. The peeping tom causes no harm, but peeping toms deny us the privacy we need to be ourselves. If we feel we are being viewed by another, we may well act differently, and be inhibited by the viewing by the other in a way that restricts us and confines us without justification.

This basic analysis can be applied to all six types of privacy. To the extent that the different kinds of privacy are seen as different bundles of rights, just as the right to property can be seen as different kinds of rights that go with different kinds of ownership, we can derive the appropriate aspect of these bundles from other generally acknowledged rights.

Based on the notion of respect for persons, we can legitimately claim the right to the greatest amount of privacy for each necessary to develop and function as a complete person compatible with the demands of social interaction.

Extrinsic arguments for privacy tend to be of two kinds. One looks at the results of violations of privacy as we have presented them. The other looks at the results of actions that many people claim violate privacy, and may do so, but are also condemned for other reasons as well. It is arguments of the second type that lead the dissenting Justices in the cases we mentioned, and philosophers such as Judith Jarvis Thomson, to question the need for the claimed right to privacy.

Arguments of the first type are most dramatically presented in novels such as *1984*, in which the state, through its surveillance, attempts to control all the aspects of the lives of those subject to its authority. The result of such surveillance is the inhibition of anything that the state or that one's fellow citizens might consider inappropriate, the squelching of originality, innovation, spontaneity, and ultimately personal value. Without any zones of privacy, people and their lives are externalized, as are all values. If this point is conceded, then the need for privacy is acknowledged and the harm to individuals and to society that result from its absence follows. What remains is to discuss the degree to which privacy is necessary, and the means that lead to infringement of personal development and personality, that undermine the values of families and friendship, that destroy personal relationships. Some take the strong line that any steps in this direction are to be resisted. Others argue that some encroachment on privacy is tolerable with the resulting damage that we have described, and that there may be reasons for acceding to such encroachment.

The other line of defense says that for any abridgement of the supposed right to privacy, we can find some other reason to condemn that action without invoking the right to privacy. Failure to respect one's space or body results in harm or threatened harm, and we have the right not to be harmed. Divulging private information about a person can ruin his or her reputation, which is surely a harm; and identity theft which can result from misappropriating personal information is equally a harm that can be condemned and an activity that should be illegal. On this view identity theft causes personal harm and is also a form of theft. These are better and stronger reasons, critics claim, for condemning it than claiming that it is a violation of one's right to personal information privacy. We have as well the right to development, the right to freedom of expression, the right to freedom of association, all of which are related to or considered parts of different kinds of the right to privacy, and in fact make the right to privacy unnecessary.

This last argument is too strong if it is taken to show that there is no right to privacy. For it does not touch those arguments in which the intrinsic right to privacy is at stake, and no harm or other ill is threatened or actual. But it can be correctly taken to point out that sometimes a violation of privacy is also a violation of another right as well, and that sometimes what is claimed to be a violation of the right to privacy is in fact a violation of that other right. As we have noted, sometimes this other right, such as the right not to be harmed, is taken to be included in the right to privacy itself.

The right to privacy is only prima facie and may come up against other prima facie rights. When it does, we cannot say in advance which of the two will carry more weight, even though some, such as the right to life, are generally much stronger rights than other less basic and derived rights. But the point of the right to privacy is to throw the burden of proof on those who would violate the limits of access to us that we wish to assert or maintain. Our right to set limits might be overridden by the common good,[15] the rights of others, or the fact that we have in fact allowed access. The right to privacy is alienable, in that we can give it up on occasion for various reasons, and we can give up more or less of it as we choose. But it is reasonable to give it up only in return for certain benefits – liberty, security, comfort, intimacy, financial gain, among others. How we weigh these is a matter of debate, and makes legislation in this area often contentious.

An important point is that we must often give up some of our right to privacy if we are to achieve certain ends that we wish. If we wish easy access to credit, then we have to give up the right not to reveal information about our credit history, financial status, income, and related matters. We may make such revelations only partially public, and restrict their being passed on to any one other than the person to whom we reveal them. But that will not usually provide quick and easy access to credit. To obtain that the information must be more widely shared and made accessible to the variety of parties who may extend us credit or who need that information to serve us in other related ways. How much we reveal for one purpose that is used for another is an issue we must address. But clearly there are trade-offs. A complete hermit might reveal almost nothing about himself, including keeping himself from public view to the greatest extent possible. But that drastically restricts his social interactions. These require a certain amount of publicity and the voluntary giving up of our right to limit access to our bodies or our thoughts or our communications.

Several other arguments in defense of restricting access to information about ourselves have been proposed. One is that we have property rights in our body, and that we have the right to control information about us, perhaps because we own it. But the argument does not hold up well. Much of the information about myself, for instance about my transactions with others, is owned with as much right by them, unless we negotiate otherwise. That I buy certain products at a supermarket is as much information that belongs to the supermarket as it does to me. If I charge my items on a credit card, the information about my charges belongs as much to the credit card company as it does to me. To claim otherwise needs an argument that has not yet been forthcoming. If I meet someone on the street that information belongs as much to the other person as it does to me. Claiming that I have the right to control information about me is correct only up to the point at which it belongs only to me in the sense that it is mine to reveal or not reveal. It is not relational with respect to others. My thoughts and feelings fall into this category, as well as what I do when alone. This information belongs to me and I may choose not to reveal it. I have that right.

If we accept my arguments in principle, understanding that they have to be filled out to make the case, does all of this yield any principles by which we can judge specific cases? Although the answer is yes, it is doubtful that the right to limit access to oneself (or the right to privacy) provides support for all of what most people want with respect to the protection of personal information and communication.

To deal adequately with these we need to distinguish the public realm from the private realm and join the right to privacy with the right not to be harmed, to anonymity, to informed consent, to the honoring of contacts (and with it the honoring of explicit or implied confidentiality), with which the right to privacy is related and with which it is often conflated.

▲ PUBLIC AND PRIVATE ▲

What is public and what is private is often not clear and drawing a clean line between them is not possible because they are based on conventions that are often fuzzy and are understood differently by different participants in the variety of practices at issue. The distinction itself sometimes gets confused with the distinctions between private and governmental, individual and social, and secret and open. The public and the private do not necessarily delimit different spheres, and one can and does enjoy a certain amount of privacy in public. Based on the justification we have given, one's privacy results from a recognition of the respect due each of us as a moral being. We deserve this respect from all others, as they do from us. The public sphere is the impersonal sphere in which we carry on the affairs of everyday life with others. We each give up some of our privacy to make social interaction possible. But in that sphere we remain ourselves, persons worthy of respect. Although we cede much of the right to limit access to ourselves so that we can engage in social life and activities to the extent that others do also, the right to privacy remains presumptive. In public spaces, although we give up some privacy rights, exactly which we cede is often a matter of unstated convention and tradition, and new conditions raise issues of where to draw the line. In the workplace and in the quasi-public space of a business one's right to privacy may come up against competing rights of the employer and of the owner of the shop or business. The presumptions on the Internet are yet to be agreed upon. But even there we can argue from analogy to a certain extent.

Two instances tend to be paradigms of what is public, namely, performing some act in public and information that is part of the public record, and even they are not completely clear.[16]

Consider first what we do in public, e.g., walk down a public street or drive down public roads. If anything is done in public, these seem to be. To do something in public is not to deny that we continue to have and exercise our right to privacy. By wearing clothes we conceal our bodies to some extent and maintain our bodily privacy. When I walk down the street I have no basis for setting limits to access to myself such that people are not allowed to look at or notice or remember my presence. For they have as much right to be in public places as I have, and none of us is required not to see, observe, remember what transpires on a public street. That is what we mean by saying it is public: it is shared by all and all have access to it. If this is so, then there seems nothing wrong with someone taking a video of us on the street, and nothing wrong with a government mounting a video on the public street to record who appears there and what they do. If there is nothing wrong in principle with videotaping one street, there is nothing wrong with videotaping every street.

Now suppose that there are surveillance cameras on every street, put in by the police to monitor possible crime and to help guarantee the safety of all. And suppose it is possible for the pictures from each camera to be correlated so that my walking down a variety of streets, looking in windows, saying hello to friends, driving my car from place to place, are all tallied and recorded. This may be done by the police for me only, or it may be done for everyone who walks or drives on the streets of a city or town. There will therefore be a record of all our appearances on every public street every time we appear on one. How can that violate our privacy? If public plus public equals public, it would seem it cannot. Yet many people feel uneasy about any such procedure and feel that it invades their privacy. This sounds very much like the surveillance that we argued above sends a chilling effect on what I would do and how I would act that is offensive to me as a responsible being worthy of respect. My being scrutinized inhibits my way of acting. Yet if what I do in public is public, how can I protest a violation of privacy? If I am doing nothing illegal, I should have nothing to fear and am in no way threatened by harm. Nonetheless, my uneasiness about surveillance is tied to my knowledge that the government can do people harm in various ways. It can attempt social control; try to influence our behavior; lessen our political freedom; make us worry about our expression of political dissent, our associations, or vote, or reluctance to be pressured to conform, or about being opened up to ridicule or punishment. Most people in a free society wish to prevent such interference and too much social control and manipulation.

In this case the objection is not simply to the videoing taking place but to the identifying individuals in the video, correlating the many videos to produce a trace of their activity, for some unknown governmental motive that is at least threatening to the individuals. What we seem to claim is not only that our privacy is invaded, at least in the sense that my actions are inhibited in an unjustifiable way, but that the purpose of the videoing, which was to promote safety on the street, does not require the additional actions of identifying individuals guilty of no crime, correlating videos to track their movement, and preserving the videos for unknown amounts of time for unknown or unstated reasons. If such videoing is justifiable on the grounds of promoting safety, then that use should determine the limits of the videoing. Arguably, safety does not require viewing such videos, much less identifying the people videoed, unless some crime has been committed; it does not require the correlation of different videos or the tracking of individuals unless they have committed some crime; and it does not require the preservation of the tapes for more than a brief time to make sure no crimes have been committed requiring their use. Hence, even though the streets are public, we can justifiably demand that individuals not be identified unless a crime has been committed, that there be no tracking, and that the tapes not be kept more than a brief time. Whether we can demand that the same conditions be met if the videoing takes place within the premises of a business, and whether by analogy that demand can be extended to other kinds of identification and tracking, are at this point open questions.

As long as I am not violating the law or under suspicion for good cause, there is no reason for the government to track me. Although I am in public I am not completely vulnerable to others, including the government. While I am in public others are not allowed to accost me, I am not required to speak to anyone, divulge my name or anything else about me that is not publicly visible. What it means to be in public is limited and restricted and my reasonable expectations are violated by tracking. Since our right to privacy allows each of us to set limits on access, the tracking is allowable only if we citizens allow it and it is reasonable for us to do so only if we know the benefits we may achieve and believe they outweigh the benefits of privacy.

Moreover, what I often expect in a city of any size is a certain amount of anonymity. Some people may see and recognize me. Most will not. Is my anonymity threatened by the surveillance? Clearly it is, if my picture is connected with my name. Do we have a right to anonymity? I do not see how we could claim any such right in any strong sense. Such anonymity is not available to those who live in small towns and whose every action in public may be observed by someone who knows them, and may be recounted to others who know them. Their privacy is not thereby violated in small towns; but lacking anonymity their actions are public in a way that they are not when performed in public places where no one knows them and no one pays particular attention to what they do or do not do, at least as long as they remain within certain bounds of accepted behavior. Although anonymous, people remain accountable for what they do, and can be witnessed, identified, and so on, should they break the law.[17]

Whether anonymous or not, people may rightly be fearful of how the agglomerated information about them may be used. They are certainly not required to identify themselves when under public surveillance. So if we object to the surveillance and the record of all our actions, it may be on the basis of invasion privacy insofar as it inhibits our actions, or it may be on the basis of failure to consent to the practice, and/or on the legitimate fear of harm. Tracking individuals from location to location through video cameras is not required for public safety. Doing so is justifiable only if necessary to determine the whereabouts of some possible criminal suspect.

If we had a guarantee that the film or video or disk would not be looked at routinely and without cause, that we and the other individuals would not be tracked, and that the tape would be completely erased each day or within a suitably short period if no crime has taken place on the streets in question, then both our claim of inhibiting our action and our fear of harm should be for the most part put to rest. Failure to erase must be justified by some argument that is strong enough to allay our concern about possible harm.

Nonetheless, in June, 2001 Acme-Rent-A-Car tracked James Turner, who was driving one of Acme's rental cars, across three states and fined him $450 for three speeding violations that they caught during their tracking. Although the Connecticut Attorney General said the practice was illegal, Acme claimed it is legal, was stated in the rental contract, and prevented catastrophic claims from accidents caused by speeding. The tracking was done by a Global Positioning System (GPS) installed in the car to help drivers find locations and directions, and to help the rental company locate cars that are not returned or are stolen. Moreover, the FCC requires that as of October, 2001, cell phone companies be able to specify a 911 caller's location to between 50 and 300 meters. This means that one's location can be determined by the cell phone service whenever one turns on one's cell phone. Advertisers are eager to use this capability. Law enforcement agencies might also be interested. Legislation has been proposed, but not yet passed, requiring that customers be informed of when they are being tracked, and that no information about them be provided or sold to third parties without the customer's consent.

The second plausible paradigm I mentioned of something being public was public records. It would seem that if any information is public, these are. Records of birth, marriage, death, purchase of real estate, felony convictions, and licenses are all public information. Much else is also a matter of public record, such as (in most states) the salaries of state employees. Yet even here, although the records are available to the public, in the past one had to go to the records office and search through the written records to obtain the information. Public meant available through a search, and the search was sufficiently difficult and time consuming that the ordinary person did not have to worry about the public information on him or her being collated and correlated, bought and used in unknown ways by interested parties, commercial, governmental, or private (i.e., nonpublic).

Such information is now kept on computers, it can be easily stored or shipped, and it is easily collated with databases from a large variety of sources. It is now technically possible for the government or a company or an individual to get all the public records on each of us fairly easily. Computers can receive the large databases and produce the matching, ending up with comparative ease with a profile of each of us. From this inferences, which may or may not be correct, may be made. Is this the purpose of public records? It clearly was not when public records started being kept and prior to the development of large computers. Does making public information about us more readily accessible violate our privacy? We have already seen the argument to the effect that public plus public yields public. Whether or not it violates our privacy, however, it may make us uneasy because of fear of how the information may be misused, and clearly it does not seem to be what we as a society originally intended when we authorized public records on people for certain limited purposes. Some public officials understand this problem; others feel that if documents are public that automatically means that they should be made available to anyone by the simplest and most convenient means possible. In a computerized society that means making all records available on-line freely to everyone. Yet it does not seem that the intent of recording births for public purposes – establishing citizenship, eligibility to vote or receive government benefits, etc. – was to supply businesses with the names of people in certain age brackets so they could be sent ads or promotional information, much less to identify those who might be vulnerable to scams or to satisfy the idle curiosity of someone about someone else's age.

Salaries in some companies are considered by the company as a trade secret, not to be divulged, even by one employee to another. But the salaries of state employees are a matter of public record. We all know or can easily learn the salary of the President, or of the state governors, or of the members of the national and state legislatures. The salaries of each faculty member at the University of Kansas is a matter of public record and can be accessed by anyone wishing to view the university budget document. Until now, that document has been accessible in book form at selected places and one must make the effort to look at it in some public place (where one can be seen looking at it and perhaps may have to ask for it and even sign for it). This makes casual or curious viewers rare. Is the information more public if the State of Kansas were to make the university's budget available on the World Wide Web, freely accessible to anyone wishing to access it on-line and able to choose individuals by name? It is no more public, but it is much more accessible, and the information might well be taken and correlated by any number of businesses. Having one's salary publicly accessible is a cost to the individual of working for the government, and the publicity aspect is justified because the money spent is taxpayer money. One might argue, however, that although the publicity condition on the salaries of state employees is justified in terms of accountability, making the records available to casual surfers or to data collectors on the Web goes well beyond the requirement of publicity, and is a practice the state should not adopt. For the information is as much information about who receives it as it is information about the way the state spends its money. Might the same purpose be served by simply identifying the members of the university by department and some designation as Professor 1, Associate Professor 1, 2, 3, and so on? Are individual names required by the publicity condition on the expenditure of state funds? That is debatable. One might argue, nonetheless, that publishing the information on the Internet goes beyond what accountability requires even for government spending. Publicly accessible need not mean indiscriminately available. We should rethink public records in the computer age and determine whether public in this case means readily accessible to all on the Internet.

Some states have passed legislation prohibiting the state department of motor vehicles from selling drivers license photographs and information to businesses. The best argument in defense of such legislation is that in requiring such information the state does not get permission from the licensee to sell that information, and that the information is given for a specific reason and should be used only for that reason. To use that information in additional ways, by selling it to increase revenue, goes beyond the need of the state to collect it and the licensee to submit it as a condition for receiving a license. A second reason is that it opens up the licensee to possible damage and harm, as the rising number of identity thefts confirms.

▲ ANONYMITY, CONFIDENTIALITY, AND ▲ INFORMED CONSENT

Let us leave the street and go into a bank. This is private property, yet I am in at least semi-public view. If I stand in line to withdraw a certain amount of money, my presence at the bank is public in that anyone who is there can see me. When I come to the counter, however, I expect my transaction to be confidential, a transaction between me and the bank, mediated by the teller, who, as an agent of the bank, I expect to respect the confidentiality of the transaction and not reveal to others whether I deposited money or withdrew it or in either case how much was involved. Yet if the person behind me in line hears me say to the teller, "I would like to withdraw a thousand dollars," it is not clear he or she violates my privacy, depending on how closely they were listening. I am engaged in a transaction whose conditions I do not set. The transaction is private in the special sense of being confidential. What I reveal in confidence is not public. Confidentiality is a state of affairs in which the parties to a transaction agree not to divulge the details of the transaction (or perhaps even the transaction itself) to any third party, without the consent of the party revealing the information. The confidentiality relation is not a reciprocal one. A doctor–patient relation may impose on the doctor the obligation not to reveal without the consent of the patient to a third party the details of a patient's condition or words, but the patient is free to tell anyone he wishes about his visit and about what the doctor said without the doctor's permission. There is some information that we legitimately expect is revealed in confidence and will be kept confidential – our bank transactions, for instance.

In a professional relation I reveal information because it is necessary to obtain the help or service I desire. I tell my doctor about my health or lack thereof in order to get treatment. To gain the greatest benefit, I have to be as frank and open in discussing my symptoms as possible. I reveal my condition with the understanding that I am doing so to him or her only, and with the understanding that the record of my visit and of my condition will be kept confidential. This means that he will not share it with others without my permission. I may tell whom I wish. If he tells others he breaks the condition we explicitly or implicitly agreed to, namely the confidentiality condition. Nonetheless, others may legitimately have access to his records of me – the secretary who types up the report, the records librarian who files it, the nurse who refers to it when I make my next appointment. Each of these is expected to respect the confidentiality of the material and not reveal it to others. An individual may keep something completely private by excluding all others from access to it. Confidentiality requires at least two people, and usually applies to information that is necessarily disclosed. Nonetheless, violations of confidentiality are often considered violations of privacy.

The right to confidentiality in the case of both the bank and the medical setting is one of implied confidentiality, and can be considered part of an implied contract. In some cases it may be part of an actual contract. Whether implied or explicit, the bank or medical institution is bound by the confidentiality agreement not to divulge the transaction or information received in confidence. It may do so only with the consent of the customer or patient. And, of course, the consent should be the informed consent of one who knows and understands what he or she is doing, and the consequences thereof. Hence before any bank information or medical records are revealed to any third party, explicit informed consent should be given. Although people often assume that this is the case, they are frequently asked to routinely sign consent forms that are often very vague and very broad, allowing the bank or the medical facility to release their records to a large number of unspecified third parties for very vague purposes determined by the bank or medical facility. And once released, the individual no longer has any control over their use. They often find their way into a variety of compilations of data on the individual without the individual knowing that such compilations exist, and therefore without being able to inspect them and so to correct them if they are inaccurate.

Now leave the bank and go to the supermarket. The supermarket is privately owned, and so private in that sense, yet open to the public. Presumably people may be excluded for good reason. The store has a security camera, just as the street has. In this instance it is to assure that no one is stealing, possibly to improve the store's marketing, as well as possibly to help serve the customer. Our selection of items to purchase, as well as the items we look at and do not purchase, may all be viewed and used for whatever legally allowed purposes the store wishes. If our identity is known, e.g., through my having filled out a form of some sort or if I previously used a credit card there or cashed a check, or if the store uses a shopper's card system, the store may attach a name to my likeness. Does this violate my privacy? We have no right to set limits on what the store may observe about us while in the store, since after all it is the store's space that we are in, and anyone else in the store could see as much by observing us. We are acting in quasi-public space. Any claim to privacy seems ill-founded. If we feel somewhat uneasy about this, it is once again because, at least in cities, we expect a certain amount of anonymity in our shopping. But that is not something we have a right to, and our anonymity is lost when we are observed by those who know or recognize us.

Nonetheless, even without my likeness, if the store records that I buy two dozen eggs a week, and this becomes known to my insurance company, and it links it to information from other sources that I drive everywhere and have no recorded transactions with any health club, might the company infer that I am a poor health risk? If this is done, I am unwittingly, indirectly, and unavoidably revealing more than I wish and intend. Being forced to reveal this information can be seen as some sort of violation of me, whether of my privacy or of my right not to be harmed. When I enter a store it is not part of the expectation that a great deal of information is necessary for the transaction that I engage in by purchasing items in the store, and it is not part of the general expectation that I give up very much information about myself. The shelves at which I look and the products I touch may be used for marketing purposes when joined in aggregate with observations of other customers. But that legitimate use does not require identifying me as an individual.

As I check out, the clerk or the person behind me may know me and may note what I purchase. I cannot control their seeing this and I cannot control what they do with that information. It is not private, even in the tenuous sense that my bank transaction is private. But my expectation is that for the most part if I use cash the transaction is anonymous. However, if I use my credit card to pay for my purchases, the store itemizes each purchase and my total purchase is charged to my credit card. The store now has a record of my purchases, and my credit card company in some cases does as well. If I had paid by cash, unless someone who knew me joined my name to the list of purchases rung up (or I had been tracked by the store camera and my name and face correlated), my transaction would have been anonymous. The price I pay for using a credit card is some loss of anonymity. Do I have any right to limit what the store and my credit card company record about my transaction? Since they are parties to the transaction, one could argue that the information is as much about them as it is about me. But the store does not need to know my name, and the credit card company does not need to know the items I buy. What the store appropriately records is the sale of certain items so it can restock and the credit card company notes the debit of a certain amount of money to my account. The computer makes the capture of much more information easily available. But that does not mean that businesses may therefore capture as much information about their customers as they can. Once again we can invoke a claim to the right to informed consent in a transaction. Customers should know the cost of the transaction which means not only knowing how much they must pay for the items but what else they are giving or revealing to the seller which will be used in unspecified ways.

Can I claim that when I use my credit card the action is, if not private, at least confidential, just as when I make a bank transaction? Or, since the purchase of those items was publicly done, does that make the transaction public? Can I legitimately control the information about me that I made those purchases, since I made them publicly? If not, then I cannot complain that the credit card company that receives this information does not treat it as confidential information about me. The intuitions of people about whether the information is public or private or confidential vary, which is an indication that there is no clear consensus on the matter. As a society we did not in the past make any clear determination about exactly what is private or confidential and what is public in this area. The ambiguity caused no problems. With the advent of computers and the vast possibilities of record keeping and collating, we are now faced with unclear intuitions and with blurry lines between what is public and what is private, what is confidential and what is not. The unclarity and the blur are the stuff of which some of our moral and ethical puzzles in this area are made. Although the claim of complete privacy with respect to credit cards is too strong, the claim of confidentiality is not.

If I feel uneasy about either the store or the credit card company having the information, it might be for three other reasons, which could serve as a basis for complaint. The first has to do with the use that will be made of the information. The second has to do with claims of lack of consent. The third has to do with possible harm. The worry about the use that will be made of the information hinges on the fact that this information about my purchases in one store can be sold by that store or correlated by the credit card company with all the other purchases I make with that card. This information can be further correlated with other information available about me from any source in which I appear by name as part of a database. The result is that much more is revealed about me than I intend to reveal by individual purchases. Before all the information in databases could be so easily correlated, the fact that I performed any particular act in public or in semi-public, such as a store, might be noticed or even correlated with a limited amount of information available about me. But the trouble and cost of doing anything of the sort which is now easily possible tended to preclude any serious concern. The information remained fragmented, and so the threat it posed was minimal. This is changed with the growth in the use of computers, and the ease and low cost of collecting and correlating data. It is doubtful that the public has consented to these practices, even if they have been vaguely aware of them. The fact that they are possible and have become actual does not mean that people must simply accept them and modify their expectations accordingly. People need not accept whatever is technologically possible. Technology can be used to serve the interests of all rather than the interests of those who use and control them.

Are credit card transactions confidential transactions such that they should not be revealed by the credit card company without the consent of the credit card holder? Present custom is unclear on this point. Some customers may think this is the case. But there is usually nothing in the contract that goes with the credit card that specifies this, and so there is a presumption against that expectation. The claim that the general public has tacitly consented to the practice on the part of stores and credit card companies because the public has not complained hinges on the lack of vocal complaint. In that case it can be undone by vocal complaint. The harm threatened, we have already noted, stems from the possible use of such information to adversely affect our employment possibilities and our insurance prospects, among others. We have no access to the databases we do not know exist and cannot correct errors therein. *Should* our credit card transactions be confidential? That answer does not depend on any claimed right to privacy. If customers feel strongly about this, then they can unite to express their views and expect that some credit card company will seek to attract them as customers by offering confidentiality as part of the package, and perhaps charging for the cost of enforcing this and for the loss of revenue incurred from not selling credit card information as their competitors do. Customers can also seek protection, if they feel threatened, by legislation enforcing confidentiality on all such transactions. The US Congress, in reaction to video rental information publicized about Justice Robert Bork when he was being considered for the Supreme Court, made video rentals confidential. It could take similar action in other realms.

Although we act in public, we might make out a case for confidentiality, justified on grounds of an understood basis for a transaction (as the doctor–patient transaction is assumed, often incorrectly)[18] to be confidential, or by consumer pressure or legislation that protects us from possible or threatened harm.

Just as the notion of confidentiality can clarify some issues couched in terms of privacy, so can the notion of informed consent, as we have already seen. When I fill out warranty forms for a new product I purchase, I give information about myself. When I fill out a questionnaire promoted to "help serve me better" and as a reward I am entered into a sweepstake and become eligible to receive the grand prize, I have in effect sold that information about myself – my likes and dislikes, my preferences, perhaps data about my salary level, home ownership, and countless other things. Have I thereby given the recipient the right to use that information in any way it wishes, to sell it to others, to combine it with other information about me, and so on? It seems so, unless the questionnaire notes otherwise or has an opt-out box for me to check if I so desire. When I place a magazine subscription, do I give the magazine the right to sell my name and address and the information that I am a subscriber? These are ambiguous cases in which the right to informed consent has not been raised. But as the sharing of such information, given for one purpose and used for another, has grown, one can argue that the right to informed consent can and should be asserted as a means of defending our privacy as well as our right to be free from fear of being harmed (e.g., by identity theft or by a poor credit rating based on misinformation) and our homes invaded by intrusive phone calls, ads as we visit websites, and so on.

▲ CONSUMER VERSUS BUSINESS ▲ INTERESTS

Any attempt at restricting personal information as presently practiced will affect the way business is done, and businesses can be expected to assert their rights in these matters, as well as argue against any radical changes on the basis of the great costs that any changes will impose.

Let us then consider what some of the arguments on behalf of business interests are.

One argument is that the information of any business transaction belongs rightfully to both parties, and hence in a purchase the information belongs as much to the seller as to the buyer. Surely a legitimate limit to any claim to privacy on the part of the customer must be balanced against the right of a business to use its information as it wants. The business may claim that the facts of the transaction – to whom it was made, what was purchased, and other details of the transaction – belong to the business and are part of its records, with which it is allowed to do as it wishes. It may save them, collate them to get customer profiles, or sell them. Although customers may feel that the transaction is a private one between the two parties, and that by making the purchase they give the business no right to use the information about the transaction and the customer as it wishes, businesses can plausibly claim that customers are simply mistaken. With most transactions that involve a computerized record of any sort attaching the customer's name to the transaction, the customer is not informed of what is done with the information – whether it is stored, sorted, collated, sold, or otherwise used. Many businesses feel that this is not anything they have to reveal to the consumer because the information is part of the transaction and belongs to the business.

A second argument on the part of business claims that the information is not personal in any sense relevant to privacy. There is nothing sensitive about a company knowing that I purchased a refrigerator, or a quart of milk, or any number of other products. Some items, such as medications, might be sensitive and could be considered personal. But the vast majority of items do not fall into this class. To claim that my privacy is violated because a supermarket records that I bought a quart of milk borders on paranoia. Hence with respect to most purchases, any claim that one's privacy is violated by a recording process is without foundation. Finally, even though the supermarket may record my purchase, and if I charge it the purchases will be reported to my credit card company, neither of them makes this information public in any usual sense of public. Both and all other businesses that gain access to it will treat it as proprietary, not available to the general population, and not public.

Third, business can legitimately argue that there is ample precedent for their collecting, correlating, selling, and otherwise using the information they gather through records of a variety of business transactions. Such use is justified, they can argue, on the basis that it is long-accepted practice. Knowledge of the various uses to which information about transactions is put has been discussed in the newspaper, has been the subject of various articles, reports, and so on; it is certainly not arcane or specialized knowledge available only to those in special positions. Since there is a long tradition of doing business this way, it is clearly accepted practice.

Fourth, consider the cost of changing the practice. The cost would be prohibitive. Not only would businesses lose the revenue that they presently receive, but their marketing strategies would have to be drastically changed. In addition, if each business had to inform its customers of its new policy and had to get explicit permission for each use of the information it solicited or obtained, the cost would be prohibitive. Overall, the cost would be very high both to individual businesses and to the general American economy. The cost, as all costs, would have to be borne eventually by the consumer. The overall result would really benefit no segment of society and so would not be worthwhile.

Fifth, any changed set of rules about business's ability to use the information it gathers from customers would result in customers getting less and poorer service rather than more or better. The fact that someone is interested in fishing might be gathered from their purchases and magazine subscriptions. They would now be targeted to receive ads and promotional information and discount coupons having to do with fishing. Given their interest in fishing, they may well find some of what they receive useful and be happy to receive it. The advertisers would target their ads to those who would most likely be responsive. Thus both the sender and the recipient benefit. If the information on individuals' interests were not available in this way, advertisers would have to send information about their product much more broadly in the hope of reaching those with an interest in fishing. The result is more money spent on advertising, and more people receiving what they will consider junk mail because they have no interest in the product. Changes in what information may be gathered and used will thus result in more junk mail, more intrusions on one's time by such mail, perhaps more marketing calls (if these are not prohibited), loss of efficiency, and increase in general expense for all.

Finally, the present policy respects the freedom of all. It respects the freedom of the market and of those in the market to market their goods efficiently and as they see fit. Those that wish to opt out of the system are being given a chance more and more to do so. More and more firms are sending customers their privacy policies and most often they have an opt out provision. This respects the freedom of all parties. If in fact the percentage of those who do opt out is rather small, that presumably indicates that they are not bothered enough by the system or not sufficiently worried about possible infringement of their privacy so as to do anything to change the current practices.

As an example of how this works in practice consider the fact that I am a subscriber to a magazine. That information is as much its information as it is mine. Hence, since that information legitimately belongs to the magazine, it may use it for its purposes, including selling the fact that I subscribe to it to another business. On the other hand, I can just as plausibly argue that I have not given the magazine the right to do that. All I implicitly contracted for was for them to send me the magazine I requested. The fact that I am their customer means that they have the right to use that information in connection with my subscription. They may send me renewal notices at the proper time and even send me renewal notices after my subscription lapses. The fact that I subscribed to their magazine in the past is information to which they appropriately have access. But in subscribing I did not in any way give them my name and address to use in any way they chose. I did not both subscribe and authorize them to sell my name and address or the fact of my subscription to them. If the publisher of that magazine publishes or produces another product, they may feel free to use the subscription list of the magazine to which I subscribe to send me information about the other magazine or product. Such a practice does not seem to violate my privacy. Few people seem to object to this and it has become a standard marketing practice. Many firms consider their mailing lists one of their prime assets. Truly informed consent would require that when I enter my subscription, or sometime thereafter, I indicate that the company may use my name and address for the purpose of sending me information from the company about other products and that I give them permission to sell or trade or in other ways make my subscription information available to some or indiscriminately to all others the company wishes. This is not the present practice. The present practice is to inform the customer of the possibility that the mailing list will be used in a variety of ways, and then require that if the customer wishes to opt out of the practice, they take the necessary steps to so inform the company. The present practice, then, assumes consent instead of requiring that it be explicit, and the company need supply only as much information as the company wishes. But, the magazine can argue, if I do not opt out, I have been informed and I have willingly accepted their use of my name and address on their subscription list.

Sometimes when I subscribe to a magazine or order a product through the mail, the business will include a card stating that it sometimes sells its customer list to other firms and stating that unless I so indicate, my name will be included. The assumption here is that if I reply in the negative my name will not be included. A current debate exists over whether the inclusion of my name is something that I must explicitly choose for inclusion in the list, or whether my name is automatically included and I should be allowed to have it excluded. The first approach says that including my name on a list that is sold is something I must specifically permit; the second says that permission is implied and that at best I have the right to request that my name be excluded. Of course, even the second option implies that I will be informed that the magazine or business sells its list. Is this required or does the fact that I have subscribed or placed an order give ownership rights of that information to business? The magazine or business has a right to the information that I freely supply it.

When I order clothes by mail I indicate my size. It is not clear that I give that information in confidence; nor is it clear that I do not. Is that information about me that should be added to the many databases about me, and the size of my clothes added as I change sizes? This certainly is not the general expectation. But once again it is information freely given for one purpose, with no explicit restriction on how it is to be used. If implicit consent is assumed, then there is no objection to its being stored, sold, or used for marketing or any other legal purpose. Although one's right to privacy is limited by the other party's right to information that comes from a legitimate transaction, there is room to argue that present practices favor business at the expense of the consumer, and that information supplied for one purpose should not be used for any other purpose without the explicit consent of the individual supplying it.

Some have argued that since the information we supply is sold or in other ways has commercial value, it is only fair that we be paid for the information. It is obviously valuable, and that therefore the customers should in some way be recompensed for that value. One obvious reply is that they already are and that the cost of the magazine or product would be higher if the company did not have this additional source of income. A second, similar argument, is that the customers benefit from receiving information about products that they are plausibly interested in, given the interest evidenced by the initial subscription of purchase. Of course, companies could make this transaction explicit, by perhaps having two prices, one a non-discounted full price and the other a discounted price for those who do not deny the use of their information for any purpose other than the explicitly stated transaction. Alternatively, companies that forgo using the information they receive from a transaction might use that fact to gain a competitive edge.

Despite the fact that information about and contained in a transaction belongs equally to both parties, it would be clearly unethical for either party to harm the other through the use of the information about the transaction, assuming it is ethical and legal. Whether harm is done to a consumer whose transactions – purchases for instance – are recorded, collated, and sold is not entirely clear and is a point of contention. In most cases, the lists are used to send advertisements for products that match the consumer's interests as evidenced by the pattern of purchases. Whether simply getting what might be considered by the receiver as junk mail is harm is debatable, and again in most cases would amount to being a nuisance, rather than a serious harm. Some consumers might be pleased to receive discount offers, information about bargains, or updated information on a product they use. If one could be sure that this is the only use to which information would be put, then the anxiety on the part of most people might be allayed. But there is no guarantee about who will use the information or how, and that is a cause of worry to many people.

Much information about individuals, of course, is freely given by them. Most products that come with a warranty have a registration card enclosed. The registration card need not be filed for the warranty to be valid. But if the product is defective, unless one returns the card, the producer will not know whom to contact with warnings about defects and with possible recall notices. This requires only that the purchasers identify the product and supply their names and addresses. Anyone willing to forgo such notification need not return the card (although the purchase may be recorded in any number of places if it was paid for by a credit card). Nonetheless, most registration cards ask for a wealth of information including range of income, number of persons in the household, and all sorts of spending, recreation, and business activities – many of which are completely unrelated to the product purchased. Some consumers may believe they must complete the card and answer all the questions to ensure their warranty. Businesses should not mislead customers into so thinking. The defect there is not invasion of privacy but misleading presentation. The cards do not state this, and some indicate that registration does not affect the warranty. Some forms indicate that the information will be used to send those who fill it out information of interest to them, and a few might have a box at the end which customers may check if they do not wish to receive any ads and if they do not wish their names and addresses sold or passed on to any other business. Even in cases where the customer checks the box, it is not clear whether, if a manufacturer is owned by a parent company, one's information will be passed on to the parent company or other affiliated companies.

In the United States, as we have seen, the assumption on which most businesses operate is that customers allow the use of information about their purchases and of the information they supply unless the business is informed otherwise. Some businesses make requests to opt out relatively simply, e.g., by checking a box. Many do not.

Since there are competing claims, it seems only fair that both sides be considered. If information about transactions is to belong presumptively to the business supplier, at the very least this should be public knowledge, and consumers should have some way of indicating that they do not wish the information about the transaction attached to their names or used beyond billing for that transaction. This might be done by checking a box, for instance, on a credit card form. With respect to information submitted in questionnaires, product registration forms, and the like, there should be a statement of how the information will be used, and there should also be a box to check if the purchasers do not wish the information sold or released to another company. Both of these are simply ways of trying to introduce the notion of informed consent into practices that are now often perceived as taking unfair advantage of the ignorance of consumers as to business practices made possible through computerization.

This approach gives the benefit of the doubt to business. The opposite approach, that gives the benefit of the doubt to consumers, would require that information on a transaction not be used for other purposes unless the consumer check a box authorizing such use. Placing the burden of authorization on the consumer favors the privacy of the consumer, and is preferred by those who worry about consumer privacy.

Whichever system is adopted, what is ethically demanded is that all parties to the transaction know what they are entering into, including knowing how the information of the transaction will be used, and that they agree to that in entering the transaction in the way in which they do.

▲ PERSONAL INFORMATION PROTECTION ▲

What conclusions can we draw from the above discussions? One on which all parties seem to agree is that personal information is important and deserves protection. In the abstract it is hard to disagree with that statement. But there are important differences on the questions of what constitutes personal information that deserves protection, on whether in fact that protection is forthcoming in the United States, on whether or not legislation is necessary to achieve that protection, and if so what that legislation should be like. There is also general agreement on the principles pertinent to the issue: there is a right to privacy, and in particular to personal information privacy which both business and government should respect; individuals have a right not to be harmed, and so not to be harmed by the misuse of information about them; individuals have a right to confidentiality, at least in certain transactions, where this is either a contractual right or one that is implied; informed consent is appropriate whenever one releases delicate personal information to a business that will sell or share it with others; tracking and collating one's actions need special argument to be justifiable; and anonymity, if not a right, is something that people hold is important in many situations and can usually assume that their actions will not be made public in the sense of widely available. But once again, there is great variation in how individuals and businesses apply these principles to particular cases and circumstances.

Personal information has received legal protection in the European Union. The US approach has up until recently been based almost exclusively on the notion of self-restraint. Critics claim with some justification that reliance on self-restraint has proven confusing and ultimately ineffective. Hence, we as a society should reconsider our right to protection of personal information in the Information Age, in which conditions have changed sufficiently that the old assumptions no longer clearly apply.

The result has been many calls for legislation that will clarify the situation and protect the individual's privacy. Although legislation will help settle some of the issues, the question remains as to what is ethically demanded. What does ethics say that can guide legislation? Although there is no clear consensus on many aspects of this issue, due in part to lack of information about what actually takes place, in part to disputes about what ownership rights are involved, and in part to the rapidly changing ways in which information is gathered and used, some general guidelines are helpful.

The larger question is how much information on individuals should be collected, collated, and made available as profiles and to whom such profiles, or files, should be made available. Purchases are only one part of the information. Preferences and habits as either stated or inferred are another. Information supplied by an individual may, of course, not be accurate or truthful. In filling out a questionnaire attached to a warranty for a new hair dryer, there is no way of knowing whether the individual fills in his or her preferences accurately, whether the salary range checked is higher or lower or actually representative of the person's salary. If one's profile is made up of partial misinformation, and then inferences are made on the basis of the available data, the room for error increases. How valid is inferred information? Of course, the answer is, it depends on many factors. Does inferred information potentially harm one? Does it violate one's privacy or other rights? Once again no blanket answer is possible. But the questions and the resulting answers demonstrate two other rights that people assert can be derived from the right to privacy and the right not to be harmed, namely the right to know that files are kept on one that result from collation of information and the right to inspect and correct such files.

Especially sensitive information poses special problems. Medical records, bank records, possibly even donations to various causes seem importantly different from the purchase of routine items. It is easy to imagine people being categorized as to their religion, sexual preferences, political leanings, and so on, on the basis of what they subscribe to and what they donate money to, and it is easy to imagine groups, government, insurance companies, potential or actual employers, neighbors, and enemies using this information to stigmatize, harass, fire, refuse to hire, refuse to insure, blackball, and in other ways harm the person in question. It also seems clear that social security numbers, which are frequently used for identification purposes, should not be available for sale, nor should the maiden name of the mother of any individual, since that is also used as an identification check. The only reason for selling these is so that someone may access another individual's accounts. When these are validly used they are supplied by the individual to the user and should be used only for the purpose of identification by the user to which they were revealed. To make them available to others is to violate what most people would consider an implicit agreement on the conditions for which they were submitted. Similarly, most people feel that their medical records should be kept confidential. If they are not, then people will be reluctant to reveal their symptoms to doctors for fear of who might find out about them. This would undermine the doctor–patient relationship. Individuals may release their medical records to others for specific purposes, such as to insurance companies when applying for life or health insurance. But they usually do so with the assumption that they are releasing them only to the company in question and only for that company's use in determining whether or not to issue insurance. They are not releasing their records to the company for further use by the company. For companies to use such records in ways other than the one for which the patient released them is to act unethically, even if there is no statement made by the insurance company that it will not use the records in other ways. The presumption on the part of applicants is that they will not be otherwise used.

It is the justified fear that many people have about the misuses of collated unchecked, possibly erroneous information, profiles, and files, kept by firms on them and distributed to any paying inquirer, that argue in favor of the option of consumer rather than business control of transaction information.

The generally acknowledged right of employees to know that their employers have files on them and the right to access the information therein and to correct misinformation and counter false or disputed claims seems appropriate with respect to consumers as well. Consumers, and so the general public, should know what files are kept on them that are made available to business and others, should have access to them, should be able to correct them, and should be able to add their version of disputed claims. The three leading credit bureaus that gather and make available a wealth of information about individuals, their credit and bank ratings, income, employment and marital status, driving record, court records, and other personal information, are TRW, Equifax, and Trans Union Credit Information. Each of these has provisions that allow individuals to check their records on them and to add corrections, but people have had their credit rating ruined by mistaken information, and have had a very difficult time remedying the damage. The agencies argue that since they handle records on 120–150 million people the harm done to a few should be weighed against the benefit to the many who are given instant credit when opening accounts, applying for a mortgage, and other benefits that would not be available without such centralized records.

There is also good reason to argue that centralized records should not contain information that may be used for discrimination not allowed by law – race, national origin, religious affiliation, age, and sexual orientation.

Most companies have given too little thought to the rights of consumers with respect to information collection, to the possible misuse to which information they sell might be put, or to adopting explicit information to inform the consumer of the true nature of transactions and the uses to which information supplied will be put. Yet ethics demands at least that much.

▲ LEGAL PROTECTION VERSUS ▲ SELF-POLICING BY BUSINESS

In the fall of 1998 the European Union adopted a set of laws concerning personal information privacy. The laws, which have to be accepted in principle by the individual nations, have already been enacted by several of them, and must be implemented within three years by the others, specify that information provided by customers for one purpose cannot be used by the receiving firm for another purpose and cannot be sold or given to any third party without the consent of the customer. These provisions are just the opposite of what is the case in the United States, even though Americans often think of themselves as champions of privacy.

In the United States, by law first-class mail is private, as are telephone conversations. Student records of educational institutions that receive federal funds are protected by law, but not the records of students at other institutions. Records of the sale or rental of video tapes are private, as are bank records, and in some states records of library loans. Privacy of records does not in fact legally extend very far, and varies from state to state. If one charges prescription drugs that is not confidential, but if one rents Bambi from Blockbuster TV that is confidential. Renting X-rated videos, if made public, might prove embarrassing. The law has not cut down on video rentals, and may even have bolstered the number of rentals. But it has prevented selling the information of who likes what type of videos to other vendors. The law shows that the American Congress and the American people are not opposed in principle to protection of personal information when it comes to selected areas. There is evidence that large numbers of Americans feel their privacy is being threatened, even though most are knowingly or unknowingly giving it away themselves.

The position of the European Union can be interpreted as standing on several fundamental precepts that we have already seen most American individuals and business also acknowledge. One is that people have the right to know what information is being collected on them and what collections of such information exist that may adversely affect them, and they have the right to access their data and make corrections if there are errors. The second is that the right to informed consent applies with respect to information that one reveals about oneself. The third is that there should be some enforcement mechanism and remedy for breaches of the principles of the protection of personal information. The European Union's law is addressed to the collection and use of information by business or commercial enterprises, and excludes issues bound up with state security or criminal law. The data on individuals is to be accurate; where necessary, it is to be kept up to date; and it may be kept for no longer than needed for the purpose for which it was collected. The requirement that the "data subject has given his consent unambiguously" (Sec. II, Art. 7), is especially noteworthy. In the United States, the assumption made by most businesses and one allowed by law is what is termed the "opt out" approach. That is, the assumed default position is that any information given or legitimately obtained may be used any way the collector wishes, unless the data subject has "opted out" of either giving information or about its being used in specific ways by making a specific request to that effect. Even if made, however, there is no legal requirement that the data collector need respect that request. The system is said to be self-policing. Because of the "opt out" default, no informed consent is required, which means information may be collected without one's knowledge, much less one's consent. Forms and information-gathering techniques need not be and often are not made public.

The US default position is in favor of personal data collection in almost all areas of business, with the opt out option only sometimes available. Hence the argument for federal legislation comparable to the protection provided by the European Union can be made on the dual basis that all concerned parties agree on the principles, and the self-policing and opt out process have proven ineffective. The argument holds that the interests of individuals and of society as a whole can only be served by federal legislation that provides each person and each business with accurate standards that apply to all and that are enforced. This is the only way that individuals can know what their rights are and what they can expect. All businesses are placed in a similar situation, keeping competition fair. If, as some rightly say, this will be costly, then the burden is shared by all businesses, and the members of the society realize that they must in turn bear the cost of maintaining their personal information protection. This will not prevent firms from requesting information or from using information they are supplied. But it puts the burden on them to solicit and get permission, rather than on receiving permission by default as is presently the case. If informed consent is to have any real meaning, it cannot be given by default by those who do not read the fine print in questionnaires and forms that offer them the opportunity to opt out. The default position is most likely the one that will be most often taken. Hence it is important that the default be opt out.

In 2001 federal action moved in the direction of protection of personal information on two fronts: the medical and the financial.

The need for the protection of personal medical information is obvious and clear to most patients. Until recently, any protection of such records was provided by state law and varied from jurisdiction to jurisdiction. There was no federal legislation of regulations. That gap has only recently been addressed. Shortly before leaving office,

President Clinton issued new rules on medical data privacy after Congress failed to produce any legislation that could command the necessary majority votes. President Bush on April 12, 2001 directed the rule to stand and be implemented by the Department of Health and Human Services, with an enforcement date of April 14, 2003. The key provisions of the rules limit the use and exchange of patient information by healthcare providers, health plans, health data clearing houses, employers, and insurance companies, among others, and it gives patients the right to review their medical records and request corrections of errors. But critics point out that the safeguards provided are far from complete and allow individually identifiable information to be used without the consent of the patient in a variety of cases including payment and treatment. Public health and governmental health data systems are excluded, as are law enforcement coroners and judicial and administrative proceedings, as is non-individually identifiable information. The basic intent was to prevent marketing uses of medical data without the consent of the patient. The law does not allow patients to sue for violation of their privacy rights, and exactly how the new rules will be enforced remains to be seen.

Three aspects of the legislation are pertinent to our discussion. One is that the country and the various constituents thereof are sufficiently divided that Congress was unable to agree on legislation. The second is that the executive branch of government, under both Democratic and Republican Presidents, felt enough public pressure to take some action in the direction of federal protection of individual medical records. The third is that the action fell short of what many privacy and consumer advocates desire, and that it was restricted to medical records – leaving all types of other records vulnerable to commercial use and possible abuse.

In the financial area Congress acted in November 1999, passing the Gramm-Leach Bliley (GLB) Financial Services Modernization Act. Title V of the Act concerns the protection of personal financial information. It requires that banks, credit card companies, insurance companies, mortgage companies, collection agencies, and other financial providers and institutions annually provide their customers with the institution's policies for collecting, disclosing, and protecting non-public personal information. They must state what information of this type they collect and the conditions under which they share this information with third parties. Non-public information includes information not available from the media or governmental records and includes social security numbers, account balance information, account numbers and credit card purchase information, among others. The financial institution must also provide the customer with specific information on how they can opt out of having their information disclosed to non-related third parties for marketing purposes. The law allows the sharing of customer information with affiliated companies. Information shared with others may be used only for the purpose requested by the financial institution, and no reuse or sale of the information by the third party is allowed.

Although the GLB Act can be seen as a step in the protection of personal information privacy, it fell far short of the kind of protection provided by the European Union. In the spring of 2001 customers received a small torrent of official notices from their banks, credit card companies, the department stores at which they charge accounts, their insurance companies, and all the other financial institutions required to send out their policies. The information varied greatly in the details presented and in the manner of presentation. Some firms included an opt out form and return envelope; some only a form; some only listed an address to which to write or a phone number to call. The burden to take action was on the customer, and the customer had to act in each case as indicated – which required reading each form fairly carefully. The result, as informally reported, was a very low rate of return of the opt out forms or notifications. Even some bank officials reflected surprise, and indicated that they would opt out. The reason, of course, for their reaction is that they were fully informed about what was at issue; while most consumers, unaware of the existence of the GLB Act or of its provisions, suddenly started getting what seemed like routine legal notices in the mail from a variety of sources. Being neither a bill nor anything that obviously seemed to require action, it looked like the standard forms one periodically receives from credit card companies and was probably discarded without much thought. A notice requiring one to opt in would probably not receive the same treatment, because it would be attractively packaged by the institution, with some incentive provided both to read it and to reply affirmatively.

The overall result is that American consumers have little in the way of legally enforced protection of their personal information, even in the sensitive areas of medical and financial information. The argument that with other ordinary purchases the only result of collecting information on consumers is an increase in junk mail and phone solicitations is by no means an accurate one, even if those results are the major consequences. Interestingly, the European Union also prohibits such soliciting unless authorized by the recipient. Many Americans fume through such calls at meal times, but there is no legislation proposed to prohibit it. It is worth while pondering why this is the case.

What is noteworthy about the European approach and its model of personal information protection is that it is general in its application. It applies to all means of obtaining and using personal information. It is not written especially for the electronic data (which is the emphasis of the Medical Data Directives) and does not attempt to control the Internet or its development beyond the protection of the rights of individuals. It allows all the practices that businesses wish as long as they are clearly and explicitly stated and agreed to by the informed participants. Customers who value their information or their privacy more than the services they may receive by giving or trading information about themselves are protected. Competition in personal information protection or privacy protection is as valid as competition in other areas, providing the competition is kept fair through full disclosure and informed consent legislation.

The conclusion to which attention to the various rights of individuals leads is that from an ethical point of view the United States should follow the European lead in the area of legal personal information protection, as should other nations which have yet to adopt any policy. The market in this case is not self-correcting and legislation is required for the adequate protection of individual rights.

▲ CONFIDENTIALITY OF RECORDS AND ▲ RESPONSIBILITY FOR ERRORS AND HARM

We have already seen we must sometimes reveal certain information about ourselves in order to engage in certain transactions. We could hardly expect a bank to lend us money unless it knew something about our financial situation – employer, income, outstanding debts, and the like. We could not expect a doctor to treat us unless we told him the symptoms we are concerned about. However, we reveal this information to a specific person for a specific purpose. With respect to doctors, lawyers, and banks, we assume that the information is confidential and that it will not be revealed to others without our consent. It is their obligation to keep it secure. The same is true of any other business or agency that has information about us that it should keep from being divulged to unauthorized recipients. This is true even if individuals have given their consent to the information being used for marketing purposes by the recipient firm and its affiliates and even if the individual has agreed that the information could be sold to selected third parties by the recipient firm. Customers do not usually give personal information about themselves with the expectation that it will be made available to anyone or published in the newspapers or posted on the Web. Whatever the limitations on the personal information a business or agency has, they should be respected and hence safeguards developed to keep the information secure and out of the hands of unauthorized others.

Four principles apply to all such information. First, the information supplied for a certain purpose or purposes, and authorized for certain uses, should be used only for those purposes and uses. To do otherwise is to break at least an implicit agreement, if not a formal one (which will sometimes be the case).

Second, sufficient care should be taken to ensure that the information is not used for other purposes or made available or accessible to unauthorized persons or entities. Unless this is the case, permission to use the information in certain ways and to distribute it to certain third parties would in fact be permission to use it in any way anyone wishes and to make it available indiscriminately to anyone who wishes it. The latter is clearly not the case. Of course, if the information has monetary value, then the business that receives it has a self-interested incentive to keep it secure from unauthorized access.

Third, the information should be kept only as long as the purpose for which it was given remains. This length of time will obviously vary. Medical records might be kept by a medical facility as long as the individual is a patient – which might be decades – since one's medical history remains medically pertinent to later treatment. On the other hand, information about one's marital status, one's address, one's income, one's interests, and similar facts about individuals may change periodically. There is no specific rule about how long this information is pertinent, but clearly it possibly becomes dated after a number of years, and certainly cannot be assumed to be accurate after a decade. Marketers would not be interested in dated and obsolete information. Unless individuals know what records are being kept on them by whom, they cannot verify and correct them. Hence, either individuals should be informed that records are being kept on them and be given the right to correct them (as we have seen is the case with respect to the three major credit rating companies), or those holding the information have the responsibility to keep the records up to date or to destroy them when they are no longer useful.

Fourth, since those companies that hold records on individuals are responsible for their proper use and their protection, it does not seem unreasonable to hold them responsible for their improper use, their being divulged to or accessed by unauthorized third parties, and the harm that is done to the individuals due to the failure on the part of the companies to live up to their responsibilities. Holding them responsible may be difficult in practice, because it may not be clear who divulged information to whom, or who accessed it without authorization from where. But in some cases, as with specific medical records, it will be clear. In either case, the company has the stated responsibility and is ethically required to adopt the means necessary to live up to this responsibility. Whether or not it does can be checked.

Before the arrival of computers, records were typically kept on paper and stored in files. The fact that records were paper-bound was not insignificant and determined a great deal about records and record keeping. The sheer bulk of paper records meant that there was a natural tendency, often prompted by the necessities of space, to cull and throw out records after a certain period of time. The bulk of papers also meant that if they were allowed to accumulate to too large an extent it became very difficult and time consuming to retrieve information from them. Businesses would store records they legally needed to keep, but they were accessed only in case of need. Others were shredded or otherwise destroyed. Personnel files, like other files, were bulky. A frequent practice was to keep information in personnel files for only three years. This made for efficiency, as well as protecting employees from having old evaluations or rumors or letters or other material stay indefinitely to their detriment. Typically, employees also had the right to see their files and to rebut any adverse charges, as well as to correct any errors. Consumer files were similarly routinely culled and destroyed.

The fact that records were on paper meant that transferring them from one place to another was time consuming. Copies could be made, but that too involved copying, shipping, and so on. Consequently records typically stayed in the place of origin. Medical records were kept in the medical department or the clinic or hospital.

Police records were kept by the police. Business records were kept in the records room of the business. Public records were open to the public, but one had to go to City Hall or the public records room of the department that kept the records to see them. Most people and most businesses did not bother to go through the trouble to access such records unless there was a pressing reason to do so. Banks kept records of their customers' transactions, but these too were kept on paper.

The overall result was a wide decentralization of records on any one person. An investigator with a great deal of time could piece together information on someone. But much of it was in the hands of individual firms, hospitals, banks, and so on and not available to outsiders except with a court order. Paper records were kept in file drawers. Anyone wishing access to those files had either to make an official request to see them or have them sent, or had physically to appear and inspect the files on site. Confidential files were kept in locked drawers, and after working hours they were in locked rooms. Anyone wishing to see them either had to have legitimate access or had to break and enter. The latter were guilty of physical trespass and took the chance of a face-to-face encounter with a security officer or a late-working employee. The deterrence to casual attempts at seeing someone else's file was considerable. Similarly, tampering with and making changes on paper records is fairly difficult to do in such a way that the changes are not detectable. Erasures, whiteouts, and other attempts at changing the contents are reasonably easy to detect.

A consequence of the wide dispersal of records was a certain anonymity that each person enjoyed *vis-à-vis* the general public, friends and acquaintances, employers, and even the government. Much of this has changed fairly rapidly as computers have replaced paper as the medium on which to store records.

Similarly, prior to the widespread use of computers and credit cards, most purchases were made either in cash or by check. Checks were also written on paper and filed by banks under individual accounts. No routine record was kept of whom the checks were written to, and there was no profile of one's spending habits. It would have been too costly to be worth the effort. Cash transactions were, and still are, anonymous. One might get a receipt. But unless for a significant amount, the purchaser's name was not recorded. One could buy freely at supermarkets, discount houses, and department stores with no one keeping track of what the purchaser was buying.

The change from keeping records on paper to keeping them on computer has dramatically changed the nature of records. Records kept on computers suffer from few of the disadvantages – if they were disadvantages – of paper records. There is no longer a problem of space and bulk. Records that were too bulky to keep in paper form can now easily be stored in computers. Accessing data on computers is much simpler, faster, and more convenient than with paper files. There is also little difficulty in copying information, as well as in sending it to another user. As it becomes easy and cheap to store information, the incentive to cull out old information lessens. Keeping all information requires no screening, no decisions about what to keep and what to discard, and no time on the part of any operator to delete information. Hence there is an incentive not to review or cull or destroy or delete information on individuals, contrary to the third principle above.

Keeping confidential information that is stored in a computer to which many people have access is possible. But it takes special care and training on the part of all users. It is much easier to divulge passwords that give access to restricted areas than it is to give away one's office key. Someone with the password has access to files without the fear of confronting anyone during the search, and without physical trespass. The possibility that someone will browse out of curiosity to find out information about a fellow worker is much greater when the access is a few key strokes away than when it requires physically going to file drawers in some office. It is relatively easy to change computer files, and it can be done so that there is no record of the change, unless perhaps someone checks against a backup of the document made before the change. Copying is also easy and leaves no trace. Stealing is much less difficult than it is with paper records, physically guarded and kept under multiple locks and keys guarding doors and drawers. Hence there is an even greater need than before to guarantee the security of records containing personal information on individuals, both internally from employees with no need to know the information in questions and externally from hackers, other companies, predators, and other third parties. That is a responsibility of those who collect and maintain records of personal information on individuals.

Clearly the movement of records from paper to computers

changes how people and businesses should think about and treat files and it imposes on record keepers the burden of making sure that they preserve personal information so that it is kept secure and confidential.

▲ NOTES ▲

1. Many people freely give away personal information about their preferences to marketers through questionnaires. Some do so for a chance to receive a prize in a draw, some out of lack of realization of what they are giving away. Some even install cameras in their homes to display whatever they are doing 24 hours a day on Webcam sites accessible to anyone, sometimes for a small fee.
2. "Universal Declaration of Human Rights," in Ian Brownlie, ed., *Basic Documents on Human Rights*, 2nd. edn. (Oxford: Clarendon Press, 1981), p. 253.
3. Samuel D. Warren and Louis D. Brandeis, "The Right to Privacy," *Harvard Law Review*, Vol. IV, No. 5 (December 15, 1890), pp. 193–220.
4. *Griswold et al. v. Connecticut*, 381 US 479.
5. *Roe et al. v. Wade, District Attorney of Dallas County*, 410 US 113.
6. Judith Jarvis Thomson, "The Right to Privacy," *Philosophy & Public Affairs*, Vol. 4, No. 4 (summer 1975), pp. 295–314.
7. See, for example, Thomas Scanlon, "Thomson on Privacy," and James Rachels, "Why Privacy Is Important," in *Philosophy and Public Affairs*, Vol. 4, No. 4 (summer 1975).
8. W. A. Parent, in his article "Recent Work on the Concept of Privacy," *American Philosophical Quarterly*, Vol. 20, No. 4 (October 1983), pp. 341–55, wrote that "the current state of privacy research is in hopeless disarray" (p. 341). State statutes on privacy vary greatly from state to state.
9. Ibid, p. 346.
10. Julie Inness, "Information, Access, or Intimate Decisions about One's Actions? The Content of Privacy," *Public Affairs Quarterly*, Vol. 5, No. 3 (July 1991), pp. 227–42, criticizes such views on grounds other than those I raise.
11. See Parent, "Recent Work on the Concept of Privacy," pp. 343–5, for a review of those who hold these positions.
12. The courts have ruled that if employers own the computers that their employees use, the owners have the right to access and monitor the computers and their use. The law does not recognize any privacy claim on the part of employees with respect to what is on their computers or to what they do with their computers. Whether from a moral point of

view employers should recognize some privacy rights of their employees is a debated issued.

13. The issue of character *vis-à-vis* public officials raises this in a dramatic way.

14. Julie Inness,"Information, Access, or Intimate Decisions about One's Actions?," reconstrues all privacy in terms of intimacy, but concludes with the need to analyze intimacy in the same way that others analyze privacy.

15. Amitai Etzioni, in *The Limits of Privacy* (New York: Basic Books, 1999), argues forcefully the limitations on privacy that the general good demands .

16. Helen Nissenbaum, "Protecting Privacy in An Information Age: The Problem of Privacy in Public," *Law and Philosophy*, 17 (1998), pp. 559–96, develops the notion of "privacy in public."

17. This distinguishes anonymity on a street from anonymity on the World Wide Web, which raises different issues related to privacy. There, anonymity achieved through anonymous servers makes it possible for people to avoid accountability and responsibility. Encryption, which is another means of protecting privacy for electronic transmissions, raises similar problems.

18. Until recently there was no federal legislation guaranteeing privacy of medical records. The amount of legal protection of such records varies from state to state.

chapter three

Employees and Communication Privacy

Olivia Cruse, Vice President for Human Resources at Westbury Tech, Inc., could hardly believe her ears. Greg Woody, the CEO of the 700-plus employee firm, had just said, "I'm thinking of firing Jack Ridder and Patricia Hutt." Jack was one of the firm's best salesmen and Patricia was tops in the marketing division. Both of them were under consideration for promotion just last week.

"I don't understand," blurted Olivia in a shaky voice. "What's happened?"

"Well, you know that we just recently installed the Desktop Surveillance program that lets us keep track of what everyone is doing on their computers. Since we were thinking of promoting Jack and Pat I asked our IT people to do a quick check of their e-mail and Web use. I got the report today, and I am sorely disappointed in both of them. Jack has been staying late evenings, and I thought he was putting in more hours. Instead he's been looking at porn on the Web and downloading it. Pat, much to my amazement, spends several hours a day – some of it her own lunchtimes – shopping on the Web or chatting with friends. They are both good people in their own way. But they are both abusing our trust and not working as hard as they should. I don't think they deserve promotions, and I think it would send a clear message to everyone if we made examples of them by firing them."

"But that's not fair," countered Olivia. "Before firing them we should warn them about their behavior and give them a chance to stop. They're too good to make them sacrificial lambs. Besides, the message you send will be that we don't trust our employees, that we snoop on them, and that we're out to get them on any pretext. We have no stated policy on e-mail or Internet use. Obviously we need one."

Greg didn't hesitate in replying. "You mean to tell me that people don't know that they are hired to work and not shop or gossip or look at porn? Do you expect me to believe that people like Jack and Pat have to be told the obvious about what's right and wrong? If we found that either of them had lied on their résumé, they would be out of here in a flash, even though we have no written statement that says that is our policy. Why is this any different? You also know that other companies are doing it, so there is precedent. The New York Times fired 23 employees for inappropriate e-mails and Dow Chemical fired 40 for downloading pornography and sending obscene e-mails. Why shouldn't our ethical standards be as high as theirs?"

Olivia hesitated a few minutes. "Well," she said, "let's consider Jack first. Granted he used the office computer to surf the Web for pornography. But he did it on his own time, after hours; he didn't create a sexually hostile environment or pass what he downloaded onto anyone else; and what he did didn't affect his productivity in any way. There's no reason to think that if we published explicit guidelines about e-mail and Web use, he would violate them. If he did, that would be another story."

"And what's your defense of Pat? I supposed it's that she shopped on her own time, e-mailed friends no more than most others chat on the phone, and that her productivity is among the top in her division. I've thought of all that, but I still don't like the attitude her actions project."

"But, Greg, do you really want to fire two of our best people because you happened to choose them for screening because they were being considered for promotion? Is that fair? Others may be doing far worse. Do we want to find out? Is that why you had the new surveillance programs installed? Do we really want to treat our employees that way?"

"Well," Greg continued, "that seems to be the way most companies are going these days. Improper use of the Web and of e-mail is getting out of hand and we have to do something to control it."

"I don't disagree. But give me a chance to come up with a proposal for a set of guidelines for proper e-mail and Internet use by everyone in the company. And let me talk to Jack and Pat before we do anything more about them. After all, that is HR's job!"

Greg shuffled in his chair and thought a minute. "OK, let's see what you come up with. But I want it fast, before I change my mind.

And I want it to have some teeth, so if anyone is found in violation we can get rid of them."

Olivia left and on her way to her office wondered, "What would a really good set of guidelines for e-mail and Internet use be, and from whom should I get input?"

When any company hires an employee it is usually to fill a certain position and do a certain job. But whether that job is to perform routine repetitive work or one with great flexibility and responsibility, whoever is hired is a human being and so carries with him or her the human rights that all human beings have. This, as we have seen, includes some right to privacy. But the extent of the privacy that employees can legally claim on the job in the United States is in fact severely limited. According to the law, if a company provides the premises in which the employees work and if it owns the equipment, including the computers on which they work, then the company has to right to monitor what the employees do on the premises and how they use the equipment. The exceptions are surveillance of rest rooms and locker rooms or dressing areas. Hence any legal right to physical privacy, to the extent that this refers to the right to restrict physical observation of oneself, is extremely limited. This comes as no surprise to most employees, since they know they work in the company's facilities. Except for those who work in private offices, what one does is usually visible to others, and is often supervised.

A similar analysis applies to communication privacy, if the communication is transmitted over the company's computers or phones or faxes. As we shall see, the employee still maintains some right to personal information privacy, but this is protected not so much by any legal claim to privacy as it is by legal claims concerning discrimination. We can nonetheless raise the issue of the ethical rights to privacy and to respect that employees have as human beings and inquire as to what kinds of corporate policies in fact respect those rights.

The major issue concerning employees and information technology is surveillance – of employees themselves, of their e-mail, and of their use of the Internet. The advent of the computer has opened up new possibilities of surveillance and of communication, with the attendant temptations of abuse on the part of both employers and employees. Many companies are still struggling with the new issues and with a reasonable and ethically defensible policy.

▲ EMPLOYEE PRIVACY AND ▲ SURVEILLANCE

We have already discussed surveillance of individuals in public and the collecting and collating of information. Many of the principles applicable to that discussion, however, find little place in the workplace. In the vast majority of cases, the workplace is not public space and those who work within it are paid employees. They work on company premises, using company tools, machines, furniture, and supplies. They are paid to do certain jobs for a certain period of time. Although they do not belong to their employer, during the time of work they have little claim on privacy. Those who employ them have a right to keep track of the work they do, of how they do it, and of the time it takes them to do it. Some people work under constant supervision. The image of a foreman looking over the piece work of factory workers and applying constant pressure to increase the pace conjures up images of sweatshops. The kind of close surveillance associated with blue collar workers, factories, and assembly lines is now readily available as well in the office with respect to typists, keypunchers, data inputters, and anyone who uses a computer, with the concomitant dangers. Surveillance is of many types and we can distinguish security surveillance from personal surveillance.

Security surveillance is probably brought to its peak in casinos. Other places of business often have similar, although not as comprehensive, security. Cameras cover parking lots, entrances to buildings, foyers, and the business premises themselves. When the purpose is security, guards monitor the screens for any sign of attempted unauthorized entry or suspicious activity. This is similar to comparable cameras in semi-public areas. And as in the case with semi-public areas, the capacity to view and track individuals, who as employees will be known by name, becomes a possibility. This leads to the question of personal surveillance.

There are three types with which we will be concerned, and each raises somewhat different issues. The first is physical surveillance, the second e-mail surveillance, and the third Internet surveillance by an employer of employees.

Physical surveillance

Two types of physical surveillance concern us. One is via cameras and the other via the monitoring of computer keyboards. Aside from security purposes the cameras might be seen as replacing the shop foreman, and used to keep track of who is on a break, how long they take, how often they take breaks, whether they are working while at their desk. There is no issue of privacy here and in most cases such physical monitoring via cameras is not necessary. Nonetheless an employer has the right to know that his employees are working and when they are not.

If employees see that surveillance cameras are being used, they will most likely wonder to what use they are being put. An employer might trade on the fact that if employees do not know, then they may well assume that they are constantly under scrutiny and will act accordingly. Whether this will produce the desired effect or whether it will have an inhibiting effect that impedes efficiency as workers wonder how certain of their movements or actions might be interpreted is debatable, and is likely to vary depending on a great many different conditions.

One operative principle is that respect for persons would lead a company to at least notify its employees of the use made of its surveillance equipment. Leaving them in doubt shows a lack of trust and might well tend to promote an unpleasant and hostile workplace environment. On the factory floor the workmen saw the foreman and knew they were being watched. The surveillance was open and above board. Office workers deserve at least that much respect. They ought to know the conditions under which they work. Beyond that, any surveillance that does take place via cameras should have some justification behind it. That it is possible is not a justification. There may be plausible and defensible uses of constant surveillance – as one can possibly argue in the case of money handlers, although even here there are usually other methods of enforcing accountability.

The other kind of surveillance is via computer keyboards. There are now programs available that can track every keystroke, every correction and backspace, and the speed of entry. It is possible for a manager to track the speed and accuracy of those inputting data not only by the end result but also by a minutely detailed record of the process. It is possible to use the tracking to record not only key-strokes but also which keys are hit, and so to track not only data entered but also e-mail accessed or sent and the URL of Internet sites accessed and used.

Some such software is also sold for individual, personal use and advertised for parents to check up on the use of their computers by their children or for a suspicious spouse to check on the computer use of his or her mate. The latter use clearly indicates lack of trust. In the case of corporate use, this may not necessarily be the case. There may be legitimate corporate uses of such programs, for instance to gain information on what common computer practices of their employees are and how these might be streamlined and made more efficient, or to try to ascertain why one unit that does comparable work with another is more productive or less productive, or some other comparable and reasonable work-related purpose. Most such purposes do not require that the surveillance be conducted secretly. Employees should know the standards which their work is expected to meet, and they should know what measures are used to determine whether they meet those standards. Using such programs to put more and more pressure on employees to produce more and more quickly is not the most effective incentive and tends to come close to reproducing the unreasonable expectations and pressures of sweatshops.

E-mail

E-mail is an especially vexing problem for many firms. Since employees' computers belong to the firm for which they work and since they are hired to do certain tasks, the law (or at least court decisions thus far) gives the firm the right to both control the use of its equipment and the right to the contents thereof. It is therefore perfectly legal for companies to monitor all the use made by their employees of their computers and to access whenever they want all the information on the computer, including e-mail. The exception would be in the case of a unionized location in which the union had negotiated some restriction on a company's monitoring as part of the contract specifying conditions of employment.

Since this is the legal situation, it would appear that there are no difficulties. Employees in effect have no legal right to privacy with respect to their e-mails or computer use, and that should be known and understood by all. The difficulty comes from the fact that it is not known by many employees; that not all companies exercise their legal right to monitor or even randomly read their employees' e-mail, thus undermining the claim that all employees should know that it is done or might be done; that in many cases there is no reason for companies to do so; that doing so may be counterproductive from the point of view of the company's interests; and that there are ethical considerations that militate against companies monitoring all employee e-mail.

Many employees erroneously believe that e-mail is comparable to US mail and is private in the same way that regular mail is private. They know it is a violation of the law for anyone to tamper with another's personal mail, to intercept it or open it or steal it. What one person writes to another and sends through the US mail is thus considered private, and is in fact a private communication between the sender and the receiver. Since e-mail is in many ways a comparable type of communication between a sender and a receiver, it is natural for people to assume that similar rules apply in the two types of communication. By analogy they assume that their e-mail is private, just as their federal mail is private. Although perhaps natural, the assumption is false, and the analogy does not hold in several important respects. Legally their e-mail sent or received on a company computer belongs to the company. There are no copies of an individual's letters sent or received that are automatically archived by companies. E-mails are not only not privately owned by the individual employee, they may pass though other systems on their way to or from the sender or recipient and can be intercepted and read by others. In this regard they are more like postcards than like sealed letters. They are not destroyed simply by being deleted and they cannot be shredded by an individual the way a letter can. There are other disanalogies that are also pertinent. Many people regard letters as something rather formal. E-mails are often treated much less formally. They are so easy to write and send that they are often sent quickly, and without the thought and care that goes into a letter. They are not checked the way letters are. They are easily sent to the wrong recipient or to multiple recipients when only one was intended. Whereas the phone replaced letters for many purposes, e-mail has replaced the phone.

Another analogy that also does not hold is between the telephone and e-mail, although the analogy is closer here than to the federal mail. People in general know that although phone lines may be tapped, and although some employers may listen in on employees' phone conversations to make sure they are not using the phone for personal use, or perhaps to monitor certain types of phone manners or effectiveness of presentations, phone calls for the most part are private communications.

Most firms have some policy about the use of phones and about the use of federal mail. They expect that employees will usually not make personal calls on company phones or on company time, and that they will not spend company time writing personal letters. With respect to phones the rules are usually stricter with respect to long-distance and other toll calls than to local calls of short duration. Company postage stamps should not be used for personal letters, nor should company stationery. These rules are common and widely known.

There is some logical and legitimate transfer of expectations from regular mail and phone use to e-mail use. Since using company time for personal correspondence and phone calls takes one away from one's work, it is obvious that this is not the appropriate use of an employee's time, when they are supposed to be doing the work for which they were hired. The same is true of the use of e-mail.

Most employers do not rule out emergency personal calls, or short calls to check on the state of a sick child or similar personal calls.

As is true with respect to letters and phone calls, so also with e-mail; it is not always easy to separate out completely personal from business use. Each of the categories is clear at the extremes. A purely personal letter to a friend is personal. A business order is business. There are grey areas when the communication is a business one but the person is also a friend and one includes information of a personal nature.

What makes the greatest difference between regular mail and e-mail from a legal point of view is that the law that applies to regular mail simply does not apply to e-mail. So far the courts have decided that because computers at work are the property of the employer provided for business purposes, whatever is done on them is the property of the employer. This has been taken to include employees' e-mail, which employers are legally permitted to read if they wish. What is sent on e-mail is not private between the sender and receiver, but is available at various stages to various people who may legally read it. Moreover, most companies make backups of all messages sent and received by e-mail, and usually archive them. They are thereby saved and may be retrieved and read. In cases of criminal investigation they may be searched and turned over to the police. This all comes as something of a surprise and shock to some employees, who felt that their passwords provided security from their messages being available to others and who did not know about backups and archives and who thought that their e-mail messages were sent to a certain recipient and that when deleted by the recipient and by the sender, they were permanently deleted without a trace. That this is the not the case comes as a surprise because they do not understand the technicalities of the transmission process, who may access the transmission at various points, and the backup and achieving procedures. Many consequently feel that their privacy has been violated if and when they find that someone either has read their e-mail or that someone might do so. Employees who have complained about their supervisors or their company in e-mail messages have been surprised when they have been penalized or fired for what they thought were private messages. Corporate executives themselves have also sometimes been surprised when their internal e-mails have been subpoenaed in connection with lawsuits or government investigations.

It would clearly not be cost-effective for a company to have anyone read all the e-mail generated by all its employees. But this is not necessary to accomplish most of the aims of a company with respect to e-mail. What are the major corporate concerns and complaints? One is that e-mails that go out from their employees are identifiable as coming from the company, usually through the return address that accompanies e-mail. Hence the reputation and possibly the liability of the company are tied to e-mails that employees send. Clearly, illegal activity, such as an employee sending child pornography as attachments to e-mail, would not be tolerated at most firms. Nor would sexually harassing e-mail, hate e-mail, or other such use of e-mail be tolerated. Using e-mail to circulate sexual jokes to fellow-workers is not uncommon, but does open up the possibility of creating an environment that is legally characterized as "hostile-environment sexual harassment" for which the company is legally liable. It is very easy to hit the wrong send button or in other ways to missend e-mail to those other than the intended recipients. It is also prima facie inappropriate for employees to use their company computers to circulate or exchange such jokes. The company therefore reasonably argues that it has the right to protect itself from abuses of e-mail by its employees and may legally and ethically take measures to protect itself. This includes the option of reading employees' e-mails – either randomly, or by looking at employees suspected of something, or by using software that scans all the e-mail on the company's server for certain key words or for certain addresses or addressees.

Companies also are concerned about other uses that they consider abuses. One is the spreading of discontent or disaffection by use of the company's e-mail; another is the disclosure of a company's trade secrets either intentionally or unintentionally; a third is the abuse of a company's e-mail for excessive personal correspondence; and a fourth is possibly the use of a company's e-mail to search for a position at other companies.

With the possible exception of the fourth, these are all legitimate concerns and are arguably abuses that any company should be able to protect itself against. The questions are whether monitoring e-mail is the best mechanism for accomplishing the company's aims, and, if so, what is the best way to accomplish the monitoring.

The considerations on the other side are the privacy of employees and the effect of monitoring on the morale, actions, and productivity of employees.

From an ethical point of view we can start with what is the least that can be expected of company policies and actions. At the least, employees should be fully informed about the policy of the company for which they work, which provides them with their computers and e-mail access. Because it is legal for an employer to monitor and read employees' e-mail, it is difficult to say that it is unethical for the employer to do so. But it is unethical for the company to either mislead employees into thinking that their e-mail is private when in fact it is not, or to let them make that assumption and then penalize them for what they say. At a minimum, what a company that wishes to be ethical should do is inform their employees of its policy. So far, in the United States this is a legal requirement only in the state of Connecticut. If the company archives all incoming and outgoing e-mail, employees should know this. If it archives such communications but accesses them only if someone raises a legitimate complaint, or if they have cause to think that something illegal is contained in them or that accessing them may help them in investigating illegal activity, that is very different from routinely or randomly monitoring e-mail simply to check that there are no personal messages or what management might consider abuses of the system. Doing the latter is not unethical in itself, but employees should know the rules under which they are operating. They should not be held responsible for breaking rules of which they were not informed, nor should they be penalized if they are the recipients and not the originators of private or improper messages.

If the company does monitor or possibly access e-mail communications, the company should let employees know under what conditions this is done, and who is authorized to do the monitoring or accessing. Such monitoring should only be done for business reasons in pursuit of business interests. A company that does a great deal of its business with customers through e-mail might well wish to monitor how customers are treated, how orders are handled, and so on. When much customer service is done over the phone there is frequently a message that customers hear informing them that the call may be monitored to ensure quality service. A policy that also informs employees when their e-mail has been read would both let people know that the policy is enforced and that they will know when the monitoring might affect them.

Some firms prefer both not to monitor and not to inform their employees of the policy. By not monitoring, they feel they are respecting their employees. But they feel that the lack of information about the policy may incline employees to monitor themselves, that clearly stating that employees are not being monitored might lead to abuses that would not take place otherwise, and that by not stating a policy the company leaves open the option of whether or not to read or monitor in specific cases or at a later time. It is therefore to the company's advantage not to state a policy, and at the same time its not monitoring shows respect for its employees. The only difficulty is that the latter is not really the case. For the respect it shows its employees is conditional and subject to change at will. It trades on assuming and profiting from employee ignorance – which is hardly an indication of respect. It may well be the case that a company does not feel it can anticipate and spell out all the conditions under which it might have a business obligation to read or monitor specific e-mails. Its policy can state this, at the same time indicating that its general policy is not to do so, and indicating, if special conditions arise, who does the monitoring or reading and what, if any, protection the employee has. Many companies have the policy of not going through an employee's desk or files without at least two persons present, one of whom is the employee's supervisor or superior, or a representative from human resources. A similar policy, suitably modified, can be adopted with respect to e-mail.

Developing a policy that clearly informs employees of a company's policy may still leave some areas open to interpretation. It would be unreasonable to refuse to let employees use e-mail for any personal messages, such as emergency communication with their children. What constitutes excessive personal use may also be open to interpretation. But as with other evaluations, employees should be evaluated on how well individuals do their jobs. Any use of e-mail that interferes with one's job and lessens one's productivity is something that a supervisor may rightly talk to the employee about. The ground of the complaint is the interference and the lessening of productivity. And if the cause is use of time spent on personal e-mails, then that is something that can and should be corrected, and about which the employee may be warned.

Surely, if as a result of monitoring or reading an employee's e-mail a manager discovers private information about that individual – a love affair or something else of a personal nature – the manager and the company have no right to disclose that information to others. Just because the company owns the e-mail, it does not thereby have the right to do whatever it wants with the contents. Even though it legally owns the contents, the individual's right to privacy precludes disclosure of personal information that has no business relevance. Moreover, some content is protected, and even if accessed, cannot be prohibited. The National Labor Relations Board has ruled that employers cannot restrict the use of e-mail used by employees to organize or to discussion of organizational activities and workplace conditions.

The other abuses listed above – such as sending off-color jokes or spreading disaffection or revealing trade secrets – should be fairly obvious actions that employees should know would be abuses of the company's e-mail system. Nonetheless, specifying actions of this type as improper use seems to be fair warning of what is not allowable use. This does not mean that all improper uses must be made explicit, nor does it imply that any use that is not specified as unacceptable is therefore acceptable. But the policy should be explicit enough so that ordinary workers using their common sense know what the company's policy is.

Using a company's e-mail to look for another job is an example of borderline use. Many companies are not happy about their employees seeking other employment and using a company's facilities to do so. This is understandable. On the other hand, if a corporation is known to be planning to downsize, it can hardly blame its employees if they to try to find other employment. In all cases the job-seeking must be kept within reasonable bounds and employees are still expected to do their jobs. Nor does it seem completely inappropriate for someone to e-mail his or her résumé upon request, any more than it would be inappropriate to make or receive a short phone call. In this as in other cases, the complaint should not be the nature of the e-mail so much as the question of whether it interferes with one's performance.

So far all that we have argued is that the company's policy, whatever it is, be made clearly known to all employees. What more might an ethically defensible e-mail policy for a company contain?

Although a company can legally prohibit employees from using e-mail for any personal use and it can legally monitor all employee e-mail, and although we have argued a company should notify employees of its policy, some policies are better than others, and some can be challenged on both pragmatic and ethical grounds.

Consider, for example, a policy that prohibits all personal use of e-mail. Such a policy, I have argued so far, is both legal and seems to be ethically justifiable, providing the employees are informed of the policy. Now consider the pragmatic consequences and the reasonable reaction of employees. If they are not allowed to use e-mail for personal use, they will probably not do so; but they may well use the phone more to accomplish the same purpose, or they may find other more time-consuming means to achieve what they wished to achieve by their e-mails. They will internalize the company's rules and might well exclude from e-mails anything that might be considered personal, lest they be censured by their employer, even though the personal aspects might help relations with customers or suppliers or others with whom they carry on official e-mail contact. And they may well feel that the company policy is unreasonable, and that the company does not trust its employees to act like responsible adults. The kind of atmosphere that such feelings generate can scarcely be expected to increase productivity or loyalty to the company or promote the kind of environment that encourages employees to give their best at work.

The ethical consideration brings into question whether it is sufficient from an ethical point of view simply to make known the company's policy, without also considering what that policy is. Although legally a company may do whatever it wants with respect to employee e-mail, surely both considerations of employees' right to respect and of their privacy will preclude certain policies. To read all of an employee's e-mail certainly demonstrates lack of trust.

Screening all e-mail for key words or random screening or reading of e-mail are both less costly, but as a policy also indicate lack of trust. We have already noted different kinds of activities – monitoring for quality control of customer contact is different from routine monitoring of internal or external e-mails. If someone is suspected of leaking or selling the company's proprietary information, that is a matter of concern and is a plausible justification for monitoring that individual's e-mail. But the suspicion precedes and does not follow from the monitoring.

In a well-publicized case, the New York Times Company in November, 1999, fired 22 of its employees in its Norfolk, Virginia, payroll processing plant for sending "inappropriate and offensive" e-mail in violation of the company's e-mail policy. The e-mails were considerable in number and contained sexual jokes and items involving "a graphic display of sex." The discovery of the violation was not the result of any routine monitoring of employee e-mail but was uncovered as the result of an investigation into the use by an employee of company stationery to help a friend get unemployment benefits. As a result of a mistaken address, the letter was returned to the Times Company, and that in turn set off an investigation of that matter, which in turn led to the uncovering of the improper use of e-mail by others. An additional 20 employees who received the e-mails in question but neither reported nor forwarded them to others, received warning letters. A refresher on the Times Company policy had been sent to all employees only four months before the incident.[1]

The suspicion that an individual is using e-mail to look for another job is not adequate cause to monitor that person's e-mail. Employees frequently look for other jobs. They typically do not use a great deal of company time to do so, and if they do, that interferes with their work – which is the proper cause for complaint. The use of e-mail in this case is similar to other personal uses of e-mail. If such use interferes with doing one's job, lessens productivity, causes one to fall behind, and so on, then that is a problem that one may be called to account for by one's boss or supervisor. But monitoring the person's e-mail does not add any new pertinent information.

The general rules that apply to the use of the telephone seem to work in most businesses. A line may be tapped in case of criminal investigation. Otherwise, with the exception of quality control monitoring, phones are not tapped and excessive personal use is obvious in the lack of productivity. Simply because there is technology that enables a company to monitor employees' e-mail is no reason that it should be used. Because of the respect due employees as individuals it is the use of such technology that needs justification rather than failure to use it.

Because companies have adopted a large variety of different rules about the use of e-mail, it is all the more necessary for companies to establish their policies and inform their employees of them. A policy that places heavy emphasis on monitoring e-mail will lead to employees using the system more cautiously and will tend to inhibit what they write, since they know it might be read, might be misinterpreted, might be taken out of the context in which it was intended, and so on. If one of the benefits of e-mail is rapid and informal communication that makes meetings and phone calls less necessary, some of the benefit is lost if employees are inhibited in their use of the medium. On the other hand, if there is free use for personal as well as business use, there is the danger that some employees will spend a great deal of time on e-mail to the detriment of their other work. Where and how to draw the line and what policy to adopt depends on the nature of the company, its employees, the nature of their work, whether their work is closely supervised or relatively unsupervised, and other similar considerations. No matter whether the policy the company adopts is restrictive or permissive, employees should know that no company can guarantee complete privacy, since e-mail records are open to subpoena in criminal investigations. E-mail is of course vulnerable to being seen by others accidentally on either the receiver's or the sender's monitor, or if they are downloaded to hard copy, to access in that form. It is also possible to missend e-mail messages by pushing the wrong button, or by sending the message to more than the single individual intended. Also, no matter what the company's policy, employees should realize that if they send messages to persons outside the firm, the recipient's firm might have different rules, and what is considered private at one's own firm might not be at the recipient's end, or vice versa.

In general, the less restrictive and the less intrusive the policy, the more it indicates respect and trust for employees and the easier it is to defend from an ethical point of view. In some kinds of business, we have already seen that routine reviewing of e-mail may be necessary for quality control and optimal customer service. In many cases, no routine or random accessing and reading of employees' e-mail is the appropriate policy. Accessing and reading e-mail might be triggered by a complaint or by some suspicion of wrongdoing from another source. But then proper, announced procedures should be followed. Routine inspection of e-mail by subject heading is less intrusive than reading the contents of the e-mail, and so preferable. Indications of problems might be flagged in still less intrusive ways – such as a program that reports e-mail use that is excessive in number, given the assignments and responsibilities of the employees; or programs that indicate internal forwarding of a large number of e-mails. In such cases, the e-mails do not have to be examined for a supervisor to contact the employee involved and inquire about the large numbers or other aspects that indicate a possible problem.

The situation gets even more complicated if an employee uses the company's server to receive personal e-mail at home. They can access their mail from home on their own computer, which may not belong to the company. They could, of course, subscribe to a separate server on which to receive their e-mail. But if they do not, should their e-mail be read? The answer seems implicit in what we have already said. The employee should know the rules of the company. Does the company allow such use? If so, what are the stated conditions for monitoring? If employers allow home use of the company's e-mail server, then they should respect the privacy of e-mails generated to and from an employee's home. Yet if a company's e-mail is routinely monitored for key words or randomly monitored, then all e-mail going through the server will be monitored, and distinguishing between e-mail generated at work or at home may not be possible. Employees wanting greater privacy would in this case do well to subscribe to services such as AOL for their personal e-mail. If they do, then the reverse consideration also applies. They may then access their personal e-mail on their personal account from work. But if they do, and if it is received through the company's server, it has a status similar to e-mail generated on the company's server.

There are other variations that more technologically sophisticated employees may use. One is to encrypt their e-mails for personal use. This would prevent their employers from reading them, but it would not prevent them from knowing they were being sent, and to whom and with what frequency. As encryption becomes more common and easier to use, its frequency of use will increase. It may be used for internal memos as well as for many business transactions in addition to personal use. Governments are worried about encryption as a means of evading criminal investigation. Employees may see it as a means of protecting privacy. But companies may worry about it as a means of preventing accountability on the part of employees. The solution to this and other technical means of employees' protecting their privacy such as by the use of anonymous mailers is to not follow the technological imperative from the start. Just because monitoring is possible does not mean it must or should be used. If it is, are counter-measures by employees to protect their e-mail ethically justifiable? The answer is the same as the one we have given all along. Companies should make clear their policies. Will a company's outlawing of employee encryption of e-mail be taken as a lack of trust and respect? It probably will, unless the company itself has not pursued an aggressive monitoring policy. Eventually, encryption may be used widely even internally. Whether this is a wise move from a business perspective is difficult to predict, because it depends on the ease of use and cost in time and convenience. From an ethical point of view, it is necessary to include the intent of the one encrypting and the conditions under which it is used.

The ethical issues that have accompanied the use of e-mail have been in part a function of the technology involved, and the ethical quandaries that arise reflect the fact that our intuitions have not had a chance to develop adequately with respect to the new possibilities and consequent scenarios. We can expect this state of affairs to continue as the technology develops, both for electronic communication of new kinds and for technological means for protecting privacy.

The sanctions for misuse of a company's e-mail should be proportionate to the offense. Unless the action is illegal or so obviously wrong (such as spending all one's time on personal e-mails) that employees know their behavior is not allowable, it is only fair for employees to know that there are sanctions and what they are. Terminating someone on the spot simply for sending a message to other employees is not justifiable, and sends the message that the company is arbitrary. Employees should not be penalized for violating rules they do not know exist. Nor is firing someone appropriate when a letter of reprimand would do.

Internet

Our analysis of e-mail in part carries over into the use and monitoring of employee use of the Internet.

Just as there are many firms that have not drawn up clear guidelines on employee use of e-mail, so many have not drawn up clear guidelines for what is and what is not allowable use with respect to the Internet. Whether they are allowed to use the Internet for their personal needs or wants – be it entertainment or shopping or pursuing one's hobby or other personal interests – is often not made clear to employees. Perhaps they should know that on company time they should not pursue personal interests. But what about during lunch time or breaks or after hours? Ethics does not dictate any particular policy. But fairness requires that employees know the rules they are expected to obey with respect to the new communications media, lest they be penalized for breaching rules they did not know existed, or feel unjustly treated when they indirectly learn that their Web browsing is being monitored by the company.

The Internet problems we are primarily concerned with here relate to employee use of news groups, chat groups, and the World Wide Web.

An enormous amount of information is available on the Internet on almost every subject imaginable. There are also a wide variety of interest groups, many professionally oriented. Someone interested in business ethics or computer ethics will find a great many resources available, as will someone interested in pornography. And there is no easy and completely satisfactory way to allow employees access to information that helps them perform their jobs more efficiently and adds value from those that do just the opposite.

Legally the situation is the same as with e-mail. The computers belong to the company and anything on them belongs to the company. Their use is allowed by the company and may legally be monitored.

Server logs, which record all Internet activity on a network, will present an account of which computer accessed which website for how long and where the user went next. A little detective work can piece together patterns of who is doing what with respect to Internet use. Some companies use such logs either to determine whether they have problems or abuse by employees, or to catch particular employees whom they suspect of misusing the Internet while at work.

Various studies and polls, however, indicate that personal use of the computer at work is more the rule than the exception. A survey by Vault.com in the fall of 2000 reports that only 9.6 percent claimed not to spend time surfing non-work related websites during an average day. The question that companies face is how much such surfing is tolerable, what kind of surfing is intolerable, and what can be done in either situation.

Programs are available that can keep track of what sites employees are visiting. Others are available that can block access to specific types of sites. One such program, Websense, which claims to have 8,500 corporate customers, including 244 of the Fortune 500 companies, provides a variety of services. Its filtering software covers more than 2.4 million sites, is updated daily, and can block or selectively block certain groups, and time-limit access to more than 75 categories.[2] So technologically it is possible both to track and to block. Each poses somewhat different problems, both from a business and from an ethical perspective.

Employees have the ethical obligation to do the work for which they are hired while on the job. It would be stealing time from their employer to spend hours chatting in chat groups or playing games on the Internet or doing personal shopping, or even browsing sites on the Web that may be tangentially related to one's job, but far from central and an easy way to pass time rather than to do whatever else one should be doing. The latter is especially difficult, since it hinges on a judgment call about when one has enough information for the task required and how much peripheral and ancillary information it may be important to know and have.

But taking some slack time, chatting with one's office mates, spending time around the water cooler, or shopping on a long lunch break are not unknown among white collar workers. One estimate by a management consulting firm claims that the average office worker actually works only about 60 percent of the day.[3] Whether checking one's stocks, buying a present, or looking at the sports returns on-line is more time consuming and disruptive of an employee's work depends on how much time they spend on such activities and whether they would in fact spend more time at doing their jobs if they did not have Internet access.

Given the fact that the employer owns the computer and pays for whatever Internet connections it allows and establishes, employees can claim no right to unlimited access to the Internet at any time they wish and for however long they wish. The issue is not one of censorship, as it would be if the employee were using his or her own Internet connection at home. It might seem so obvious to employers that their employees should not spend time on non-job related activities on the Internet, that they do not specify any restrictions. Nonetheless the same general sort of thinking that applies to e-mail applies as well to Internet use.

Companies should determine what their rules are with respect to Internet use: whether the Information Systems manager will monitor what employees are accessing, downloading, and communicating; whether there are restrictions on use; whether use is closely restricted to business purposes (usually broadly defined, since the line, as with e-mail, between business and non-business purposes is often blurred); how infractions of the rules will be dealt with, if there will be any penalty; and any other rules of use that the company adopts. Some companies, such as Lincoln National Corp., have installed a message that appears each time an employee connects with the Internet, that reminds them of the company's policy that access is to be used only for company business and that their connections will be recorded. This makes clear each time what the rules are, and gives fair warning of what is allowed and what is not allowed.[4]

Managers and supervisors will be aware of whether someone is getting his or her work done, or if there is a dramatic falloff in productivity as a result of overuse of the Internet. Addiction to any aspect of Internet use should be handled as any other addiction that interferes with employees doing their jobs. Of course, illegal activity on the Web, such as trafficking in child pornography, should be as little tolerated as other sorts of illegal behavior, such as trafficking in illegal drugs.

Accessing legal pornography in many places of business is not tolerated, not only because it is not business related, but also for two other reasons. One is that such access associates the business with the pornographic site (the site must have the address of the computer to which it sends the images) and makes likely the further receipt of pornographic spam and advertising. Second, and even more importantly, if the computer is visible by anyone other than the user – as it is in most situations – pornographic images create what is legally a sexually hostile environment and opens the company up to legal suits, should any employee complain. Compaq fired 20 employees and Xerox fired 40 for surfing pornographic websites often and for considerable periods of time, as have other firms.

Prohibiting access to pornographic sites is easily justified because accessing such sites opens up the company to legal suits. Similarly, prohibiting the downloading of MP3 music files and movies is also an easy call because such downloading takes up so much bandwidth that it may clog the system, and because of the danger of legal suits in case the music downloaded free is copyrighted. Bell South blocks access to sex sites, hate sites, and gambling sites.

Other personal use, such as shopping, checking on the stock market, looking for vacation sites and bargains, pursuing one's hobby, chatting with people with similar interests, and the like, do not pose the same sort of legal problem for the firm. But they raise the issues of appropriate use of the Internet and appropriate times for different uses.

Some companies simply do not provide access to the Internet, at least for a large number whom the company feels have no business need to access it. If there is no business need, then there is nothing wrong with not providing access.

As with the use of e-mail, the company's policy should be clearly stated, and in this case whether personal use is allowed during lunch periods or other non-business hours. As with e-mail, a policy of trust, unless otherwise counter-indicated, is the ethically preferable approach. Complete monitoring or monitoring by specific websites or by key word indexes is possible, but the considerations are similar to those we have already seen with e-mail. Moreover, once one establishes a policy of monitoring, then one's legal liability might increase unless one continues to monitor, does so effectively, and takes measures to prevent such misuse as might lead, for instance, to charges of a sexually hostile environment. A company cannot both claim to monitor and plead ignorance to its employees accessing sexually oriented sites that may be offensive to other employees.

Two important differences between Internet abuses of work time by employees and other kinds of abuses are the greater possibility of abuse from the point of view of one's use of time and the possibility of blocking sites.

The problem of idling away one's time on the Internet, we have already noted, is only one way in which employees can spend their time in non-work related ways. But the difference from other ways is that one may appear to be working while surfing the Internet for one's own personal interests, that people often get carried away by the activity of surfing itself and lose track of time, spending much more time than they intended, and that for some people surfing the Web seems to be addictive. One can spend many hours surfing sites that are not problematic, but are simply not business related. Such use clearly amounts to abuse, and employers have every right to complain about such abuse and insist that it be stopped. This means that they must know it is taking place, that the fact that it is an abuse is clear to the employee, and that they take some action to inform and warn or train the employee on proper use.

What is somewhat surprising it that some employees are able to spend so much time on the Internet pursuing their own interests. It would seem that they could not do so and get the work done that they are hired to do. It would seem further that either they are able to get their work done in less time than their managers believe, or they make up for the time they spend on the Internet by staying late or in other ways compensating, or that their managers do not manage very well. What constitutes abuse is not getting one's work done while pursuing one's own interests. But then one can and it seems should rightly be called to task for not doing one's work. The fact that one does not do one job's because of the Internet is secondary to the fact that one does not do one's job. The Internet, in such situations, is only part of the problem.

The other difference between other abuses by employees of their work time and abuses involving Internet use is that in the latter a company may block access to certain kinds of websites. Blocking will prevent access to certain sites, and may be justified in some cases to employees, who may nonetheless feel that it implies a lack of trust and a paternalistic attitude on the part of the employer.

Aside from this reaction, there are at least four difficulties with the use of any blocking programs. The first is that, although it may be obvious that one wants to block pornographic sites and MP3 music downloading sites, it is not clear what more than these makes sense. Blocking all shopping sites prevents those who makes legitimate company purchases on-line. Blocking sports sites may interfere with getting information someone legitimately needs. Blocking sites and then making individual users request access from the Information Technology manager is time consuming and may be seen as not worth the effort of pursuing.

Second, any means of screening and blocking sites relies on blocking sites with certain key words or on the judgment of those who provide the blocking program. The purchaser is not told what the key words are or which sites are blocked, since that is considered proprietary information. So the user is uncertain about exactly what is blocked and whether it is more or less than the company wishes. To the extent that it under- or over-blocks, it fails to achieve the purpose for which it was installed. Thus, the third problem is that blocking may actually prevent employees from accessing legitimate sites that may be of business use to them. The usual example is that if any site that has the word 'sex' or 'breast' is blocked, then many medical sites will be blocked, as well as literary, movie, art, and other kinds of sites. The same is true of any category one chooses. Many sites supply the standard search engines with a fairly large number of key words under which to index the site so that users can find it no matter which aspect of the site they might be interested in. Blocking in some cases causes more difficulties than it solves. The fourth difficulty is that new sites appear everyday, and unless the program is constantly being updated, it will not catch some of the new sites that one may wish blocked. An employee wishing to access forbidden sites and knowing this will be somewhat deterred, but will spend more time than otherwise finding what he or she wants.

Blocking will, of course, catch many of the sites one wishes blocked and a company might decide that despite the negative consequences, these are outweighed by the positive ones. If employees know that certain categories of sites are blocked, most of them will not try to access such sites. But that is true even if they were simply told that they should not access those categories. So for most of them the blocking is unnecessary.

For those more knowledgeable, there are ways around any attempt at blocking. They can access another, perhaps an anonymous server and then access the sites of their choice from there. The technological game then escalates, as it does with encryption and e-mail. But companies needn't go down that path in the first place, and a sound policy, with justification provided for it, will serve most companies well and make their employees feel they are trusted and respected.

Use of the Internet also raises the issue of what is on an employee's hard (or floppy) drive. Texts, documents, and pictures can be downloaded to one's hard drive from the Web for easy access at later times and can be kept until deleted. Even after deleted, it can be accessed if it is not overwritten. In addition the computer saves a great deal of information about one's Internet use. Most browsers keep a record of the sites one has visited in a history file. In addition the pictures and text one accesses are saved at least temporarily in various cache files, and most sites place identifiable cookies in the cookie file. There are other traces as well, including listing in "favorites," "documents," and a variety of temporary files. Anyone wishing to see what sites one has visited and knows what to look for can find this out. It does not require any monitoring or special program. All one needs is access to the computer. What is the ethics of snooping in this way? It is clearly not allowable for those unauthorized to have access to one's computer to do this. That is a violation of both property and privacy. But what of those who have authorized access – one's supervisor or boss? The computer belongs to the company and so access to it is not illegal by representatives of the company. This comes close to looking in an employee's physical files or in their cubicle or desk. The guiding principle is whether there is a business-related purpose that such a search requires. Idle curiosity or personal animosity are not sufficient business-related justifications.

Knowledgeable computer-using employees may also thwart such attempts at snooping by downloading and using programs that erase one's Internet tracks, that clean up the caches, that overwrite Internet files. Is there anything unethical about their doing so? If what they are covering up is unethical activity, then what is unethical is the original activity. Using programs to erase evidence of what one has accessed is in itself not unethical. Should companies prohibit the use of such programs, or ignore them? Specifically prohibiting them both calls attention to them and indicates that the company wishes to be able to search the computer's record of Internet access. While it would not be unethical to do so, it would send a clear message of lack of trust and perhaps make employees fear snooping that will never take place and inhibit their use of the Internet beyond what is reasonable.

There are more intrusive programs that make such tactics by employees useless. One program, "Win What Where," records all computer use: keystrokes, record files and applications opened, menu items chosen, and the browser's history. "Silent Watch" can not only log keystrokes but send to a manager's screen what is on an employee's screen. "Spector" records everything that shows up on a computer screen and so sees passwords, secret files, and encrypted files. All of these can be placed on employees' computers without their knowledge, and their existence on a computer does not show up in the standard ways that other programs on a computer are displayed. Such "snoopware" is surprisingly widely used. Unless there is strong reason to suspect wrongdoing on the part of an employee, it is difficult to justify from an ethical point of view, and clearly shows a lack of trust and respect. As an investigative tool, it is obviously most effective when the employee remains unaware of its being used. As a routine means of keeping track of all employees, it smacks of a corporate version of Big Brother.

The key in all cases is supplying clear information to the employee about what is and is not appropriate Internet use and providing some justification for any restrictions imposed. Some firms that are serious about instructing their employees in this area, provide training sessions in which the policy is demonstrated, in which grey areas are discussed, and in which the rationale for the company's policy is explained. Treating employees with respect in this context means that they are not simply told what they may and may not do, but are also provided with the reasoning behind the rules.

The issues will get more complex as the Internet is more and more integrated into other applications, such as spread sheets and word processing. Many senior managers tend to turn policy development as well as implementation over to their Information Systems or Information Technolgy departments. But the members of those departments are frequently technically skilled people, not managers, and neither trained nor equipped to make the decisions and set the policies involved. The decisions are managerial, and senior managers have the responsibility for developing reasonable and ethical Internet use policies.

▲ EMPLOYEE RECORDS ▲

There is no reason why employee privacy should be diminished when records are kept on computers rather than on paper. Whatever rights to privacy they had before the widespread use of computers they still have after their widespread use. The principles that are applicable are the same. The confidential nature of material remains the same. The right to see their files and enter corrections remains the same. The appropriateness of culling files and eliminating material that is no longer pertinent, that is dated, that is inaccurate, is still the same. The sheer bulk of paper files was an incentive to destroy those no longer necessary. That incentive disappears with computers, on which huge amounts of data can be stored with ease, taking up no more physical space than the size of the disk or storage device. The fact that the records are on computers and that it is easier for employers to keep everything once entered on them rather than spend the time removing data does not change the rights of employees in this regard.

Several principles continue to apply, even though their implementation with respect to computer records as opposed to paper records requires some rethinking and different ways of doing things on the part of many employers.

(1) *Records should only be kept when there is a legitimate reason for doing so, and they should be kept only as long as the reason continues.* The justification for this principle is that obsolete and unjustified

records can harm employees, and they have the right not to be harmed. In general, letters of recommendation written before a person is hired, have served their purpose once the person is hired. They may prove useful for a short while after the hire, but there is no need to keep them permanently. If such letters were written in confidence, with a waiver by the person about whom they were written, then they should not be shown to that person. The less such confidential information is kept in a file, the better.

A general rule of thumb that some companies follow is to cull records after a three-year or a five-year period. Either term is long enough to judge continuing performance and any trends that are appropriately considered in evaluations. If performed fairly, the past three evaluations should be enough to judge competence, perform-ance, and potential. Evaluations, commendations, and reprimands older than five years have dubious relevance to current appraisals. Whether such records are on a computer or on paper makes no difference in this regard.

If this principle if followed it is often easier to keep on computer records permanent information about employment that may be accessed by a larger number of people rather than information that is confidential or sensitive and may properly be accessed by only certain people. Health records might be of the latter kind. Melding the two kinds of information may compromise confidentiality. Employee records are properly accessible only to those who need to know, and some may need to know one kind of confidential infor-mation and not another kind.

Some confidential information may even better be kept in a separate paper file rather than on computer to avoid the problem.

(2) *Employees should have access to their files.* The justification for this is to prevent erroneous, detrimental information from remaining in the file. Unless the employee can see what is in his or her file, the employee has no way of correcting misinformation or of refuting allegations or negative reports that the employee believes are unjus-tified. The employee's side of a dispute or statement of disagreement should be included in his or her file.

The employee does not have the right to see confidential infor-mation if this is, for instance, a letter of recommendation which the employee has requested and has waived the right to see. Nonetheless, the employee has the right to know that the document exists and is in his or her file.

Similarly, there may be other confidential material in a file that the employee may not see for some good reason – for instance possible promotion or career development plans for the employee that management is considering but to which it is not yet ready to commit itself. In general, however, employees have the right to know what is in their file and to refute what they believe erroneous.

(3) *Employees have the right to have confidential information about them kept confidential.* If records are paper records this is often easier than if they are on computers. Nonetheless the employees' rights in this regard are not diminished. One of the benefits of computers is that they can give access to records to many people without the records being physically accessed or sent or moved. But that benefit carries with it the dangers that access is too easy for too many people, that confidential records may not be properly separated from non-confidential, that the records may be accessed by unauthorized employees or managers, or that they may be compromised through intrusion by unauthorized persons in or out of the corporation.

Most managers are familiar with the ways to safeguard the confidentiality of paper records. They are kept in secure offices and are filed in locked file cabinets to which only appropriate people have or are given access. One difficulty with computer files is that many managers do not know much about securing such files. They are not able to say how the security should be established, they are unfamiliar with how it may be breached. They must rely on others, who may or may not know enough to adequately safeguard the files. Computer files are also easily compromised if some unauthorized person gets or guesses a password used by an authorized user. Thus there are several levels at which a company and the mangers in charge of the records have the responsibility to make sure that the records are kept confidential. They must make sure they are organized so that information that is appropriately only available to certain people is kept separated and made only available to them, from information that is general and more readily available. They must make sure that there are proper safeguards on access to each of the kinds of material. They must ensure that all who have access are conscious of the need not to divulge either passwords or the contents of private records.

Keeping records confidential thus becomes more difficult rather than less so when records are kept on computers. The responsibility of those charged with keeping the records and keeping them confidential requires that they know a good deal about computers and computer security in order to know that those entrusted with the mechanics of keeping the files secure are both given clear instructions and are held accountable for doing their jobs properly.

Confidential information should not be divulged to any outside entities without the consent of the employee. Health records, for instance, unrelated to company-provided insurance, should not be given to insurance companies without the knowledge and consent of the employee. Similarly, information on wages should not be given to credit companies, except as a result of the employee's request.

(4) There is a corollary to this principle: *confidential information about an employee or potential employee should not be sought or gathered by an employer.* An employer only has the right to know information about an employee or a prospective employee that is job related. Thus, in job interviews employers typically should not ask potential employees about their marital status, whether they have or plan to have children, their sexual preferences, and other information about the job candidate's personal life. The reason is that such information is not pertinent to most jobs and that such information is often the basis of job discrimination. Candidates for a position have the right not to be turned down for non-job related reasons, and they have the right not to be discriminated against because of their race, gender, age, religious affiliation, and national origin. By like reasoning, they should not be discriminated against because of other non-job related information – for instance, how much in debt they are, or what their credit rating is – unless this is somehow pertinent to their prospective position.

Because it is inappropriate for employers to ask these questions during an interview and pre-job selection, it is also inappropriate for them to try to find out this information through other means, e.g., by requesting the candidate's credit information, or by utilizing databases on individuals that contain information of the kind that they may not ask directly about. That such information may be available in some databases does not mean that it may be used in making determinations about prospective employees. Nor should it be used to make decisions about current employees. An employee's private life is precisely that, private. Evaluations, promotions, and other on-the-job decisions about employees should be made on the basis of job performance and not on the basis of the employee's private life, even if some of this information is available in some external database. This does not preclude appropriate background checks to verify information supplied by candidates.

(5) *Employees have the right to know what the rules are concerning*

their files and who properly has access to the various kinds of material they contain. The four previous principles prescribe general rules. They do not specify particular rules, for instance, about what kinds of files should be kept. What the employee has a right to know is what files are kept, what the company's policies are with respect to culling and keeping records, who in general has access to them, how they are kept confidential, and to what external agencies, persons, or companies their files or portions thereof are given.

▲ EMPLOYER PRIVACY ▲

Is there some notion of corporate privacy that must be considered as a counterweight to claims about employee and consumer privacy? If corporations are considered legal persons, existing only in contemplation of the law, then the argument in favor of any sort of privacy claim, in a sense comparable to that made for individuals, cannot be made. Individual human beings are moral persons and as such deserve respect. Included in this is respecting their thoughts and feelings, and allowing them to develop their independence and moral autonomy. This is part of what is protected by privacy. Also protected is the opportunity and environment to develop personal relationships, free from intrusion and prying. Neither of these meanings of privacy applies to corporations, since they are not moral persons, even though their actions can be morally evaluated. Moreover, as legal entities, they are open to the scrutiny of the law. If they are publicly held, then they are open to scrutiny by their shareholders and they must make pertinent information about themselves available for potential shareholders, and so they must make that information public.

Nonetheless, corporations have the legal right to protect information that they have developed and that is valuable from a competitive point of view. Such information is covered by trade secrecy laws. This usually includes product development, strategic planning, take-over plans and the like. There is also much information that a company has that is not strictly a trade secret, but that it wishes to and may legitimately keep confidential. Although the salaries the corporation pays to its top executives are a matter of public record, what it pays to its other employees is not. This does not mean that a particular employee cannot divulge his or her salary, but that the salary of others is usually considered a confidential matter, known of course to the individual's supervisor and to the compensation, human relations, accounting and other offices that deal with payroll and wages. Those with access to these records are usually expected to keep the information confidential, not only from outside sources but also from other employees that do not have a reason to know that information. Such records are different from an individual's records, since they are corporate records. The corporation may of course take whatever measures it wishes to keep those records confidential, as it does to keep records about customers and orders confidential. That these records are kept on computers does not change their status, although it does make them potentially available to more people more easily, both within and outside the corporation.

The employees have an obligation to protect the confidentiality of their employer's records, just as the employer has the obligation to protect the individual employee's records. The reason is not privacy, but the fact that the information is proprietary, even though it is not a trade secret. The inner workings of a corporation, of its day-to-day problems, difficulties, headaches, are not governed by trade secrecy laws. Nonetheless, this is not the sort of information that employees should make public. Such information does not enjoy the protection of trade secrets, and the confidentiality required is less. Unless precluded by trade secrecy, employees may discuss problems and difficulties at work with spouses and friends. This is different from revealing them publicly to the media or to competitors or over the World Wide Web. Such information may be embarrassing, and may be costly to the corporation in question. It is not information pertinent to shareholders or to potential shareholders and so need not be made public. Yet since it may cause harm, such information may be made public only when there is good reason for doing so.

On the other hand, when for instance a company uses the Internet in ways that are not widely known by those on whom they gather information or to whom they send junk mail, there is nothing wrong with that being divulged by anyone with access to that information, since that information is pertinent to the targets of that practice, who have a right to know so that they may, if they wish, protect themselves and help preserve their privacy.

Such revelation and the absence of any strict right to privacy on the part of corporations does not, of course, justify either espionage, unethical intelligence gathering, surreptitious entry into a company's computers, or any other action that violates the company's property rights.

The issues of privacy in the workplace are evolving. A great deal of legislation in the United States, both on the national level and on the state level, has been drafted and introduced that would protect employee privacy. But as of 2002, such legislation has made little headway. Businesses understandably are opposed to different laws in different states, which makes any general corporate policy for companies that have a presence in more than one state difficult. The opposition on the part of business interests to national legislation is part of the opposition to any legislation that restricts their marketing practices or decreases their autonomy. Nonetheless, it appears likely that sooner or later some legislation requiring at least informing employees of the practices a company uses will be forthcoming.

▲ NOTES ▲

1. *Wall Street Journal*, February 4, 2000, pp. A1, 8; *New York Times*, April 5, 2000, pp. C1, 10.
2. See http://www.websense.com/products/about/howitworks/index.cfm
3. Reported in Alan Cohen, "No Web for You!" *Fortune*, October 30, 2000.
4. "Employees Ordered to Curtail Internet Surfing," *Lawrence Journal World*, March 9, 1997, p. E1.

chapter four

New, Intellectual, and Other Property

When VCRs first became available in the United States, both the movie and the TV industries felt them as a threat to their commercial interests. They sued to block the use of VCRs, arguing they were a tool devised to violate copyright laws. The courts ruled otherwise, finding that VCRs had many legitimate uses, even though they might be used to violate copyright laws, and holding that users could legally make copies of material presented on TV for personal viewing and use at a later time. They justified this under the "fair use" clause of the copyright law, which allows individuals to make certain reasonable use of copyrighted material for personal use. The commercial use of such copies is illegal, as is the copying of rented movies and other copyrighted material available in tape format. The movie and TV industries responded creatively by turning the presence of home VCRs into an additional profit stream through the sale and rental of movies and TV programs.

Last evening Joe taped the popular movie *The Sound of Music,* which was playing on one of the TV channels. He was away for the evening and intended to look at the movie when it better fitted his schedule. This is both common and legal. He may tape as many programs and movies as he wishes for later viewing. His taped version is his to use, even though the same movie is also available for rent or sale at his local video rental store. His friend, Richard, intended to tape the movie, but by mistake set his VCR to the wrong channel, and hence taped some other program instead. When he learned this, he asked Joe if he could copy Joe's tape. He reasoned that since it was legal for him to copy the movie directly from the TV, and he would have if he had not made a mistake, there seems to be no difference in principle for him to copy Joe's tape. Another friend, Tom, also meant to tape the movie, but forgot to set his machine. Rather than phone friends to see if any of them had taped it, he simply went to the Internet and asked if anyone had made a copy from the TV broadcast that they would let him copy. His reasoning was similar to Richard's. It was legal for him to make a copy from the TV, there is no difference in principle between his recording it directly or his getting it from someone else who recorded it directly, and it does not make any difference whether or not the person he copies it from is a friend, as long as he or she copied it legally. Now whether this reasoning is correct from a legal point of view is questionable, since lending a copy of one's tape for someone else to copy does not seem to be "personal use." Yet the reasoning of Richard and Tom does seem to have some plausibility. For if they could have made legal copies directly themselves, then there is nothing wrong in their having the copy from that source, and getting it second hand rather than first hand does not seem pertinent from an ethical point of view. No harm is done the commercial interests of any of the parties. The small number of viewers who did not tape directly and got their copy second hand would not likely change the station's Nielsen ratings, and neither Richard nor Tom would buy or rent the film, nor would Joe. They simply wanted a copy of that and other films to look at when the TV offerings on a given evening were not to their liking.

In addition to taping *The Sound of Music*, Joe also taped some songs that were being played on MTV. He not only videotaped them, but he also taped just the audio part on his tape recorder. Since he could tape the whole video, it seems he is also allowed to tape only a portion of it. Richard and Tom, having the same tastes as Joe and being in the same situations as they were with the movie, copy from Joe or from whomever has a copy and is willing to share the videos and the songs.

Since he may make copies for his personal use, Joe reasons that he may also make copies of music played by DJs on the radio or that he gets via the Internet. The principle of fair use seems to be the same, whether one uses a VCR or a CD writer on one's computer.

Napster is a firm that carried this scenario one step further. It developed technology that would allow anyone using the Internet to request a certain song, and Napster would serve as an intermediary between the requester and someone willing to supply the song. There were two important differences, however, from the cases of Joe, Richard, and Tom. First, although some of the songs that were supplied and copied were not covered by copyright, others were so covered. They were copies on CDs that the owner had purchased. And purchasing the CD gives one a right to listen to the songs on it, but it does not give one the right to copy the songs or to allow others to copy them. The same is true of rented or purchased tapes of movies. They may not legally be copied and such copying does not come under the doctrine of fair use. The second important difference is that the service provided by Napster proved to be so attractive that it was used by millions of people to download music free that they would otherwise have paid for. Why buy a CD when one can get the same songs free? Why buy all the songs on a CD when one is only interested in one song and one can download it free?

The rock band Mettalica sued Napster for copyright infringement. A US District Court ordered Napster to shut down its services. In October 2000, a US Appellate Court affirmed the lower court's action and ruled that Napster could only provide access to those songs that were not protected by copyright, and that it had to find a way to do this before it could continue its operation. Some music companies then sought to enter into various agreements with Napster whereby they would get a fee for each of their songs downloaded. On July 1, 2001, Napster shut down to integrate the technology the courts mandated it have installed to block the trading of copyrighted material.

In the meantime, however, other programmers devised programs that did not require an intermediary such as Napster, and that allowed individuals to contact each other and trade or download music on a peer-to-peer basis. Gnutella was one of these programs, which users could download free and then use to contact and trade music with others who used the program. Gnutella, like Napster, can be used to download the newest amateur band that wants to get an audience by giving its music away, as well as copyrighted music. By mid-July, 2001, six alternative services had sprung up and were providing peer-to-peer copying capabilities involving no intermediary. Over a million users downloaded Music City's program Morpheus, and over 900,000 downloaded Audiogalaxy's Satellite program. The companies, which hope to make money by running banner ads, claim that they are not responsible for what users do with the programs they provide.

Two questions arise. First, is the development of such technology itself ethically defensible, and does the same kind of argument that justifies the use of VCRs justify its use as well? Second, is the copying of material, such as music, from someone else's hard drive using this technology ethically defensible if the material, for instance, is played over steaming audio sites on the Internet?

Central to answering these questions is the notion of property and its ethical and legal status.

▲ PROPERTY ▲

Property implies ownership of something, is of various kinds, and is dependent on an accepted system or set of laws. Hence the notion of property varies somewhat according to the society in which it is located. In a strictly communist system, for instance, there is no concept of private ownership of the means of production – no privately owned businesses or factories. All productive resources are socially or state owned. Some American Indian tribes had no concept of the ownership of land, any more than we have a concept of the ownership of the air we breathe. Some societies have a different view of so-called intellectual property than do others, questioning whether there is any such thing. Ownership is in turn best understood as a bundle of rights. The bundle varies according to the different kinds of property, and the different bundles are usually designated as tangible, intangible, real, and intellectual property, respectively.

Tangible property, as the name implies, includes all those things one can touch. Real property refers to ownership of land and the structures built on it. One has the right to destroy one's own tangible property if one wishes, but the notion of destroying the land is clearly not the same notion and hence the bundle of rights making up real property will be different from the bundle making up tangible property. Intangible property refers to financial claims that one has – stocks, bonds, money. Paper money represents a claim on a government for the value indicated on the bill. But when one deposits money in the bank and then withdraws it, one does not expect to receive the same bills back. On the other hand, if one puts one's diamond ring in a safe deposit box, one expects to get back that same diamond ring. Intellectual property differs from all of these in significant ways.

Intellectual property refers to certain products of the mind or intellect that a society decides can be owned in some sense. One trait that distinguishes intellectual property from other types of property is that intellectual property is infinitely shareable. If I have an idea I can give it away and still have it. Unlike other kinds of property, someone can borrow or take or steal my idea and I still have it. I no longer have exclusive use of it if others have it as well; but their having it does not preclude my also having it. It is this key feature of products of the mind that make discussions of intellectual property significantly different from discussions about other kinds of property. One may have the right to exclusive use, but not the right to destroy it (which would make no sense), and one's possession of the intellectual property is compatible with others having the same property. Because I can have an idea and you may independently come to have a similar idea, ideas in general are not considered the type of thing that can be owned. There would be no way of knowing if someone else had an idea first and, if so, whether the idea belonged to that person. There would be no social utility in trying to have ownership of ideas. Nor would there be any social utility in trying to assign ownership rights to mathematics or to facts or to scientific discoveries and theories. But "idea" is a very broad term and covers some things to which some societies give property rights. What is usually proprietary is the expression of an idea in some tangible form, such as a book or an invention, although this is a rough characterization, since it is debatable whether one can have an idea that one does not express in some sense.

A second feature that influences the bundle of rights that constitutes intellectual property is the fact that any expression of an idea builds on prior knowledge that is not of one's creation. Newton and Leibniz hit upon the calculus independently, and there was a dispute about who had the idea first. But it makes no difference to others who had the idea first since both shared their insight and made their mathematical discoveries available to all. The more or less simultaneous development of the calculus demonstrates the notion that ideas are built on other ideas. By the time of Newton and Leibniz mathematical knowledge had developed to the level where the next step was the calculus. Had Leibniz and Newton not developed it, someone else within a reasonable amount of time would undoubtedly have done so. We each stand on the shoulders of others who have gone before us and who have passed on their ideas. We absorb them and in turn build on them before passing them on. So we cannot make complete claim to them, the way we might with physical objects we build or make our own.

The third aspect of intellectual property that makes it distinctive is that such property is fundamentally social. It is not only socially developed but information and knowledge are most useful when shared, because sharing allows others to develop them further. For this reason some societies do not and have not recognized any property right to the products of the mind or to any claimed sort of intellectual property. Those that do recognize intellectual property must balance the social nature against individual claims to certain rights with respect to it, and this directly influences the bundle of rights any society assigns to intellectual property.

These three characteristics form the foundation for the widely held belief that each generation has the responsibility to pass on to the next generation the knowledge that has been socially acquired and developed. It is this aspect of human beings – the ability to develop and pass on knowledge – that clearly separates them from other species. Colleges and universities in turn are established in order to preserve, transmit, and develop the social knowledge base, and they have the responsibility to do so.

This social view of knowledge informed the early development of the computer and the mind set of the early programmers, who freely shared their work. It similarly was an important aspect in the early development of the Internet, which was seen as free and open to all. It is also the basis for the movement among some people in the computer community called the "open source movement."

"Open source" refers to software that is distributed free and whose source code, or the programming instructions or code that underlie the program, is made available for others to study and improve. The point is to tap into the potential of a great many users working to improve a program and sharing their improvements for others to build on in turn. Clearly, not everyone is capable of or interested in working with source code, and those who are can sell their services to tailor software to the needs of users.

Supporters can point to the success of this approach in developing the Web, based on open software called the Mosaic browser, which led to Netscape. Apache, which is software for Web servers, and the operating system Linux, are other examples of successful open source software. Early programmers in the 1970s freely shared their work. Richard M. Stallman has been and remains a strong proponent of the position that all software source code should be free.

Netscape followed Microsoft in giving away their browsers free. Netscape also made available its source code to those interested in debugging and improving it in a project called Modzilla. In each case there is a licensing procedure so that those who take part in rewriting code agree to share their results without charge and submit their improvements to those running the project for it to be tested and tried before being incorporated into the program for general use. Some companies, such as Red Hat Software, package, distribute, and support the Linux operating system, which customers can download free. But they will pay, e.g., $50.00, for Red Hat documentation, support, and assurance of the quality of the product.

Open source is popular among academic scientists who share their programs and who supply their source code as part of the scientific requirement that others be able to check and replicate one's work.

Despite the importance of open source historically, in the academic world, and as an alternative and a goad to improvement of commercial software, and despite the claims of some leaders of the open source movement, commercial software is not unethical and it legitimately constitutes part of what is considered intellectual property. There is a basis for holding that some products of the mind do deserve protection, at least for a limited amount of time.

▲ PROTECTION OF INTELLECTUAL ▲ PROPERTY

Since what constitutes property in any given society is at least partially determined by the legal structure of that society, the ethical considerations concerning property are to that extent based on the law. Although stealing is unethical in every society, since stealing involves unjustly taking someone else's property, what is considered property is pertinent. If land, for instance, cannot be owned in a society, then it cannot be stolen. It might be misappropriated or illegally and unethically used, but it cannot be stolen. If the air we breathe cannot be owned, it cannot be stolen. If some society does not recognize intellectual property, then similarly it cannot be stolen. Most societies do not go so far as to acknowledge no right to any intellectual property; but the views of exactly what kinds of rights are appropriate and the extent of one's claims to intellectual property do vary.

In the United States the legal basis for the protection of intellectual property comes from the US Constitution, Article 1, Section 8, which includes under the Powers of Congress the power "To promote the Progress of Science and useful Arts, by securing for limited Times to Authors and Inventors the exclusive Right to their respective Writings and Discoveries." Two aspects of this basis for the protection of intellectual property are noteworthy. The first is that the main purpose of the protection of intellectual property is not the right of the author or inventor but the progress of science and the useful arts. The purpose of the protection is the benefit of the common good. The second is that unlike other property rights which exist indefinitely, the rights granted for intellectual property are limited in time.

The major ways of legally protecting intellectual property in the United States are through copyright, patent, and trade secrecy laws.

Trade secrecy is simply an extension of the right of each individual both to think for him or herself whatever thoughts he or she wishes, together with the right to keep one's thoughts to oneself. We can think what we want and have no obligation to reveal our thoughts. By extension, groups or businesses or corporations have the right to pursue whatever research they wish, attempt to develop whatever knowledge they want, with no obligation to reveal what they are doing to anyone else. If what they are pursuing is valuable to the company, and if they take appropriate measures to keep the knowledge secret – such as protecting the information, restricting access to it, informing those with access that it is secret, and so on – then the law protects this secrecy and provides legal recourse if someone who had access reveals that information to a competing firm, or if those without authorization steal or attempt to steal the protected information. The most famous and one of the longest kept trade secrets is the formula for Coca-Cola.

Since trade secrecy is recognized in general, it would seem that those who work with computers or programs are similarly allowed to think independently if they wish and to keep their results to themselves. Some see this as an anti-social approach to take and contrary to the origins of programming in which programmers exchanged their work freely. But even this is an exaggeration, for no one was expected to share all their mistakes, false starts, and incomplete results, since doing so would not help but probably confuse and send others on the mistaken track on which they themselves were proceeding. Even if one claims that one has an obligation to share the advances one makes since everyone builds on others in computing, nonetheless, even here one can keep one's work to oneself until one feels it is sufficiently developed to share.

Copyright, as the name implies, governs the exclusive right of the author to reproduce or copy the work, distribute it, display or perform it publicly, prepare derivative works based upon it, and authorize others to do these things. We have seen that ideas cannot be owned. What one can have a legal right to is the protection of the expression of one's ideas, and it is this that copyright grants. We can express our ideas in a variety of ways. Language is the most obvious, and copyright covers verbal expressions in books, articles, plays, poetry, and other written media. Copyright includes also the expression of ideas in other forms – music, film, video, painting, recordings. It protects authorship in that it makes it illegal for anyone but the author to claim authorship. It also gives the author the exclusive right to sell the expression of his idea or to otherwise profit from it. This in turn prohibits others from copying it or from selling or profiting from it without the author's permission. The exception is fair use which allows certain uses, such as quoting a portion of a work in a review or in a scholarly publication (giving appropriate attribution), or making a partial copy for legitimate personal use. Copyright is automatic when one expresses one's ideas, but registering the work makes it easier to enforce one's right legally. When a copyright applies, as opposed to trade secrecy, the work is made public or available to the public. It is to society's advantage to have many different works of a large variety available to it. So it is reasonable to grant those who express their ideas some proprietary rights. On the other hand, we have already seen that everyone's ideas come from the general social store and build on that store. Hence, the proprietary rights should not continue indefinitely, and the rights appropriately expire after a certain amount of time. How long should that time be? The amount of time has varied under US and international copyright law.

Until 1978 copyright was granted for 28 years, and was renewable for another 28 years. After 28 years if the work was no longer in print or of commercial value, the copyright holder did not bother to renew the work and allowed it to fall into the public domain, where it could be copied freely, although the claim to original authorship still applied. This covered most cases. Twenty-eight years seemed a reasonable amount of time to allow an author the chance to recoup any investment of time, energy, and money he or she or a corporation may have invested in producing the product. In 1978 the law was revised to bring US law in line with the international agreement on copyright (the Berne Copyright Convention of 1928). Copyright then was granted for a period of the life of the author plus 50 years or for a corporate owner, a period of 75 years. Any specific length of time is arbitrary. Was life plus 50 years more reasonable than 28 or

56 years? Clearly 75 years for a corporation was longer than the previous maximum of 56 years. Was the extension necessary to promote more or better works for society? It seems hardly likely. In 1998 the period of protection was again extended, from the life of the author plus 50 years to the life of the author plus 70 years, and for corporations from 75 years to 95 years. The justification given once again was to bring US law in line with the European Union, which had extended the term of copyright in 1995. But the justification for the extension is not clear. A group of US lawyers challenged the extension, claiming that it was a violation of the "just takings" article of the Constitution, since the government was taking from the public what should have become part of the public domain.[1] Disney Studios, among others, campaigned for the change, and it occurred in time to save Mickey Mouse from falling into the public domain in 2002.

The ethical justification for copyright is twofold. The first is a basically utilitarian justification. This says that since society wishes to encourage the production of such works, the best way to promote such production is by making it possible for those who produce them to benefit financially therefrom. We have the history of the development of works that are covered by copyright that tends to show the result has been to society's benefit. Of course, we do not know what would have been produced without the financial incentives copyright provides, and we do know that people continue to have ideas, to develop mathematics, to develop scientific formulas, and to produce knowledge that cannot be protected by copyright. There are some societies that deny any protection for ideas in any form and hence do not recognize the validity of claims of intellectual property rights. For centuries there was no copyright protection, yet works of art, literature, music, and so on were produced. Shakespeare borrowed many of his plots from others and had no copyright protection for what he produced. Nonetheless, in modern societies the financial inducement is certainly at least one motivating force encouraging the production of literary, artistic, and other works.

The second justification for copyright is one of fairness. It says that those who expend time, energy, and money on developing the expression of their ideas, deserve recompense for that time, energy, and money. Moreover, if such protection did not exist, and the item were sold commercially, then those who did not expend the time, energy, and money would reap the rewards instead of the originator of the work. The one who did profit without the prior effort and expense would be a free rider, and since the free rider had no prior expenses to be recouped, could undersell the legitimate producer. This would be clearly unfair.

This argument is challenged by some who contend that the claim of authorship is legitimate, but that there is no inherent right to any reward from the production of any such work. Despite the possible and actual objections by some, the justifications are widely accepted and ground the legitimacy of copyright worldwide.

Should copyright law be extended to computer programs?

Initially the answer was not clear. Computer programs are not literary or artistic expressions of ideas in the ordinary sense of these words. They are instructions to a computer to do certain things. They are written for computers and are not to be read in an ordinary sense by ordinary people. They are a hybrid, not quite a literary work and not quite a machine, even though they make machines work in certain ways. Computer programs are usually written in a computing language that produces what is called a source code, which is then translated into a machine-readable form of zeros and ones called an object code. When the US first decided to grant copyright protection to computer programs, it extended that protection only to the source code, which could be read by people, and not to the object code or the strings of ones and zeros that constituted the machine-language version of the program. But it was soon seen that this did not make much sense, since the machine version is simply a translation of the source code. If the machine version was not also protected, then anyone could legitimately copy, use, and sell the machine version – which would reduce the protection of the source code to little if any protection at all.

In 1980 the US Congress amended the copyright laws to cover computer programs. Not all countries recognize copyright protection for software. Hence we have what is called software piracy when software copyrighted in the US and other countries is duplicated and sold without paying any royalties in a country which does not extend copyright protection to software; it is not illegal to do so in the country in question.

There are also some in the United States and other countries which issue and recognize copyright protection for software who claim that copyright protection for software is not only unnecessary, but counterproductive. They argue that the utilitarian argument does not hold with respect to computer programs and that instead of promoting the common good by encouraging the development of programs, protection has been counterproductive and has led to poorer programs and greater inefficiency than would otherwise be the case. This is the argument of those who endorse open source code.

The same period of protection as for any other copyrighted item applies, of course, to software programs, even though producers of programs admit that most programs become obsolete in about five years. Since copyright law allows others to write programs that perform the same function as another program as long as one does not copy the code of the original, the point of such long protection is not clear. On the other hand, if the program is in fact obsolete, granting it continued protection does no harm, since it would not make much sense to copy obsolete code rather than writing new up-to-date code.

Because software can be copied so easily by individuals, some argue that the law prohibiting such copying cannot be enforced and so is both ineffective and leads to building disrespect for law in general. For a short period software companies tried to add "disk protection" code to the software disks they sold, making copying impossible for the ordinary user. But the result was great customer dissatisfaction, and companies found they could make a profit without such protection. Companies have also learned that once customers become accustomed to using certain kinds of software, they tend to continue using them, and the company makes a profit by constantly improving the product and selling the improved or upgraded version. By the time competitors had had a chance to duplicate the new innovations, the original copy had leaped ahead with a new version. Hence, the argument goes, copyright, at least as it presently exists with respect to software, is in part anachronistic and is based on a model appropriate for written expressions but not for software.

Hence a number of critics have asked the more general question of whether it makes sense for one kind of protection – in this case copyright protection – to be applied to all the various kinds of products to which it has been extended.[2] A computer program, as we have noted, is not like other kinds of products, although it resembles a number of them in various ways. It is not a book, although it can be described as a linguistic expression of an idea. Yet it is a list of instructions to a machine, and in some ways seems to act like a machine.

Once one buys most copyrighted items, for instance a book, one has the right to treat the physical object just as one would other items of tangible property. You may resell it, lend it to someone else, write on the pages, throw it away, give it away, and so on. Although you do not own what the words on the page say and may not reproduce them, the book is yours to do with what you will. The same, however, is not true with purchased commercial software. The reason is that strictly speaking one does not buy the disk with the program. Rather the holder of the copyright licenses the use of the program to the purchaser with certain restrictions. Whether one buys the program on-line and downloads it to one's computer or whether one buys a disk and loads the program into one's computer makes no difference. What one purchases is limited use of the program. The limits are set by the seller as part of an agreement. But the limits which are justifiable and those which are not are disputed, and raise problems, ranging from the unenforceability problem with respect to individual copying, to the fairness of agreements set by the seller and forced on the buyer of shrink-wrapped products.

Just as we as a society have not adequately discussed the changing nature of privacy, society has not adequately discussed the changing nature of property applicable to the Information Age. We have sought to use traditional laws about copyright and patents, and have in the process caused a great deal of confusion. Instead of rethinking intellectual property in the Information Age, we have tried to make do with concepts and legal doctrines that were not constructed with intellectual property such as software in mind. In 1998 the US Congress passed the Digital Millennium Copyright Act in an attempt to address the new aspects of copyright raised by the Internet. It makes it illegal to break through passwords, encryption, and other defenses used to protect Internet content. But it does not address the general issue of copyright protection for software.

The doctrine of "fair use," written into the copyright Act since 1976, has had to bear more and more weight and instead of legislative action the courts have decided what is and is not fair use. What the courts decide, however, is considerably different from the practice of many people, and actual practice in some cases leads to practical changes in the way business is done.

▲ COPYRIGHT AND SOFTWARE ▲

The great confusion about intellectual property on the part of the general public concerning software, which we have noted, is a result not only of the fact that software is a relatively new concept and a product that does not fit comfortably within present copyright law, but also that we must necessarily deal with it by analogy, and our analogies are often as misleading as they are illuminating.

The ethical rules concerning software are not in some Platonic or other heaven waiting to be found. They cannot be derived from analyzing software or intellectual property in the abstract. From a moral point of view whether we use a utilitarian, a deontological, or any other approach, we must consider how the judgments we arrive at and how the various rules we apply concerning software cohere with our other moral rules. This is in fact the process we as a society have been engaged in since the invention of software. The arguments that carry primary weight in this discussion ultimately involve us in arguments from coherence and from analogy. Although philosophical analysis can help sort out some of the difficulties, what is right and what is wrong in much of this area can only be determined in conjunction with working out the appropriate specific legal parameters. Any number of different decisions about rights in this area are equally defensible from an ethical point of view.

The concept of intellectual property is itself based on an analogy with other kinds of property, although there are significant differences between what we generally consider property and the nature of ideas and knowledge. The Lockean justification for property has for the most part been ignored in justifications for copyright protection. Locke argued that since everyone has property in his own person, his labor is his, and when he joins his labor to something found in the natural state, he makes it his property, as long as there is enough and as good left for others. Anyone who has engaged in any intellectual endeavor knows that the hardest part of any intellectual task is getting an original idea. That is the most work, and according to the Lockean view what we can claim some property right to is that which is the product of labor. From an intuitive naive point of view, if one were to identify anything as intellectual property one would be tempted to say that the most important products of the intellect should have that status, and these would plausibly be original ideas. The more fundamental, basic, and far reaching, the more valuable they are and the more they should be worth, whether we follow the model of Locke and a labor theory as the right to property, or a social utility model, or any number of other models. Yet it is precisely the most important intellectual products – ideas, concepts, equations, laws of nature – that by law are not protectable as intellectual property. We have seen why one cannot claim exclusive right to an idea, and since equations, laws of nature, and facts are of the greatest social utility, it is appropriate that the social good of these outweighs the claim of any individual to their exclusive use.

Copyright was originally intended to protect the written word, which was considered in legal terms the expression of ideas, as if one can have an idea that is not expressed, or as if a novel is simply an expressed idea. Yet we know the difference in some rough way between having an idea and working out its implications and spelling it out in detail. When we get an idea for a book it is different from writing the book, which fully expresses the idea. If it is true that getting the idea is the more difficult of the two from the point of view of labor, why protect the expression and not the idea? On Lockean grounds that makes no sense. Yet we can only copyright the expression of the idea not because that takes more work but because for practical reasons that is the only thing that we can identify in such a way as to be able to prove originality. The basis is not ownership rights of a Lockean type but social utility and pragmatic commercial claims.

A machine can as correctly be called the expression of an idea as a novel can. Legally a machine can be protected by patent for 20 years; a novel can be protected by copyright for the life of the author plus 70 years. Whether either type of protection really makes sense for software is still debatable. Although there is nothing unethical in granting such rights, there is no reason in principle why we cannot have a different kind of protection for software, and there are good reasons for developing this different kind of protection.

Since copyrights were originally developed to protect the written word, when extended to software the tendency is to take works of literature as the paradigm, and to compare computer programs to them. This yields one set of analogies. If we take mathematics as the paradigm and compare computer programs to that, we get another set of analogies. Which is the proper set of analogies to follow? Lawyers who push the literature analogy wax eloquent about the art, structure, and beauty of computer programs, and argue that just as these features are found in literature, they are found in software.

They argue further that since literature is protected, so should software be, as if people buy software for the beauty of the programs instead of for the utilitarian results. One of the most eloquent such defenses is Anthony Clapes's book on *Software, Copyright, and Competition*.[3] The same claims of eloquence, structure, and beauty, however, can be made about mathematical proofs. Yet mathematical proofs are not protectable. Moreover, software seems as much like mathematics as like literature. The often used analogy captured in the term "algorithm" is borrowed from mathematics. In mathematics it has a definite meaning. Stretched to apply to computer programs it is no longer clear exactly what people who use the term mean and different people mean by it different things. What the term means is slowly being decided by the courts. But since the term "algorithm" is used, and since at present one cannot copyright a mathematical algorithm, the analogy with mathematics limits the protection of parts of the software. The reason for the limitation is not based on some ethical theory or on some view of property rights, but once again it is pragmatic.

If one asks about the relation of intellectual property, ethics, and copyright protection, four different moral intuitions are applicable and represent four different perspectives. The perspectives represent the four major parties involved in copyright issues.

The first intuition is that from an ethical point of view what is appropriate in this domain is not property rights but honesty of attribution. This is the view of scholars and of some authors. One should not claim that an idea is one's own when it comes from another. But ideas are not the sort of thing that we can or should in general restrict. They can be shared and if useful can be built upon and developed. Since ideas and knowledge are infinitely shareable, the general rule is that we all benefit from correct ideas and knowledge, and the way to make sure the ideas and knowledge are correct is to test them against other ideas and knowledge claims that are contrary to them. This is the view of ideas prevalent in most areas of a university, where ideas are usually shared rather than sold or traded. To take one area, in a university teachers of philosophy share their philosophical ideas with their colleagues, in their classes, at meetings and conventions, in articles, and in books. They do not steal each other's ideas by using, criticizing, or developing them. But they cannot ethically claim them as their own when they are not. Most philosophy journals do not pay for the articles they publish, and most books in philosophy are not written with the intent of making a great deal of money. If that is the goal, it is rarely achieved. That does not prevent articles and books from being written and published. This is the point of view adopted by many of the writers of programs, who argue that software should be treated the same as many other products of intellectual activity and that this is the best way to guarantee their development.

A second widely shared ethical intuition is that of the entrepreneur. Just as one should not copy another's work and claim it is one's own, if a product is sold it is prima facie wrong simply to copy that product and sell it as if it were one's own. Selling it while acknowledging that it is not one's own satisfies the criterion of honesty of attribution. It violates property rights if these have been developed in a legal system of property, such as the one we have. Vendors of software want people to buy their products, and are not interested in simply having others acknowledge the source. They spend money to develop and market the product, and they want a return on that investment. It is blatantly unfair for some other company simply to copy and market the product, under the same or a different name, and get the profit without having invested in the development. Even worse is undercutting the original producer and driving it out of business. Hence if a society wants commercial products, they should be protected at least until the original producers can recoup their expenses. This intuition is part of the basis for the claim of legal protection by the commercial vendors of software. They argue in addition for continuous protection for as long as possible for them to reap profits – a claim that goes beyond the moral intuition.

The third intuition is that of the buyers of software that what they buy is their own to use in any way they like comparable to their use of other products they buy. Thus if I have three computers in my home and I buy a word processing program, I tend to feel I have the right to use it on all three machines rather than buying three copies, or physically carrying the program from machine to machine and loading it each time, as some software vendors claim I should. The rights I have with respect to most of the other items I buy are not restricted, except insofar as they violate the second intuition. But if I do not engage in selling the product or copying it for sale, it is mine to do with as I like.

The fourth group is society as a whole. And the appropriate intuition is that intellectual knowledge and intellectual products are essentially social for the reasons we have already seen. They should be used for the common good. And if there is a conflict between the common good and individual claims to property rights in intellectual property, the former may well take precedence over the latter.

Although the interests of the four groups overlap to some extent, in many ways they are importantly different. To argue either in ethics or law from only one of these perspectives is not to do justice to the others. The law has tended to favor the interests of the marketers of software, since the law has been formed in part by the claims of the marketers and the cases have involved primarily suits brought by them.

▲ UNAUTHORIZED COPYING ▲ OF SOFTWARE

The four intuitions are applicable in considering the unauthorized copying of software.

We can divide such unauthorized copying into four categories, each of which requires a somewhat different analysis, even though from the legal point of view they all similarly violate the copyright law. Since we have already seen that one has a prima facie obligation to obey the law, we could simply infer that in each of the cases the action is unethical. This is the standard approach. But if we wish to ask what the law should be or what ethics requires if we abstract from what the law says, then further analysis is required. Also, since the obligation is in each case a prima facie one, it is possible to ask whether there are other ethical considerations that override the prohibition against copying.

The four categories are (1) piracy, that is copying and reselling commercial software, with two subheadings, (a) in the United States and other developed countries, and (b) in less developed countries; (2) buying a license and then making and using more copies than the license permits; (3) copying commercial software and making it available free on the Internet; and (4) individual copying of programs for personal use from other individuals.

Pirating in developed countries

The pirating – another analogy that captures some of what pirates do – of programs by other firms or by individuals for commercial purposes is often, and appropriately, fought in court. That is a conflict among vendors and falls most often, at least in developed countries, entirely under the second intuition. We are developing a more and more coherent and comprehensive set of laws governing that practice. It is ethically as well as legally wrong to take another's product and produce and sell it as if it were one's own. Even here, however, there are borderline cases. In the development of software there has been a series of disputes among companies. Perhaps the best known is that between Microsoft and Apple about whether Microsoft stole the look and feel of its "Windows" from Apple. The courts eventually decided that it had not violated copyright, although it had clearly borrowed a good many ideas.

Pirating in less developed countries

The more difficult case is piracy of software by and within less developed countries. Here the claim is often that our second intuition must be balanced against the fourth. An example in another, related area makes the point. Drugs used to treat AIDS patients are very expensive. They are so expensive that few people in developing countries of Africa, for instance, can afford them. Yet it is in these countries that the disease often reaches epidemic proportions. Hence, representatives of these countries have argued that the common good of their people overrides the property rights of the pharmaceutical companies, and that these countries are justified in buying cheaper versions of these drugs, even if they are produced in violation of patent laws. Alternatively, they argue that if the Western manufacturers insist on their property rights, then they should sell the drugs at affordable prices in poor countries, making their profit from their sales in the developed countries. The arguments have been given a good deal of weight and have proven convincing to many. It is not unfair to have different prices for different markets, if these can be justified by relevant considerations – either of the common good, as in this case, or by economic and business considerations.

A similar type of argument is being developed by some of the less developed countries with respect to software. The Information Age is based on information and the computer is at the heart of it. The gap between information-rich and information-poor countries will only be exacerbated to the detriment of the poor countries, unless they have access to computers and software. Yet the prices at which software is sold in developed countries puts it beyond the reach of the mass of people in less developed countries. Hence pirated software, sold at affordable prices for the local population, is claimed as necessary for the common good of the developing countries – both for the development of the population and for the possibility of either closing somewhat or at least keeping the gap between rich and poor from developing further. The argument is compatible with the claim that once the economies of these countries become such that the general population can afford to purchase software at world-market rates, then the justification for piracy will no longer be present. Representatives of India have been most articulate in defending this kind of position, and claim the right to decide which categories of goods or products it will exclude from legal protection.

The attitude is exemplified by the Farooq brothers in Pakistan, which did not recognize software patent protection. The brothers embedded a virus that destroyed DOS formatted disks into programs they sold to foreign tourists. The intent was to punish those Westerners who sought to escape their own country's copyright laws by buying pirated versions of software available in Pakistan at very low prices.[4]

China has a long tradition of considering intellectual products as common rather than personal or individual property. The great masters are copied and followed, and tradition is more important as a value than innovation. Join this view with poverty and the nascent trend towards economic free enterprise and development, and it is not surprising that an estimated 90 percent of the software and videodiscs sold in China are pirated.[5] China has signed most of the international treaties against pirating, and in order to get WTO status has had to crack down somewhat on the pirating. But its laws are ineffective and laxly enforced, and practically speaking its economy has come to depend in some part on the inexpensive availability of such products. In many poor countries the cost of strict enforcement of laws protecting intellectual property is simply prohibitive, and the incentive, if any, comes from outside pressure. Once again the implicit claim is that social well-being and social development take precedence over intellectual property rights, and such claims carry some weight and cannot ethically be dismissed out of hand.

Making more copies than licensed

Also encompassed by the second intuition which applies to commercial pirating is the practice of some companies purchasing a license for the use of a commercial program on a given number of its computers and then using it on a great many more without any additional payment. Although this practice may be claimed to be justified by the third of our intuitions, it is in fact not. For the purchasing company acknowledges the right of the supplier to charge for the use of a certain number of copies of the program and receives a discounted rate because of the multiple purchase. For it in turn to ignore the provisions of the contract and the license is clearly to act in bad faith with respect to its supplier. It is not a practice that it could consistently condone or wish to generalize or universalize, and to do so would undermine the business structure.

Making commercial software available free on the Internet

The second intuition of ownership claims applies to programs such as to preclude anyone obtaining a commercial program and then making it available freely to anyone who wished to download it from the Internet. The basis for this is that we rightly feel the person does not have the right to give away indiscriminately on a potentially large scale to anyone desiring or requesting it a product that he might have bought, but which is for sale and for which the producer or distributor has the exclusive legal right of sale. Although this case is different from that of a commercial pirate who profits from the sale, the harm done to the owner is the same. Such potentially large-scale and indiscriminate distribution cannot by any stretch of the imagination be justified by our third intuition and be considered either "fair use" or personal use. Hence it is appropriate that such sites be shut down and legal action taken against those who engage in the practice. The argument usually provided in defense of such sites is either that all legal protection of software is unethical and unjustifiable, or that software is too expensive and software companies make too much money. The first argument, we have already seen, is much too broad; the second one claims without justification that individuals are the proper determiners of the value of products and what they should cost – a claim that cannot be sustained and is not accepted in any other realm of business.

Copying programs for personal use

Some of the writers of programs have opted for free exchange of software or for shareware. This is perfectly appropriate. It is interesting to note that authors of books have not objected to copyright laws, while programmers have. The reasons for the difference in attitude are significant and should be taken more seriously than they have been by the courts and legislatures. Although the coexistence of shareware and commercial programs is not obviously unfair or counterproductive to the needs of society, the protection given commercial programs must not be such as to stifle or preclude the development of shareware or of software. Claims that they do stifle or preclude the development of some software have so far fallen on deaf legislative and judicial ears.

The views of marketers rather than the views of many of the writers of software who did not market their products but shared them became the accepted legal norm in areas in which those two intuitions conflict.

The views of marketers have also trumped the views of the users of software marketed on a large scale or of the recipients of custom-designed software, and the marketers' views have been written into law. The views of the marketers of software concerning their legal claims were also put forth as morally binding. Those views almost uncritically have become the conventional ethical norm that is preached, even though widely flouted. Users of programs such as WordPerfect and Lotus 1-2-3 are told that it is unethical to share such programs with others, and there is even an attempt to make users feel guilty if they use a program they buy on more than one machine within their own homes.

Lending a book to a friend is not unethical. Lending a program is said to be. Why? The usual answer is that lending a program to a friend is not considered comparable to lending a book to a friend, since typically one retains the use of one's copy of the program. Hence lending a program is compared to photocopying a book. The argument against lending software is based on an analogy with books, copyrights of written material, and fair use doctrines established to protect written material. Although the items lent (books and programs) are very different, the analogy of copying rather than of lending or sharing has come to dominate ethical discussions. Yet the analogy between books and software breaks down at various points, and only some of these are considered, despite the arguable importance of some of the other differences. The ease of copying software is a technological boon to users and to society that one could argue should be capitalized on as a means of transferring knowledge and technology broadly. Yet that aspect of technology is precisely what mass producers of software with the help of copyright wish to stem. Insufficient thought has been given to the results.

Focusing on the third intuition above, the users of programs would like the right to use what they buy. By analogy with many other products, how one uses the product after one buys it is up to the owners. They may sell it, change it, and so on. What is precluded is copying it and selling it in competition with the original seller. What copyright grants in most cases is the right of initial sale. Thus if a students buys a textbook for a class, for instance, he or she may sell it after the course is over, and it is then resold to another student. Neither the publisher nor the author receives any compensation beyond the initial sale. After a short period of time publishers have found that the market becomes saturated with second-hand copies of the book, and sales fall dramatically. To protect their interests many textbook publishers and authors come out with a new edition of the book after three or so years, forcing the sale of the new edition and rendering the old edition obsolete and unsaleable. But the sellers of software make more radical claims for ownership and wish to prevent resale on the basis of the claim that they did not sell the product but only licensed it on certain conditions which they specify.

From a legal point of view they place a great deal of emphasis on the fact that one enters an agreement that comes with purchased software – which one does not do when one buys a book. However, the agreement is one that is forced by the seller on the buyer after having paid one's $400 or $500 if one wants to get technical support and the options to upgrade when new versions of the program come out. The borrower of a program gets neither the documentation nor the servicing – items that do not come with books, and that help justify the higher prices of programs. One typically buys a program to use it, not to read it. The extension of copyright laws to programs ignores these and other very important differences.

Since the marketers of software cannot effectively police or enforce the agreements or prevent such violations of copyright, they attempt to protect their products through moral claims. Indirectly through the agreements that are included with software there has been an attempt to inculcate a view on the morality of copying software. The moral claims do not automatically follow from the developments in the legal realm. It is not necessarily the case that everything that is illegal is immoral. Copying or lending software is not in itself immoral. It is claimed to be immoral primarily because it is illegal.

But whether a law that is neither enforced nor enforceable has the force of law, and hence whether one is ethically bound by such a legal statute, in this case is at least open to question. The argument from analogy with other items one buys provides grounds for arguing the moral justifiability of lending and copying software for personal use.

Companies that have a financial interest in software attempt to push their claims to the maximum. A software company would be delighted if all users bought a separate copy of its program for each computer in their homes. It is unlikely many people do that. Companies would like no one to lend a copy of a program to anyone else. They would like no one to copy anyone else's program for individual use. Now these practices we know are widespread, despite the letter of the law and the dislike of the large companies. We have already noted that for a short period some distributors of software made them copy-proof to preclude these practices, much to the dissatisfaction of the buyers. Not only did the sellers give way to the buyers' dislike of such copy protection, but sellers also found that those products that were not copy protected by some programmed lock sold more copies than did the others – just as IBM found that allowing clones was preferable for its place in the market to Apple's approach of prohibiting clones. Neither IBM's nor Apple's approach is ethically right and the other ethically wrong. Both are allowable and each pursued a different legitimate strategy. But since allowing clones has not hurt IBM or its place in the market, we have some evidence that copying by itself is not necessarily harmful to developers in this area. In fact those programs that are most copied are those that sell best and produce the greatest net return to their marketers.

There is no reason why the interests of the seller should take precedence from a moral point of view over the interests of the buyer. Accordingly, we can well look with some skepticism at the attempt to prohibit individuals from such practices as copying programs for their own use on several computers. This is an attempt to use quasi-moral surrogates to replace unenforceable agreements backed by unenforceable laws. Yet the copying by users has not provided a disincentive to the creation of new programs by large firms and, as we have noted, has not prevented them from garnering handsome profits. This yields some basis for reinterpreting fair use when applied to software, representing a compromise between the second and third intuitions I described.

The legal property rights one has in software are a function of the system of property and law in which the software develops and becomes embedded. It is the commercial possibilities that drive the analogies and definitions. For this reason the proper question is not some abstract notion of rights or of intellectual property. The right questions are whether the present state of affairs is satisfactory to all concerned and to society's best interests, and if not how it can be improved.

A pragmatic argument that some put forth is that unless those who produce software are both compensated and protected, they will not produce software and thus the general public – the potential users – and so society in general will not benefit to the extent it could. The further claim is that if people did not lend and borrow software, the price of software for all would fall. The difficulty with both claims is that they have not been tested, much less proven. And evidence to the contrary is at least as strong. Although it is estimated that worldwide over $13 billion was lost to the software industry through illegal copying, that figure is based on the questionable assumption that those who obtained illegal copies would have purchased the same product at its full price. Hence, although the computer software industry has undoubtedly lost some revenue due to illegal copies, it is difficult to say how much the loss is. In some instances the software companies raise no objection to students copying their programs because they hope thereby to "hook" the student on the use of the program and maybe garner him or her as a customer for years after graduation.

We in fact do not know what would happen if less in the way of protection were afforded those who produce and market programs. Arguably, society would benefit by the least protection to the vendors compatible with the greatest benefit to society. The difficulty is to determine how little protection is necessary before people stop producing and mass marketing useful programs. As a society we have not attempted to determine that point but have simply taken over copyright laws and applied them, with some adjustment, to software. The argument that this approach yields the best result for society as a whole has simply been assumed. Present procedures, moreover, tend to preclude our ever getting an answer to the question of what policy would in fact be best for society. Yet arguing from coherence and analogy is more flexible and yields a greater variety of arguments than we have developed thus far. There are at least prima facie grounds for restricting some of the claims made by sellers of software and balancing them more equitably with claims made by writers and users of software. This argument does not show that copyright laws are unfair or unethical. But it does suggest that there are alternatives that may prove to cohere better with all our moral intuitions than copyright laws presently do, and that an approach to software protection different from copyright, patents, and trade secrecy might well be in the best interest of society.

▲ PEER-TO-PEER EXCHANGE OF ▲ COPYRIGHTED MATERIAL

This brings us to the kind of case with which we started this chapter and exemplified by the legal charges brought against Napster.

When it comes to downloading MP3 music files (or eventually other copyrighted material such as movies in digital format) most people do not consider it the same as placing commercial programs on the Web for the taking. Two of their intuitions, they feel, conflict. The one is that making a copyrighted item freely available for downloading by anyone is unethical as well as illegal; the other is that one has a moral if not a legal right to share whatever one buys with a friend if one so chooses.

The courts found Napster guilty of abetting the violation of copyright law by serving as an intermediary between those wishing to swap or share copyrighted as well as non-copyrighted music. It was not seen as comparable to a VCR, which might be used for copyright violation but also had legitimate uses. It was Napster, not its 80 million individual users, that was targeted for legal action. But shutting Napster down even temporarily did not solve the problem because users quickly developed and shared peer-to-peer programs that eliminated the need for a middle man who could be identified, sued, and shut down.

Moral suasion and possible legal action have not stopped the downloading by millions of copyrighted music. While lending a copy of a song to a friend might plausibly to claimed to be covered by fair use, and while the 1992 Audio Home Recording Act allows the taping of a CD on a tape for personal use, e.g., in a car, the indiscriminate copying of copyrighted material from unknown peers on the Internet is arguably hardly comparable.

The defense of the practice that is often given is not that those who produce the music and who market it do not deserve any return for their effort. Many who engage in the practice claim that they would be willing to pay what they consider a reasonable amount for the music they wish. But the music distributors had not made available the music they want for purchase on-line, and the marketing strategy of many music companies has been to mix on a single CD a popular song with many that the customer does not want. The customer must buy the whole CD to get the item he or she wants, and to the customer the cost of the CD is greater than the perceived value of the one song. In addition, those who defend the practice argue that the music industry itself gives its music away on MTV, for instance, or by providing it on the radio or other formats available over the Internet. Vendors of computer programs do not do this. If music is provided free to the listener in these ways, and if taping videos is legally fair use, by analogy taping or downloading music should be fair use.

These arguments do not, of course, show that downloading the music one wants freely is justifiable either legally or ethically. But they do indicate that the music industry and its marketing techniques have not kept pace with technology and that there are anomalies in the way music is distributed. With the advent of VCRs movie makers found they had to adopt a different marketing strategy from the one on which they previously relied and found that they could use the prevalence of VCRs to their commercial interests by renting movies at a very reasonable rate.

The extent to which music companies and artists are harmed is a matter of controversy. One side argues that obviously those who download won't buy the music. This deprives the companies and artists of legitimate income. They will be adversely affected. Furthermore the incentive for other companies and artists to produce more music is diminished, since the rewards are less. This in turn means less music available for society and for music lovers themselves who do the downloading. The other side argues that in many cases those who download would not buy the disk anyway, so there is no lost revenue in those cases. Others download to listen. If they like what they hear, then they buy that artist's CDs, which increases sales rather than decreasing them. Forrester Research claimed that Napster increased sales. CD sales jumped 8 percent in the first quarter of 2000 over 1999.[6] Both sides can point to some statistics. Similarly, the results on society are speculative. One side argues the demise of the music industry, the other the freeing-up of creativity from the strait-jacket of the big five record companies. The utilitarian arguments hence are not decisive. But neither is the argument based on property rights, except insofar as they are presently reflected in copyright law and judicial decisions based thereon.

The problem facing the music industry and legislators in the face of the rising peer-to-peer technology that is replacing Napster is that the law is all but unenforceable. Prosecuting even a small fraction of those who download copyrighted music using the new technology from the Internet is unfeasible. Even if the worse perpetrators were caught and fined, the chance of any individual being caught would be slight, unless more resources were put into policing and prosecuting such action than it seems socially responsible to do. The alternative seeks to find some solution that does justice to both intuitions, that protects the legitimate commercial interests of those in the music industry, and that makes available at a reasonable price – determined as in most cases by the market – the music that consumers wish to download. While some question whether anyone will pay even a nominal price to download music when they can download the same music free, there are built-in incentives for users to do so. Peer-to-peer technology opens one's computer to access by anyone on the Internet, and those who download music from unknown sources take the risk of downloading viruses or other dangers. Students who download music using the fast Internet access provided by their colleges and universities open their institutions up to possible lawsuit, as well as opening themselves up to various penalties if the institution prohibits such downloading, as the institutions might do both to avoid possible suit and to avoid the need of expanding its bandwidth to accommodate the traffic and difficulties that massive downloading of music by students can create. Burning one's own CDs, moreover, requires that one buy a CD-write drive, which might more than offset what one saves from free downloads. Those who download to their hard drives do not have the portability that makes music CDs so popular.

Only so much can be legislated. It would be a great cost to society to try to outlaw any technology, such as peer-to-peer, which holds great promise as a means of easy, inexpensive exchange of all things digital.

At this stage it seems likely that accommodation will be made, that present copyright laws with reference to music and other products on the Internet is inadequate, and that changes are both necessary and will be forthcoming. The important thing is to make sure that all affected parties and their claims and arguments are adequately heard and taken into account, and that no one of the intuitions or groups is given special privilege, consideration, or legislative preference.

The great advantage of information is that it is infinitely shareable with others while retaining it oneself. Everyone in the world is thus a potential recipient of information and all can share in these benefits without depriving others of them. The Information Age thus provides an opportunity to move from individuality to community, away from private ownership rights and towards concern for sharing for the common good. Yet, paradoxically, the Information Age, by focusing on the importance of information, has highlighted its commercial value. A result has been an attempt not to share freely but to control information for commercial purposes. Technology and ownership rules are at odds in the case of the copying of software and anything else in digitized form, in the development of peer-to-peer exchanges, in the open source code movement, and in the trend towards licensing rather than the ownership acquired in purchasing.

The problem then becomes twofold. The first issue is whether the present law can be enforced if millions of users are trading copyrighted material, even if it is illegal. Is an unenforceable law a law? There is a long tradition that claims it is not. The second issue comes from the fact that downloading material easily crosses borders. If something comparable to Napster is located in a country that does not prohibit its activities, the server outlawed in the United States can perform its function from a different jurisdiction.

▲ PATENTS ▲

Patents in the United States have the same legal foundation in the US Constitution as do copyrights, and the ethical arguments in defense of the justifiability of patents are similar to those of copyrights. Patents are administered by the US Patent and Trademark Office (PTO). The PTO defines a trademark as "a word, name, symbol or device which is used in trade with goods to indicate the source of the goods and to distinguish them from the goods of others." Trademarks must be registered and may be used to prevent others from using that or a confusingly similar mark, but they do not prevent others from selling the same goods or services under a different mark.

A patent is grant of property right to the inventor "to exclude others from making, using, offering for sale or selling" the invention.

For many years patents protected an item for 17 years. The law has been changed and most new patents are issued for a period of 20 years from the date on which the application is filed. The period, as the period for copyright, is in part arbitrary. The argument in favor of that length of time is that it provides sufficient time during which the inventor can recoup the money invested in producing the item and make a legitimate profit without being undercut by free riders who could copy and produce the item without having invested anything in developing it. The length of time is the same for all patents (with the exception of design patents, which cover only the appearance of an article, not its function or structure, and which have a term of only 14 years). Thus, whether the research and testing take many years and many millions of dollars, as is the case with most pharmaceutical drug patents, or whether for a item that takes comparatively little time or investment, makes no difference. Whether it should is an issue that software patents has brought to the fore.

A patent can be issued to cover "any new and useful process, machine, manufacture, or composition of matter, or any new and useful improvement thereof." "Process" includes "a process, act, or method." In order for something to be patentable it must be (1) useful, (2) new, and (3) unobvious to "a person having ordinary skill in the area of technology relating to the invention."

Application for a patent is made to the Patent and Trademark Office and there a number of examining groups have jurisdiction over designated fields of technology. The examiners decide whether a patent can be granted, and if a patent is denied they must present the reason for the rejection. If the reason is that the item is not new, they must document this with evidence. The granting of a patent does not guarantee its validity, and patents can be challenged in the courts. The courts have interpreted the patent statutes. They have held that laws of nature, physical phenomena, and abstract ideas are not patentable. Originally excluded were also mathematical equations, formulas, and algorithms. In addition it is the courts, rather than legislative action, that have caused a good deal of controversy in the computer world by upholding the patentability of some computer algorithms of computer software and of business methods using computers and the Internet. The Supreme Court has rendered very few decisions concerning software patents, and those that have been issued have been narrowly construed.

Patents give much broader and stronger protection than does

copyright, even though the term of such protection is shorter. If an invention is described in great detail and published, it can be copyrighted. The copyright prevents anyone else from copying the text. But it does not prevent anyone from following the description and producing the product. A patent prevents anyone from making the same product. Depending on how broad the patent is, and what it covers, this prevents competition from those who would simply copy the product. Once one has secured a patent, the patented item is made public. It cannot be legitimately copied; but it can be licensed to other users. It is also possible to reverse-engineer the invention to see how it works and to improve on that invention. Those who wish to compete will have to change the product in some new and significant way. Otherwise, they may be able to license the product from the patent holder for a fee.

Copyright is the usual method of protecting computer programs. But programs are not only strings of code. We have seen that software resembles in some ways a book, and in other ways is more like a machine. Hence copyrights cover the expression of ideas in code; but what of programs that function like a machine?

For many years patents were not issued by the PTO for software. From 1940 to 1981 the basic techniques of programming were developed, and none was covered by a patent. Hence there is often no documented history of programming techniques that the patent officials can cite to document the basis for claims they reject because they are not new or original or obvious. This is part of the basis for some of the confusion and for many of the complaints raised against the growing trend to patent software. Tim Berners-Lee did not seek a patent on his invention, the World Wide Web, which forms the basis of Internet business. The basic programming languages for the Internet were not patented, nor were the basic techniques that were developed.

In addition the construction of programs involves a basic step-by-step procedure, which has come to be called the program's algorithm. Mathematical algorithms state a procedure for solving a given type of mathematical problem and are not patentable. But at least some computer algorithms, it is claimed, are more general and provide a "step-by-step procedure for solving a problem or accomplishing some end."[7] The decisive turning point came in 1981, when the Supreme Court decided the case of *Diamond v. Diehr*,[8] involving a procedure for molding uncured synthetic rubber into rubber products through the use of a computer program that controlled the curing temperature and time of rubber in a mold. Both the PTO and the lower courts have since taken the broader view of algorithms into consideration when considering applications for software patents. Although drawing the line between patentable and unpatentable algorithms is not entirely clear, in general algorithms that control the operation of hardware or that are part of an overall invention have been granted patents. Since 1981 the number of software patents has grown enormously. In 1995 alone the PTO issued more than 6,000 software-related patents. In 1999 there were 20,000.[9]

The patenting of software has proven controversial for many reasons, only one of which hinges on the definition and use of computer algorithms. A serious bone of contention for many computer programmers is the claim that patents are being issued for computer processes that are obvious and that have been used in the past, even though they have not been documented. But the reason for that is that since patents were previously not issued for software, it was not necessary to develop the documentation appropriate for patent protection. Hence, critics claim, the rules have been changed in mid-stream. Patents, they say, are being issued for techniques that have been so obvious to programmers that they did not constitute material for a publishable paper.

The result, according to critics such as the League for Programming Freedom, has been that the new rules are unfair to small and medium-sized programmers or companies. This is so for a number of reasons. One is that the cost of searching for all the techniques that have been patented but that one may develop and use on one's own is prohibitive, as is the cost and danger of lawsuits in the case of a claimed infringement. The large companies such as IBM (which obtained 900 patents on software in 1999), Microsoft, Apple, Lucent, Sony, and Motorola, they continue, are protecting themselves by securing patents that they will then cross-license to other large companies holding other patents of their own if they are accused of violating one of that company's patents. Such defensive action is not available to those with no patents to exchange – usually the smaller and medium-sized companies – and they are forced to pay the licensing fees charged by the patent holders. Moreover, some companies, such as Refac Technology Development Company, do not produce any product other than programs which it generates to secure by patent and then license. Such tactics, abetted by the patentability of software, is not promoting the development of software or of inventions as the basic notion of the Constitution seeks, but is hindering it to the detriment of society and the common good.

The other important bone of contention is the patenting of "methods of doing business." Walker Digital is a company whose business is "to invent business methods" which they patent and then license.[10] Since e-business is a new phenomenon, almost any method of doing business on the Internet can be considered in some sense new, since it involves new technology and software. The result has been a rush to obtain business methods patents – with 182 in 1998, 399 in 1999.[11] The case that received a large amount of publicity and press coverage arose in 1999 when the PTO awarded Amazon.com patent number 5,960,411. The patent was for a "Method and system for placing a purchase order via a communications network," known as "one-click." It protects the on-line ordering system developed by Amazon which requires customers to make purchases with only one click of the mouse instead of the usual two. Amazon obtained an injunction preventing its competitors, such as barnesandnoble.com, from using the one-click method. The process uses cookies technology which predated Amazon's patent and is well known. The development of the one-click process, many computer programmers claim, is obvious, even though no company had actually developed or used it before Amazon. A boycott was started against Amazon by the Free Software Foundation. In February, 2000, Amazon received a patent (number 6,029,141) for an "Internet-based customer referral system," in which other sites use Web links to refer customers to Amazon and in turn receive a portion of any resulting sale. That drew over 10,000 signatures protesting the patent, which covers a technique of getting referral commissions widely used by thousands of merchants.[12] Jeff Bezos, the founder and CEO of Amazon, responded to the criticism in an open letter.[13] He did not give up Amazon's controversial patents or withdraw its suit against Barnes & Noble for patent infringement. But he conceded that "it's possible that the current rules governing business methods and software patents could end up harming all of us." He therefore suggested changes in the patent law that would reduce the length of these patents to three to five years, that the shorter timespan be retroactive, and that there be public comment before a patent is issued. Although all three suggestions had been previously made by others, coming from the holder of two controversial patents made it newsworthy. All three make sense and are arguably fairer than the current system and so preferable from an ethical point of view .

In April, 2001 Representatives Howard L. Berman (D, CA) and Rick Broucher (D, VA) introduced a bill (the Business Method Patent Improvement Act of 2001), to "provide that where an invention differs from prior inventions only in that it is a non-novel computer implementation (i.e., an Internet adaptation of a known business practice), it is presumed to be obvious and therefore not patentable." It also requires the PTO to publish all business-method patents 18 months after filing, and it would develop a means for challenging the patent without the present necessity of filing a lawsuit.

It is noteworthy that a United States patent covers only the territory of the United States, and that patent laws in different countries differ from those in the US. All countries face the same issues of patents that we have discussed. In March, 2001 the UK Patent Office recommended that only certain kinds of software that give rise to a "technical effect" be patentable, and opposed "patents for ways of doing business on the Internet." It recommended its conclusions to the other members of the European Union, and noted the current condition of uncertainty on the issues in European legislation. Many other countries have done nothing in this regard.

While there is general agreement that patents and copyright should allow sufficient time for an individual or company to recoup the investment made in developing an idea, and that there should be room for making a profit from one's endeavors, some argue that the computer industry moves so fast that such legal protection is less useful than the spur of competition to promote development. Companies such as Microsoft have to constantly improve their products to stay ahead of the competition. And it is by staying ahead, rather than by reaping the rewards of monopoly provided by patents, that they succeed. If this is true, then patent protection for software is not needed to provide the incentive for others to develop other ideas, which help the development and enrichment of society.

Computer programs do not fit into the traditional copyright and patent models, and the courts have been forced in effect to legislate by analogy. The legislature can help to rectify the situation by considering the unique aspects of computers and software and developing appropriate protection of property rights. We have seen the issues and some of the arguments on various sides of the issues. Consequentialist approaches to the issues are uncertain because it is so difficult to foresee the consequences of different policies, and because unforeseeable innovations are occurring all the time.

There are other issues in addition that we have not raised, such as the question of when a program is a different program, and what exactly may and may not be protected. In 1988 Apple unsuccessfully sued Microsoft for copying for Microsoft's Windows program the "desktop metaphor" and other elements of the Apple "look and feel." Two years later Lotus unsuccessfully sued Borland for allegedly copying it menus and other parts of its program. But neither Microsoft nor Borland had stolen any code, and the "structure, sequence, and organization" of a program cannot be covered by copyright. Nonetheless, it is fairly clear that if Microsoft and Borland did not violate copyright law and did not steal anything, they certainly borrowed from the other companies. Yet that is allowable, and the way that progress is made. One of the objections to software patents is that they are so broad as to effectively preclude such borrowing for the duration of the patent protection period. If patents had been in effect as programming and the Internet were developing, it is unlikely either would have developed as quickly as they did.

Two issues remain which we shall discuss in later chapters; namely, the special problems related to property and the Internet, and the problem of international legal coordination.

The ethical issue is the proper extent of protection of intellectual property, and from that point of view it is not clear what the law *should* be. The issue is not simply one of property rights. Simply taking the vested interests of businesses that wish strong copyright protection as the benchmark is not a sound policy.[14] Here technology may force a rethinking of both what is in the best interest of society, and what is appropriate in the way of reward for the products that are covered by copyright and patents. Do copyright and patents serve the purpose they were originally intended to serve or are they hampering the creative development of knowledge, and so should they be rethought and changed?

The issues of ownership of intellectual property are heating up and becoming more and more complicated as technology makes the transfer of information so easy and readily accessible to all. In the Information Age information is central and its promise for the common good is that it is infinitely shareable. It is therefore ironic that in the Information Age the attempt is to limit and control the diffusion of information and its distribution through greater legal protection of claimed property rights. The question of how to properly balance legitimate commercial interests against the interests of the general public and the common good are ethical issues that have scarcely begun to be adequately addressed nationally in public debate, much less internationally.

What conclusions can we draw?

1   As we have already learned from business ethics in the Industrial Age, there are some cases in which legislation is required because market forces do not yield the ethically desirable results or do not yield them quickly enough before much harm is done. In a global economy, international legal coordination is required and the proper choice of legislation demands ethical justification.

2   Preemptive legislation is preferable to reactive legislation. In many cases, business is developing the patterns and procedures that benefit it rather than procedures that produce the most good for all or that respect the rights of all. The need for action is apparent, since it is much more difficult to change procedures once they have been developed than to correct them after they have become the standard way of doing business.

3   With respect to information and intellectual property, there is an urgent need to reconsider, from an ethical point of view, whether present US and international copyright and patent laws serve the common good as they were originally intended to do and either to revise them to the extent that they fail to do so or to adopt a new way of protecting intellectual property in the Information Age.

Ethics in business requires ethical people and ethical corporations. But they are not enough. Ethically defensible social structures, and in particular ethically justifiable legislation – both national and integrated across borders – is necessary to make and keep the competitive playing field fair and to protect the rights of all parties and the common good.

▲ NOTES ▲

1. James V. DeLong, "Business Discovers Property Rights," *Wall Street Journal*, April 26, 1999, p. A19.
2. Lester C. Thurow, "Needed: A New System of Intellectual Property Rights," *Harvard Business Review*, September–October, 1997, pp. 95–103.
3. Anthony Clapes, *Software, Copyright, and Competition* (New York: Quorum Books, 1989).
4. See Anne W. Branscomb, "Rogue Computer Programs and Computer Rogues: Tailoring the Punishment to Fit the Crime," *Rutgers Computer and Technology Law Journal*, 16 (1991), pp. 1–61.
5. For details see Craig Smith, "A Tale of Piracy: How the Chinese Stole the Grinch," *New York Times*, December 12, 2000, p. A3; Craig Smith, "Piracy a Concern as the China Trade Opens Up," *New York Times*, October 5, 2000, p. W1; Richard Behar, "Beijing's Phony War on Fakes," *Fortune*, October 30, 2000, pp. 189–208.
6. Shawn Tully, "Big Man Against Big Music," *Fortune*, August 14, 2000, pp. 186–92.
7. Webster's New Colgate Dictionary.
8. *Diamond v. Diehr*, 450 US 175 (1981).
9. Evan Ratliff, "Patent Upending," *Wired*, June 2000, pp. 208–24.
10. Geneva Sapp, "E-businesses Vie for Technology Ownership," *Infoworld*, March 6, 2000, p. 30.
11. Ibid; Julia Angwin, "'Business-Method' Patents, Key to Priceline, Draw Growing Protest," *Wall Street Journal*, October 3, 2000, pp. B1, B4.
12. James Gleick, "Patently Absurd," *New York Times Magazine*, March 12, 2000, pp. 42–9.
13. "An Open Letter from Jeff Bezos on the Subject of Patents," available online at http://www.amazon.com/exec/obidos/subst/misc/patents.html/102-4553508-4608918.
14. See Arthur Kuflik, "Moral Foundations of Intellectual Property Rights,"in *Owning Scientific and Technical Information*, ed. Vivian Weil and John W. Snapper (New Brunswick, NJ: Rutgers University Press, 1989).

chapter five

Ethical Issues in Information Technology Business and E-Business

▲ THE DOUBLECLICK CASE ▲

DoubleClick is a New York-based Internet advertising network. It displays ads on over 11,500 client sites. If someone visits any one of those sites, DoubleClick places a cookie on that person's hard drive that not only allows it to record future visits but also allows it to link that information with any data gathered from any visits to any other affiliated sites. If the person has given his or her name or address at any of the other sites, this is then added to form the individual's ongoing browsing history. Clients use the information to place ads targeted at individual Web users.

In November, 1999, DoubleClick paid $1.7 billion in stock to acquire Abacus Direct, a database marketer with names and purchase histories of 88 million households that made purchases from a large number of retail stores and mail-order catalogs. DoubleClick proposed joining this database with its browsing database. It defended its actions by saying it allowed better targeting of potential customers for on-line advertisers. It thus was beneficial for both its customers and the customers of the firms it served. Privacy advocates disagreed, arguing that DoubleClick tracked Web surfers without their knowledge or consent and then identified them not only by the IP address of their computer but also by name, enabling them to correlate a large dossier of information about the users with their surfing habits. Joining this data with the data provided by Abacus was, they claimed, a violation of consumer privacy. In March, 2000, because of the large number of complaints by privacy advocates, DoubleClick said that it had postponed linking its own database with that of Abacus Direct.

The practice of tracking by using banner ads and cookies is not illegal, nor is the matching of browsing information with the name of a user that he or she has provided at one of the sites that DoubleClick serves, nor is the correlation of that Internet information with information about the user received from other sources, such as Abacus Direct.

In August, 2001, DoubleClick came out with a revised privacy policy that allowed users to opt out of ad-serving cookies. Included in its policy was a statement that the company "may change its policy."[1] Although DoubleClick claimed that its opt out provision was sufficient to guarantee users as much privacy as they desired, critics claimed that most Web users did not and would not know about the opt out possibility and that simply making that possibility available did not constitute informed consent.

All of this raises the question: Is it ethical for a company, such as DoubleClick, to compile information on the Web-browsing habits of people without their knowledge, to link that data to other data compiled from other sources and for other purposes, and to use that new database, without the knowledge or consent of the individuals, for marketing purposes?

Every business is engaged in selling goods or services for profit, and employs human labor in the process. Business on the Internet and the business aspect of the information technology field are no different in this respect from any other business. To that extent these businesses face the same ethical problems and share the same ethical difficulties as any other business. They are governed by the same moral norms and are similarly bound not to cheat, steal, lie, and so on, as are all other businesses and persons. Nonetheless, there are special ethical problems that arise in the information technology industry and in e-business. And when the ethical issues that e-business raises are different, their solution may not be as intuitive or obvious as otherwise.

E-business is relatively new and doing business on the Internet has been touted as a great boon for consumers. E-business includes all types of interaction via the Web among businesses, customers, employees, and other businesses, including Web-based buying and selling and customer service. It is usually divided into a number of different types, each of which raises its own ethical issues. E-business is either business-to-customer (B2C) or business-to-business (B2B), which is the faster growing component of e-business. E-commerce is the marketing and selling portion of e-business.

The Internet is a vast source of information – including information about products for sale. No longer is the customer in a small town limited to the few specialized stores available there, and no longer is the customer at the mercy of the local shopkeepers' prices. Name any product, and one can find on the Web a multitude of different makes, models, and discount prices. Often available also are free assessments of the quality of different products, and users' comments. If you are interested in a book on any topic, you can probably find it quickly on the Web and you are no longer dependent on the local bookstore, with its limited inventory and access to booksellers.

Those who are invalids and the aged who want to shop from home are now able to do so. Those who are pressed for time and cannot shop during regular hours can now shop on-line at any time of day or night. In many locations one can even order one's groceries on-line, so that leaving the house becomes unnecessary. Travel information is easily available – train and air schedules and fares, cruises, hotel availability (sometimes with tours of the property, pictures of the rooms, maps and other information), and so on. No longer is one tied to a travel agent for information or service. The list is endless.

Some on-line businesses function only on-line. Amazon.com is a prime example, and quickly became known as the website to visit for books on any topic. It advertises on other sites, and places pop-up ads about travel books on travel sites, about history books on history sites, and about appropriate books on other sites. Dell only sells its computers on-line, but it heavily advertises in newspapers and magazines and through direct mail. Most businesses of any size have a website. Some do business both on- and off-line, for instance Amazon.com's competitor, Barnes & Noble, which has stores throughout the United States as well as selling on-line. Others simply have a site for information purposes. Any business of any size has a website, as do nonprofit organizations, government bureaus, and many individuals.

The promise of e-business is enormous, but is not without its drawbacks. For there are hazards and hidden costs and dangers to shopping on-line. There are unscrupulous merchants, hackers out to steal credit card and social security numbers, fly-by-night operations, companies that collect and sell personal information, intrusive pornographic sites, and others engaged in illegal, unethical, or questionable behavior.

As a result a central issue that has arisen with business on the Internet is trust.

▲ TRUST ▲

Trust is central to any business transaction, but on the Internet and in e-business it has taken on special importance. The reasons are multiple. Trust is often established between individuals through their contact and mutual interaction. In a face-to-face interaction one gets a sense of the person one is dealing with. If a new store opens in the neighborhood, a visit quickly gives one a great deal of information about the service one receives, the interest and level of precision, and a great deal more that people have learned to immediately factor into the initial impressions they form. Word of mouth, the experience of others, stories of the way others have been treated, the length of time the business has existed in that location or town, the general reputation of nationwide businesses – all go to influence the attitude one takes towards a business. One can also check with the local better business bureau, the chamber of commerce, and call references the tradesman might supply. Trust is built upon a whole host of sources, and deepens over time. One gets to know which business to trust, which brand to trust, which used car salesman or which mechanic to trust, which doctor or lawyer to trust. Employees similarly learn whom to trust within their firms, and whether the business as a whole is trustworthy, as do suppliers and those who provide services for the business. Whether the business pays it bills on time, whether it is always late, whether it performs as it promises – all of these considerations are parts of the process of building trust.

Issues of trust with respect to e-business fall into two groups. The first has to do with the general use of the Web. The second has to do with consumer or customer relations with particular businesses on the Web.

Trust and the Web

There are systemic fears that many people have with respect to doing business of any kind over the Internet. Three of them are worry about credit card theft, the question of the trustworthiness of information, and the issue of personal information privacy.

The first of these might appear to be the simplest and pose the least problem. Many people give their credit car numbers over the phone without hesitation, and they give their credit cards to clerks or waiters who sometimes go to another room to verify the card and enter the charge. Most people have come to feel reasonably safe doing this, and although there are abuses, they are not typically a major source of concern. Yet many people are still reluctant to give their credit card numbers on the Internet. Their fears are not necessarily without foundation. For the trustworthiness and security of the Internet itself are still uncertain. Scarcely a week goes by without some notice of an e-mail or other program being compromised, a warning being issued about a new breach found or a patch being offered to plug a security hole. The reports are real and not the product of a paranoid customer's imagination. The likelihood of any individual suffering harm as a result of such bugs and programming defects is probably minimal. But the number and persistence of such reports tends to undermine general confidence and trust in the security of which the Internet is capable.

Add to these general deficiencies stories of hackers entering into and stealing thousands of credit card numbers from on-line businesses, and customers can rightly wonder how safe their credit card numbers are on-line. Over the phone one knows that phone lines are protected by law, and that there is at least that guarantee of protection. On-line, there is still little regulation, and even if there were national laws, hackers can operate from anywhere in the world.

So the general issue of how safe the Internet can be made from hackers is a concern that limits the amount of trust people are willing to place on Internet transactions. There are various ways to allay such fears. Some companies allow customers to place their orders on-line and, if they choose, to give their credit card numbers over the phone. Some have customers transmit the first part of their credit card number in one transaction and then send the second part in a separate transaction. Many companies use encryption to protect the transfer of credit card information, with a lock or other symbol indicating a secure transaction. The customer, of course, is expected to understand the way encryption works and why they should trust such indications of security – which itself presumes a certain amount of trust in the somewhat arcane area of encryption and the trustworthiness of the security symbol.

The matters of security holes and of hackers entering sites and stealing credit card numbers *en masse* are matters that are only in part a function of trusting the particular firm with which one deals.

For no company seems completely immune to such problems, no matter how diligent. Hence the problems of Internet security are not an individual company's problem – although it might also be that – but a systemic problem having to do with the Internet itself.

The Internet is still new. One of its virtues is that it is open to all and in large part unregulated. But the lack of regulation means there is no guarantee of security. Trust of the security of the Internet, just as any other kind of trust, is built up over time. The Internet and e-business have not been around long enough to have generated the level of trust that people place in phone calls or the mail service.

Until the level of security can be improved in general, transactions over the Internet will carry some risk, and worry about that risk will limit the extent and development of e-business.

While security is one problem, the trustworthiness of information, including the issue of authentication, is another.

Customers, trust, and e-business

In the Information Age the communication explosion has resulted in information overload. There is more information available than any one individual can absorb. The instantaneous communication made possible by computers and the Internet opens the lines of communication to all, in an environment in which anyone can say or publish anything. There is no peer review or editorial overview before something gets published on the Web; and anonymity makes possible irresponsibility. With the freedom of speech that we cherish, more and more is posted on the World Wide Web under the guise of information, so that it is difficult to know what to believe and what to trust as reliable. Hence the need for authentication centers. In the industrial world Consumer Reports and similar groups could test and give independent judgments about products. Similar independent authenticators are needed with respect to information: which websites, for instance, that carry medical information are reliable and authoritative, and which are not. Centers of this type in all areas of information are needed if people are to benefit from the information available.

The authentication issue is not only which sites to trust, but which authenticators to trust. The level of transparency on the Web is not very great. Much goes on behind the screen that ordinary users know little or nothing about. Although the amount of information available is overwhelming, the amount of information about the trustworthiness of individual sites, including authenticators, is minimal. Search engines are necessary to find one's way about. But are the first sites listed by a particular engine those that have paid the search engine to be listed first, or is the order determined by size or alphabetically, or by date or by some other method? Usually there is no indication of the criterion or criteria for listing sites. Some search engines will list all the pertinent sites, determined frequently by the key words that the site provides in order to identify itself. Hence the issue of trust operates at several levels. Which search engines does one trust, and what does such trust mean? Bots (short for "robots") or programs that are used to search through a great deal of data (such as www.mysimon.com and www.compdirect.com) help you locate products for sale on-line and help you compare prices. But they do not guarantee anything about the sites they list. Sites that give consumer feedback (such as www.resellerratings.com or www.ratingwonders.com) may also be helpful. But once again one is asked to trust unknown respondents. There are few authenticators of the reliability of sites. A branch of the Better Business Bureau (www.bbbonline.com) has a "Reliability Seal" program and a "Privacy Seal" program, but even they can only indicate that a site has met certain specific requirements and offer no guarantee of trustworthiness. Other less well-known certifiers actually provide very little protection. Of the several authenticators that have appeared is there any way of knowing which to trust? Who authenticates the authenticators, how do they do so, and how much can they be trusted? What are the biases of the authenticators and how objective are their seals or indications of approval – be they of a site's privacy policy or of any other aspect of the site? The sheer volume of what is available on the Internet is a double-edged sword. An enormous amount of information and almost every imaginable service is available. But the difficulty of knowing which to trust, and of those, which are best from any given perspective, is daunting. Trust is built up over time, and over time some sites will emerge as trustworthy. But the risk that one takes in using possibly untrustworthy ones is a difficulty that impedes new companies and that tends to hinder the development of e-business in general.

To maintain trust it is essential to maintain a clear line between information and advertising, between information and brain washing or manipulation, between information and self-interest. The reviews of books that one sees if one goes, for instance, to Amazon.com to buy books illustrates the point. The only way such reviews will carry weight with viewers is if they can be sure that the reviews are not simply paid for by the book publisher, that the review is not planted by the author's friend, and that Amazon.com is not paid to promote the book. If the latter is the case, then it should be identified as an advertisement, as advertisements are identified in newspapers. The function of authenticator and of advertiser must be kept separate.

Systemic worries, however, are not the only source of concern. The issue of trust becomes a central issue in dealing with individual sites.

On-line, of course, there is no face-to-face contact. One cannot form an impression of the people – if there are any – one is dealing with, evaluate their comportment or the look in their eyes. The great benefit of having 10 or 20 or more different sources from which to buy a product or service becomes not a great boon but sometimes a source of uncertainty and the very ease of contact a source of uneasiness. To what extent can one take at face value what is stated or claimed about a product? Can one be sure one will actually be sent what one buys? If the product is unsatisfactory, can it be returned, and how and at what cost? There may be details on the sites spelling out the policy on all these questions. But can one trust what the site says?

People have learned over the years how to judge individuals and businesses. The physical presence of a business is an initial indication of some financing, presumably by a bank or other source that has looked into the personal history and prospects of the store's owner or the parties starting the business. Websites can be established cheaply and virtually by anyone. Which businesses are trustworthy? How can one determine this? And given the multiplicity of outlets, how does one find out about them and about which ones are more trustworthy than others? The process tends to take time, as word of mouth or of e-mail or of outside evaluations help various sites develop their reputations.

One often finds out who sells what product by going to a search engine and entering the name of the product. The number of sites listed might be very large indeed. As we have seen, one must rely on search engines. Which individual site or e-business does one trust and how is that trust established? Repeated successful experience builds trust. But trust is necessary for the first contact.

The problem of initial trust has given established businesses that have brick-and-mortar outlets and stores an advantage over those that do business only on-line. An established store already has name recognition and it is reasonable to grant an established firm a certain amount of initial trust. This is justified simply by the fact that if it were not generally trustworthy it would not have remained in business for any length of time. In dealing with an established firm, its on-line service usually parallels its off-line service. Frequently if one makes a purchase on-line and is dissatisfied, one can return the item to the nearby store. One cannot do this if the firm deals only on-line. Hence established firms have a built-in advantage when they go on-line.

This is part of the reason for the success of airline websites and travel sites that deal in airline tickets. The product is a known commodity and one can both easily compare prices and know when one is getting a deep discount from regular fares or another especially good deal. Airlines and hotels have long been making their bookings via computer. The only recent change is to open their bookings up to the general public via the Internet.

Dell is a classic example of a firm that is well established and deals only on-line. Its computers are often highly rated by computer magazines. Through ads and direct mail advertising, it has become a household name. Yet even Dell has to overcome the drawback that potential customers cannot see a Dell computer, judge the quality of its screen in person, feel the touch of its keyboard on a display model, and develop the trust that one has in products that one experiences first hand.

If an e-business sells a service or a program, it might carry on all its transactions on-line. But if it is selling a product, then even though the order is placed on-line, the physical object must be delivered – and possibly returned. How efficient and trustworthy e-businesses are with respect to deliveries, what policies they have about returns, how much extra they charge for delivery, how good they are in handling complaints of course varies from business to business, just as these do for regular brick-and-mortar stores. Worries about these issues tend to inhibit some users and make e-business less attractive than the theory about them and their benefit to customers once promised.

Trust is a central concern and businesses that act ethically as well as efficiently are more likely to succeed than those that do not.

▲ PRIVACY, TRACKING, DATA MINING, ▲ AND ONE-ON-ONE MARKETING

One of the central concerns of B2C marketing involves the issue of customer privacy, and fear of lack of privacy has been one of the deterrents to the development of B2C. Until that fear is successfully put to rest, B2C will remain hampered. Yet two trends in B2C are unsettling, raise ethical concerns about privacy, and have to be addressed in a way that guarantees the level of privacy customers desire – a level which may vary from customer to customer. One trend is data mining; the other is one-on-one marketing. There is nothing unethical in itself in either practice and both have legitimate uses. Nonetheless both have been used in ways that can be ethically faulted.

Data mining is a technique widely used beyond the marketing area. It consists of computer programs that utilize a variety of mathematical and statistical algorithms and other techniques, such as modeling, to analyze a database to discover new relationships, and so new information. It can be used on given databases and the possibilities it raises have led to programs that capture a wealth of information that was previously uncollected and so unused. It can be used to uncover trends and predict probable lines of future development, increase one's information about one's customers either in aggregate or individualized, in some case reduce or uncover fraud, and learn more about Internet use and how to make it more attractive and profitable.

One simple marketing-related use of data mining is for a company to search through its database of current customer use, glean certain characteristics among its users, and then search other databases for individuals who have those characteristics and target them as likely customers.

Data mining information used in aggregate usually causes no problems. Supermarkets have long done studies of which shelves customers are most likely to look at and they put the items they most want to push on those shelves. Stores such as Wal-Mart have done studies of which products sell best in which areas and have tailored their stores in different locations to serve the interests of the people in those areas. Supermarkets have moved into the use of "shopper's cards" or "loyalty cards" which identify a customer and when presented to the cashier yield discounts on some of the items purchased. They are often not discounts from the price competitors charge, but from an inflated price charged to those who do not use the card. The card's purpose is to collect data on individual users. One company ran correlations and found that customers who bought a lot of low-fat products did not buy potato chips. When they sent them coupons for low-calorie potato chips they had a 40 percent return, rather than the 1 percent or 2 percent return usual with the broadside distribution of such coupons.

Data collection on the Web follows similar lines but is much more complete and detailed. Sites interested in data mining can record every movement any visitor makes on its site. Information about when customers hit the Stop button can let it know if the access it provides to its information is too slow. It can record how its users utilize its links, which pages and which ads its customers react to, and so on. It can capture information about the visitor's browser, whether it uses a modem and how fast the connection is, what its operating system is, what geographical location it comes from, how much privacy the user wants, and so on, and join all this, for instance, with how much persons with the user's characteristics spend. All the information can be tallied in a wide variety of ways to uncover patterns and significant correlations. All of this information can be extremely useful to an e-business. Data from different sites can be joined in what are called data warehouses, and all the data mined for whatever purposes one wishes, revealing possible groups to target for ads or ways of doing business. Potential problems arise, however, when data mining is individualized, joined to tracking, and used in one-on-one marketing.

Two techniques especially raise issues of privacy. One is targeting, sometimes called personalization or one-on-one marketing. Targeting involves choosing a group to contact by some form of advertisement – be it a banner ad or a pop-up on-line, or an e-mail, or a mail or phone contact. A bookseller might place an ad for a travel book on sites that provide travel information. That is targeting but not objectionable from the point of view of privacy. However, when individuals are chosen on the basis of characteristics derived from data mining, which requires that the individuals be identified by name, questions arise. They arise similarly when customers are on one's own site.

Many people like and appreciate personalized service. If your local merchant knows and greets you by name when you enter the store, if they draw your attention to a particular product that the clerk knows you like and that has just arrived, if they are able to anticipate your wants and take steps to accommodate you, they are likely to be met with a favorable response and more likely than otherwise to make a sale. If this is true in brick-and-mortar businesses, why should it be less true in e-business? Hence some sites keep close track of what an individual purchases, what he or she is interested in, and what the customer's proclivities are. If through data mining they further determine that people with certain characteristics tend to have other pertinent characteristics, these can be used to provide the best service possible, anticipating needs, bringing appropriate items to one's attention, and so on. Why should anyone object?

The objection comes not from the one-on-one marketing but from the source of the information used – how it was acquired, whether it is reliable, whether it can be corrected. When we deal with the local shop keeper who gives us personalized service, we have no worry that he will sell the information he has acquired about us to parties unknown to us, or that he will collate all the information he has about us and infer information based on statistical and other types of analysis.

We have already seen the issues of privacy that must be addressed having to do with informed consent, possible misuse of information, and the uses to which the information on a person might be put and to whom it might be sold or made available without one's knowledge and consent. It is one thing to make a purchase on-line or to register at a site giving one's name, postal address, and e-mail address. It is quite another for a site to capture your IP address as you browse the Web and then correlate that to information you have provided at another website, or join all the information that can be gathered by tracking you from site to site and joining that with databases derived from a wide variety of sources off-line, such as credit history, criminal record, and public record information. All the inferred and correlated information may identify people as potential risks, or as unprofitable customers, and they may be earmarked to receive little attention or be discouraged from using a site or being a customer – perhaps by the fees charged for services to customers who cost a site more than they are worth. Clearly the point is not that one's IP address is private information about one, but that it can be used to develop a dossier of private information about the user.

The value of personal information is demonstrated by companies such as Free-PC.com which offered people free computers in exchange for a wealth of personal information about themselves – such as age, income, and hobbies – and the right to monitor all their Internet activity, as well as more or less deluge them with banner ads on-line and other ads whenever they turn on the computer. The offer had more applicants than the company wanted, and it had to limit the number it was able to accommodate. This shows both that the information collected by the company was more valuable than the cost of supplying the user with a free computer, and that some people value a free computer more than they do their personal information or information about their Web activities. Where the transaction is above board and all the conditions are known in advance and consent given to the gathering and unlimited use of such information, there is little ground for complaint.

The privacy issue arises when Internet users do not know that they are being tracked and identified, and they unknowingly become the subject of an individual and personalized database. If one gives some personal information on one site, that does not mean one gives that site the right to sell or use that information as they wish. Some sites have a privacy policy that one can consult – but only after one has already visited the site and so already been identified and after having provided all the information that goes with that simple act. It is also questionable how much one should trust explicit policy statements. Toysmart raised that issue in a dramatic way when it went bankrupt and offered to sell its database of personal information, much of it on children, even though it had declared in its policy that personal information "is never shared with a third party."[2] Amazon.com in its Privacy Notice states explicitly that "in the unlikely event that Amazon.com, Inc., or substantially all if its assets are acquired, customer information will of course be one of the transferred assets."

The present situation is the result of the technological imperative on the one hand and the Myth of Amoral Computing and Information Technology on the other. Tracking, data mining, and the other techniques that have developed are the result of what fast computers and cheap memory have made possible. But simply because the techniques could be developed and used does not mean that they had to be developed and used as they are. Both hardware and software producers made products without sufficient attention to the possible misuses to which their products could be put and to the ethical obligation to anticipate and forestall such use. Just because information can be gathered and mined does not mean it should be. In February, 1999, when Intel came out with its Pentium III chip and announced that it would transmit a unique serial number internally and to websites that request it in order to verify the identities of the website user, it was thinking only about a possible benefit to websites. Its announcement drew the ire of a large number of different groups that were so fearful that their privacy would be compromised that they planned a boycott. Only then did Intel announce it would include software that allows users to turn off the transmission and would encourage computer makers to make the default "off" in the machines they sell.

Consider two alternatives to present use that would solve the problems of privacy that have arisen. One is a reconsideration of "cookies" and similar technology. The other is the adoption of "opt out" as the default instead of "opt in."

Cookies are strings of information that a website places on a visitor's hard drive, and that are sent back to the site on subsequent visits. Cookies technology was developed by Lou Montulli in June 1994 for Netscape. As John Schwartz notes, "Cookies fundamentally altered the nature of surfing the Web from being a relatively anonymous activity, like wandering the streets of a large city, to the kind of environment where records of one's transactions, movements and even desires could be stored, sorted, mined and sold."[3] Cookies were not the only technology possible to help websites keep track of their customers, but once they were introduced they became ubiquitous. They were adopted by all browsers, and were quickly exploited by websites. There was no public protest, undoubtedly because the ordinary user was not aware of their existence or use.

There are three different basic uses of cookies that can be used to classify them into three types. The first is to keep track of an individual user's transactions on a particular site, so that the user can start a transaction, interrupt it, and go back to take up where he or she left off. This use of cookies is compatible with cookies being held only in temporary memory and not written to one's hard drive. After the transaction is closed, the cookie can disappear, having fulfilled its function. There is little reason to object to this use of cookies, since it helps customers get better service on-line and facilitates transactions. A second use or kind of cookie is placed on the user's hard drive by the website so that when the user revisits the site, the site recognizes the user. The third type is what are known as "third-party cookies," which are placed on one's hard drive not by the website one is using, but by some third party, such as

DoubleClick, which notes wherever a user browses through the use of its banner ads, which gives it a presence on all the sites on which 11,500 advertisers place banner ads. It is especially the third type or use of cookies that has raised privacy concerns, although the second also raises some concern.

Newer versions of Netscape allow users to turn off third-party cookies, as well as to choose the option of rejecting all cookies. But the user must know that this is possible. The default remains "accept all cookies." Microsoft's Explorer 6 browser has built into it a version of Platform for Privacy Preferences (P3P), developed under the auspices of the World Wide Web Consortium. It allows a user to select different levels of privacy, and is preset to block third-party cookies. It can also be set to block any cookies from sites that do not have a P3P policy that matches the one chosen by the user. But here, too, the user must know what the available options are and understand the differences between options. For true informed consent, the initial option should be to opt out of all cookies. Only after one makes a choice, based on a clear explanation of what the various choices involve, can one plausibly claim to have obtained informed consent.

There are three objections to the way cookies were introduced early on in Internet use and have remained accepted practice. First, cookies are placed on a user's hard drive. It is an invasion of property for anyone to enter into another person's computer and tamper with it in any way, including adding a string of information thereon. Yet hardware and software producers thought nothing about the practice and introduced it in all computers. Customers who purchased computers were not and are not informed that cookies are used and sites that place cookies on a person's computer do not have to inform them that they are doing it. That this practice was simply introduced and has been accepted is itself an indication of the prevalence of the Myth of Amoral Computing and Information Technology. Cookies technology is not the only technological way of being able to let customers make purchases over the Web by browsing a particular site and choosing what to purchase. If it is indeed a breach of property, as it seems to be if cookies are placed on one's hard drive without the user's knowledge or consent, then an alternative technology that does not do this should be developed and implemented.

Second, although users can search out the control governing cookies, if they learn it exists, and can choose a variety of options

(Netscape offers five options: Accept all cookies; Accept only cookies that get sent back to the originating server; Disable cookies; Warn me before accepting a cookie; Refuse all cookies), the default setting is "Accept all cookies." One must know the options exist, know how to choose a different option (in Netscape it is in the Advanced section of Preferences, indicating that those who wrote the program do not expect ordinary users to access it), and know what the result of choosing each of the different options is. A preferable approach from the point of view of privacy and of informed consent would be to make the default "Warn me before accepting a cookie." Since Netscape itself places cookies on a user's hard drive a user would immediately get a cookie message when first trying to access the Web. Users could then be informed of what cookies are, how they are used, what one's options are, and how one can change one's options, and be allowed to choose the option they prefer. That would constitute something close enough to informed consent, at least for the initial stage of accessing the Web. The same sort of analysis can be made of Microsoft's Explorer and other browsers. From an ethical point of view, if one truly wishes to safeguard individual privacy and seek informed consent, the proper default is "opt out."

The third objection comes from the use of third-party cookies and the linking of information gathered from different sites that one visits. This is a result of the way cookies technology was developed. It need not be a continuing possibility. A first step would be to make the default option on each website a refusal to supply information about access or personal information or the linking of information with information gathered elsewhere on- or off-line. Those wishing to allow a website to gather, collect, trade or sell, collate, mine, and otherwise use the information gathered would have to give specific permission for each use. Unless specific permission were given, any tracking or attempts at personal identification would be illegal and actionable. Adopting these would be no more damaging to business than similar practices that now obtain in the world of brick-and-mortar businesses. There is no reason why the same rules should not apply. The ease of tracking and the possibilities of capturing data do not justify sites or companies doing so. The general rules of privacy that we have already seen should operate in e-business as well as in all other aspects and kinds of business. There should be no secret records kept on individuals; those who are the subjects of any personal record system should both be informed of its existence and allowed to inspect and correct the data contained therein; the information should be used only for purposes that the subject agrees to under conditions of informed consent; and those who manage such records should be responsible for their use and liable for their misuse.

An arguably better alternative, however, is to get rid of cookies and develop a technology that does what all users want to do to the extent that they want it, and in such a way that it is transparent to all concerned. Just because cookies technology has been widely adopted does not mean it cannot or should not be replaced.

▲ E-BUSINESS, PRIVACY, AND RISK ▲

We have looked at the issue of privacy and e-business from an ethical point of view. If it is correct, as I have claimed, that what motivates the concern of many people is not the issue of privacy as such but that privacy is the term used to encompass their fears of various kinds of harm that may be done them from a misuse and abuse of their personal information, then it may be enlightening to look at the issue from the point of view of risk assessment.

Risk assessment usually involves some notion of harm or danger or injury and the probability it will occur, often expressed as a percentage determined mathematically or empirically. Involved in risk assessment are three questions:

1   How much safety is achievable?
2   How much safety do we want, given costs and trade-offs?
3   How do we achieve the amount of safety we want in (2)?

The first and third of these questions are at least in part technical questions. The second is a question of values, and so not amenable to a technical solution.

In order to answer the second question in some rational fashion, four conditions should be met. A person should:

•   be informed of or aware of the risk;
•   know the source of the risk and how great the danger is;
•   know how to protect against the risk to the extent possible;
•   know the alternatives.

If we apply this to e-business and privacy, different people may choose to accept different degrees of risk. Some may not worry about personal identity theft, or care if whatever is compiled on them is accurate, or worry about their credit ratings beings ruined, or their being turned down for insurance or refused a job or otherwise suffer negative consequences because of data compiled on them and inferred about them based on their Web transactions and activities. If this position is rational, they must at least know what risk they are exposed to and what harm they may suffer. This condition is only sometimes met. Although there are numerous accounts of personal identity theft in the media and of other kinds of harm that people encounter, not everyone follows such reports and many browse the Web in blissful ignorance of the possible harms. There are also the risks of hackers stealing personal information from individuals themselves and from the computers of e-businesses.

The second condition is difficult to get accurate information about. Much of the material available to the general public is anecdotal. Many negative instances receive no publicity. If a company's database is accessed by unauthorized persons and individual credit card numbers stolen, most companies do not publicly announce that fact. For a long while identity theft was not taken very seriously by credit card companies, banks, or law enforcement authorities. But even if there were accurate figures, it seems likely that to some the number of those negatively impacted by using the Web would be small in comparison to the total number of users. This is true of other crimes as well, such as murder and theft. How much risk one is willing to subject oneself to might therefore be considered a matter of temperament or individual judgment.

Nonetheless, in many other cases what is important is not only how much risk one is willing to take, but how much safety is available. With respect to buildings we know that there are certain risks that they might collapse, that we might be electrocuted by defective wires, and so on. But many societies and communities adopt building codes to minimize the risk, and those societies and communities do not simply say it is up to individuals to determine for themselves how much safety they want in their houses, and whether or not to enter skyscrapers at their own risk. The same is true of automobiles, airplanes, and other potentially dangerous products. Using any of them involves some risk. Driving an inexpensive car may be less safe than driving one that has many expensive safety features built in. But most societies adopt laws specifying a minimal level of safety that all cars must meet. What is lacking with respect to Web safety is not only any regulation, but any accurate information on how much safety is available and how it might be achieved. How secure should the records of companies on customers be, how secure can they be, and how secure should they be forced to be? Although there may always be the risk of a possible compromise of information, there can be a reasonable expectation that the risk a customer takes by engaging in e-business has been minimized in this regard by the business in question. Our cookies discussion raises another aspect of the issue. If we accept cookies as appropriate and inevitable, then using the Web will involve a certain amount of risk. But if we look at alternatives to cookies, there are possible ways of using the Web that do not pose the threats of harm that cookies do.

The third condition asks for ways of minimizing the risk. Again, taking cookies as the focal point, there are a variety of programs that one can purchase or download that allow one to manage cookies or to delete them after one signs off, it is possible to browse the Web anonymously, and so on. These are ways of minimizing risk, given the existing structures. They are often cumbersome and require a certain amount of computer facility that many people do not have. But another approach to minimizing the risk of cookies is to adopt a technology that does not employ them. The trade-off may be less information for business. But that may well be worth accepting from a societal and ethical point of view.

The last condition is to know the alternatives. Not using the Web will eliminate the risk. But this is not a viable option for many people in the Information Age. The alternatives that presently exist may well be too narrow, and a constructive approach would be to ask what preferable alternatives might be that do not yet already exist but are technologically feasible. Part of the problem currently is that the alternatives available to Web users have been devised to serve the interests of business at the expense of a feeling of privacy invasion and exposure to harm – real or imagined – on the part of a large number of users.

A similar approach to the use of software would weigh the risks of suffering the damage of lost time and aggravation versus the benefits of using the variety of computer programs that are available. In both Web-use and software-use cases, risk analysis may be used to provide an explanation of the fact that large numbers of users in fact utilize both. Yet while that would explain why this choice is a rational one, and so understandable, it does not address the issue of whether there are better alternatives and whether both e-business and computer professionals have an ethical responsibility to provide better alternatives that reduce the risks involved. Arguably they do.

The technological imperative has driven business to desire and seek to obtain as much personal information on people as possible and to use it for marketing and other purposes. It is gathered because it can be gathered. One result is some personalization of service. But the risks of abuse grow as do the databases. Is it really so much trouble to fill out one's name and address when placing an order that it has to be stored by the site or by a third party such as Microsoft's Passport? People have been led to believe that this is the case, but the arguments rarely mention the risks involved as the practice grows. This is one more instance of the Myth of Amoral Computing and Information Technology in which practices are developed, introduced, given partial defense and integrated into business practices without adequate information or discussion, as if there were no ethical implications to the decisions and practices.

▲ BUSINESS TO BUSINESS ▲

Business to business has had great initial success on the Internet because it holds great promise to increase efficiency. Through the use of the Internet companies can check on the availability of supplies from a great many vendors and check their prices. The fact that vendors make their prices available and the fact that they know they will be compared instantly with those of their competitors will be a strong impetus to price their products at truly competitive levels.

The ease and speed of this information transfer will result in lower overheads, as many layers of purchasers are no longer required to search out the information, contact individual firms, and negotiate over the phone or in person. The system obviously will work best where products are mass produced and more or less standardized, and where specifications can be easily compared. Not all products are of this type. But many are – office supplies being a prime example, and electronic equipment and components another. A centralized clearing house can eliminate the need for intermediaries and put the user in direct contact with the supplier.

B2B may be organized either to service horizontal markets – that is, a market that cuts across many industries (e.g., providing financial services) – or a vertical market, that provides all the services needed by a given particular industry (e.g., the automotive industry). Two primary forms that are emerging are those sites that use an auction approach and those that simply provide the comparative information on availability and price.

Nonetheless, just as with B2C, both types of B2B rely on the integrity and trustworthiness of the website in question. As with any auction the danger is manipulation of one sort or another. Either buyers or sellers get information that gives them an unfair advantage, or the website itself receives a payment to favor one or another party. Without trustworthiness and complete integrity the system cannot and will not work.

If the site is created by buyers, then it allows small sellers to present their goods and compete. If organized by sellers, they gather to sell to a multiplicity of small buyers. If there are more buyers than sellers, then competition favors the seller; if more sellers than buyers, the reverse is the case. So-called neutral exchanges are run by neither buyers nor sellers, but by third parties that facilitate the exchanges, much as the New York Stock Exchange facilitates the exchange of stock through a bidding process.

In addition to worries about trustworthiness and collusion, other dangers have already been identified. Some information is proprietary and sensitive. Who buys how much of what from whom might not be the sort of information a company would like its competitors to know. Preserving confidentiality is a necessary component of B2B. Excluding buyers and sellers by requiring a company, for instance, to make all its purchases through the site might restrict competition. If that seller, through its concentration of information, prevents competitors from entering its market, we again have restraint of trade. Buying only on the basis of specifications, moreover, opens companies up to the danger of not knowing whom they are doing business with. Price isn't the only factor in purchasing. Knowing a supplier, having established a relation with one, and knowing they are honest, send their goods when specified, and pay their bills on time, are all important components of purchasing. Not only is the worry about fraud a factor, but reputation and knowing whom one is doing business with is another. Accordingly some sites exist exclusively to establish payment and delivery guarantees, insure data security, and check carefully on the identification and reliability of both sellers and buyers. One such firm, eCredible, offers its service, which can be integrated into a B2B business. It checks on the credit of those in the transaction, authenticates the parties, and can even guarantee payment for a small percentage of the transaction.

There are other aspects of e-business that raise ethical issues, two of which deserve some discussion here. The first is an e-business facet of a trade market product whose primary customers are vendors. The other is on-line auctions.

The first issue has its counterpart in brick-and-mortar operations, but has come to the fore with the rise of B2B business. Most trademark items are made for sale by middle men, outlets and vendors that are not owned by the manufacturer or that are perhaps franchised by the manufacturer. In either case, the manufacturer produces a good that is sold to the vendor who in turn sells it to the customer. Grocery stores and department stores are prime examples. Such stores do not typically make the products they sell. They may sell either a number of different brands or lines made by different manufacturers, or they may deal exclusively with a single brand of product. In either case, the manufacturer's customers are the vendors. What happens when a manufacturer, then, goes on-line? Is it fair to the vendors for the manufacturer to sell its product directly to end-using customers? It thereby puts itself into direct competition with its primary customer, the vendors. Furthermore, since it eliminates the vendor, it can sell its product at prices well below what the vendor must charge to make a profit. The end-users may benefit; but if they do, it is often at the expense of the vendors, whom the customers may visit to learn about and see the product, while making their purchase on-line.

In the brick-and-mortar world one instance of the issue arises when a manufacturer opens an outlet store that carries the same items as are sold in department stores, and that sells its items at a deep discount because they are stock overruns. In order not to compete directly with the retailers they supply, many companies will locate outlets only in fairly remote locations, 30-or-more miles from their retail customers, and/or sell only "seconds" or slightly damage goods, or last year's model. They thus avoid competing directly with their primary customers, who are the vendors.

On the face of it, it is not fair for manufacturers to directly compete with their primary customers, nor is it good business. Yet every major manufacturer is expected to have a website. Since future marketing may well go in the direction of ever increasing Web sales, and that form of consumer purchasing may eventually be more important than sale through third parties, it seems like good business to establish oneself firmly and early in that market. If one charges cheaper prices to the end-user than the usual vendors do, then that is good for the customer and the vendors will have to compete by providing services that make it worthwhile for customers to buy from them rather than on-line. Some also argue that the customers who choose to buy on-line from the manufacturer are not the same people as the customers who make their purchases in the brick-and-mortar world. While this may be true to some extent, it is surely not entirely the case, and the issue of fairness remains. In this situation what is fair?

The answer must be a solution that is fair to all the parties – the end-user, the manufacturer, and the vendors. If the manufacturer wishes to do away with all vendors and operate as Dell does, completely on the Web, then that is a defensible position. But they should not both rely on their vendors as their major customers and at the same time compete with them by charging significantly less for the same products. One approach would be to maintain an on-line presence, but to list the locations of vendors and not sell directly. If the products are sold directly by the manufacturer to the end-user, then every attempt should be made not to undercut and so compete with their own vendors. If they charged prices comparable to those the vendors charge, for instance, then they may plausibly claim that they are serving a clientele other than that of their vendors.

The situation gets more complicated if their vendors also have a Web presence and sell on-line. The general ethical position, in such a situation, seems to be not to undercut their own vendors, and to make the manufacturer's site an information one that helps and doesn't hinder the sales of their vendors. When a product is sold both directly by the manufacturer and by other vendors, the vendors must be fully informed of the conditions under which they are selling the product, and these conditions should not be changed unilaterally without warning and consideration of the effect of the changes on the vendors.

Brick-and-mortar vendors will, nonetheless, have to compete with on-line buying and auctions. eBay is probably the best known of the on-line auctions. But there are now over 1,500 different auctions. Not only are individuals selling items they own, but businesses are now selling their overstock and sometimes their regular stock at auction on the Internet, thus providing consumers with the opportunity to compare prices easily and with information to which they previously did not have access. Thus a Ford Motor dealer may have to compete with other dealers and with non-Ford sources selling over the Web, but it should not have to compete with the Ford Motor Company itself.

The major ethical issues concerning on-line auctions are the trustworthiness of both buyers and sellers and the prevention of fraud. These are fairly straightforward and exemplify the problems of trust that we discussed earlier. A new question, however, is who owns bids made on the Internet. There are some websites that investigate the price for a particular item at a number of different sites and then inform those interested of the results of the comparison, indicating which has the lowest price. A similar service has developed with respect to auctions and the issue is whether the website that collects bids for the same kind of item on different sites has the right to do so. Bids are made by customers. However, they are made on the website of the company organizing the auction. To whom do the bids belong? This is a legal question, to be decided by the courts under copyright law.

A more pertinent question from an ethical point of view is who is harmed, if anyone, by the actions of the website that compiles the information. The final purchaser learns with a minimum of effort what he or she could learn by visiting all the different sites, and so saves time and knows what the bids are. Those wishing to sell an item receive greater exposure, since the information about their item is given to people who might not otherwise check the particular website on which they place their item. But they may lose a sale if someone can obtain a comparable item at a lower price. In this case, however, they are trading on the lack of competitive information on the part of the buyer. The website conducting the auction may lose a sale if the item is available for less on another site. But this is true anyway. Hence the compiler site serves the buyer and makes the market more efficient. The harm done depends on ignorance or indolence on the part of the buyer. There is no fraud, no misrepresentation, and no unjustifiable harm. If this is all actually the case, then the conclusion is that the auction is justified, just as it is in the non-auction case where a website carries the competing prices.

The objection raised by the auction sites is that this misrepresents the actual situation. Unlike a third-party site that carries information about prices, the nature of an auction is dynamic. The price on any site for any item is dynamic, not static, and may be in the process of constant change. Hence any third party that tries to capture and compare the information is always misrepresenting what may actually be the case at any particular moment. The only way not to misrepresent is to compare all the sites in real time and simultaneously, which is in fact to completely copy the sites in question, and hence would be a violation of their property rights. If the third-party sites do in fact suffer a time lag in their comparisons, then they are not providing the information that the buyer expects, unless they are informed about what the site actually does. The charge of misrepresentation would then be accurate, and the actions of the site not justifiable. But if the situation is accurately presented to the potential customer, the customer is still better off than he or she would be without the site, since no individual customer can view all the sites in question simultaneously, and so is necessarily behind the actual state of affairs at other sites when he or she visits any particular one. The claim that the comparison involves copying is an overstatement, since the third party captures what can be considered information available to the public, not the whole site itself. The conclusion, once again, with the caveats noted, is that the auction is ethically justifiable.

In addition to these issues, some of the developments of B2B have raised anti-trust concerns. B2B businesses have boomed in many industries. They provide a central exchange where companies buy and sell goods. They create, in effect, a national on-line marketplace, which replaces the need to search a great many different sources for what a company needs. The B2B businesses act as the intermediaries between buyers and sellers. The problem arises when competitors jointly own a B2B in their industry. The danger of collusion, price-fixing and the like becomes easier and more likely. Anti-trust laws prohibit collusion by companies and the fixing of prices, since they undercut the market and are unfair to consumers, preventing competition from operating as it should.

Defenders of B2B emphasize the efficiency that they bring to the marketplace by making available the most accurate information about prices. B2Bs vary greatly in their operations. Some are like auction houses, offering goods for sale to the highest bidder. Some are run by buyers in an industry, some are run by sellers of products, some are run by third-party intermediaries. Collusion is one problem. Exclusion, namely the cutting out of some competitors from the process, is another.

Covisint was the first B2B to catch the attention of the Federal Trade Commission. It describes itself as "a global, independent e-business exchange providing the automotive industry with leading collaborative product development, procurement and supply chain tools that give its customers the ability to reduce costs and bring efficiencies to their business operations."[4] The potential problem is that it was created by DaimlerChrysler, Ford, General Motors, Nissan, and Renault, which are usually competitors. They will all see the currently available prices, and this can undermine competition as well as encourage it and can lead to price fixing and other practices that are unethical and illegal. If they are all using the same information, the companies can coordinate their own prices without ever meeting or agreeing to do so. Since these companies control half of the total worldwide auto production, the FTC was understandably concerned. It finally closed its investigation, indicating that the company was still in its formative stages, but "reserved the right to take such further action as the public interest may require."[5]

▲ MONOPOLY ▲

B2B auctions are not the only potential violators of US anti-trust laws.

A monopoly is found in a situation where there is one supplier of a product who has complete control of the market. Monopolies are not in themselves unethical or illegal. There are some regulated monopolies in which a government grants monopoly rights to a company and in turn regulates the rates it may charge and the profit it may earn. The defense of such a practice is that some industries lend themselves to economies of scale and it is to the customers' benefit for there to be one large provider, so long as that provider does not take advantage of its position to elevate prices as high as it can and as high as it wishes to the detriment of the general public.

In the United States, before the wave of deregulation, a number of industries were in fact regulated monopolies. The telephone company was one, and electric companies were in general a regulated industry in which individual suppliers each had a monopoly in a certain region. From an ethical point of view, monopolies are unethical when they engage in practices that render the market so one-sided as to be unfair. The consumer is forced to buy from the one supplier, which charges much more for its product than would be the case if there were competition. If the consumer does not buy from that supplier, then the consumer goes without the product.

Electricity is necessary for modern life and if an electric company were the sole supplier for a region, it might be tempted to charge as much as it could in order to maximize its profits. Hence the need for regulation to keep the price of electricity fair.

Some people consider the notion of governmental control of monopolies and existing anti-trust laws appropriate to the industrial realm, but inappropriate when it comes to computers and computer software. The reason they give is that in these areas the notion of a restrictive monopoly does not apply because the rate of innovation is so fast and the cost of entry – especially in the area of software – is so low that it is impossible to prevent competition from developing. There are numerous stories of start-up companies that begin in a basement or garage, or software innovators who write their programs at home. Nonetheless the issue of monopoly is still of some concern and was brought to the fore in the case of Microsoft, which was charged by the government with violating anti-trust laws in October 1998. By 2001 an appellate court had ruled that Microsoft was indeed guilty of violating anti-trust laws, but had not decided on what the penalty and remedy should be.

What is of interest from the ethical point of view is the nature of the charges against Microsoft as an indication of ethical issues in the computer industry. The case initially started with the charge that Microsoft tied its Web browser, Internet Explorer, to its Windows operating system. Netscape, which was the pioneer and the leading Internet browser (with 80 percent of the market) complained that Microsoft's practice was unfair. Three main reasons emerged as a basis for the complaint. First, the Windows operating system was used on almost all (85 percent) personal computers, and hence those customers were automatically given Explorer free. To compete, Netscape also had to give its browser away free. Now this seems an odd complaint, since it would seem that the customers were the beneficiaries of Microsoft's action. They received a product free and in turn this prompted Netscape to also supply the product free. The point, however, went further. For if Microsoft were to follow a similar strategy with any number of other applications, it could control the PC software industry almost completely. This might initially seem to be to the consumer's advantage. But if Microsoft did have complete control it could more and more undercut and stifle competition and eventually dictate its own terms.

Second, if Explorer were tied to the operating system, then one could not as efficiently use another browser which had to be added on and was not integrated into the system, such as Netscape. Once agin, one might argue that such integration made the use of the Internet, the downloading of information therefrom into one's other programs, and the like, easier for users and so an advantage to them. But the counter once again was that since Microsoft controlled the Windows operating system, it had an advantage over all others who wished to write applications for the PC. Since Microsoft knew what changes it was making in its new versions of Windows it could integrate any applications it developed – such as Explorer – before the new operating systems even appeared or were made available to other programmers who develop applications. The threat of stifling competition was again a possibility, even if consumers in the short run benefited.

Third, Microsoft's Explorer was not initially chosen by users over Netscape, even when bundled with Windows. To achieve dominance in the field Microsoft developed a new and more aggressive marketing strategy, trading on its dominance of operating systems. It put an icon for its Explorer browser on the desktop of its operating system and forced companies that licensed Windows for their computers to both include the icon and not to include Netscape or any other browser in the computers they sold. Other browsers could be added after a sale if a user so desired. But this use of restrictions placed by Microsoft on what PC makers had to include or were prohibited from including prevented competition. As the case progressed charges against Microsoft came to include not only its browser but also some of its other programs and its licensing tactics and restrictions.

This led for an initial call to break up Microsoft into two companies, one that developed and sold the operating system and another that developed and sold applications, including the Explorer Internet browser. This would even out the competition, it was argued. In the operating system realm there already was some competition coming from both Apple Computers, which had its own operating system, and Linux, the free operating system. Linux is growing in popularity but still is difficult to use and cannot run some of the popular applications, such as Microsoft Office, available with Windows. The presence of such competitors shows, Microsoft argued, that it is not a monopoly.

The courts ultimately rejected the demand to breakup Microsoft.

But one result of the case was a softening in some of Microsoft's marketing tactics, as it allowed PC makers greater leeway to include what software they wished on the computers they sold.

The point of anti-trust legislation is to preserve competition, in the belief that competition is to the consumer's advantage. What is important is the benefit of consumers. It is not clear that Microsoft charged more for its operating system than it would have under conditions of greater competition, and the price of computers and software has fallen over the years rather than increased. The industry is moving so fast that the likelihood of any company gaining and maintaining dominance for long periods of time seems unlikely. Nonetheless, there are legitimate concerns about any one company dominating the software market.

Microsoft's introduction of its Passport on-line identification service only added to the worries of many users. The service allows a user to enter his or her name and password for a large variety of activities over the Internet, including paying bills and shopping. Its critics claim that it gives Microsoft the added power of controlling Web identity, as users are automatically identified no matter where they go on the Web. Not only does it permit Microsoft to be the intermediary in all commercial transactions on the Web, but it is integrated into all of Microsoft's services. Microsoft sites, moreover, require that users register, supplying a variety of information beyond name and e-mail address. Microsoft can combine all the information on any user from each of its sites, as well as all the information it garners from acting as intermediary. Reacting to complaints, Microsoft revised its terms and agreed to preserve user privacy. But it still collects the information. Moreover, in many cases, only if one registers with Passport can one get access to certain products, such as the Microsoft Reader, which is necessary to read some digital copies of books. So much power, control, and information centered in any one company cannot help but raise concern. How to draw the line between consumer benefit and harm to the consumer is a major issue that has yet to be resolved with respect to technology and software. Hence there is some reason for continued vigilance.

▲ E-BUSINESS, IPOS, AND THE ▲
NEW ECONOMY

In the late 1990s e-business seemed the wave of the future, as it may still well be. But the enthusiasm for e-business was translated into wild enthusiasm for and investment in almost any type of e-business that emerged. Investment bankers vied with each other in seeking the hot new company to place its venture capital into, and when a company became public investors were eager to buy the stock. Initial public offerings (IPOs) of Internet company stock were sometimes frenzied events. People vied to obtain part of an IPO and stock often soared in value in the first day of trading. Sycamore Networks rose from $38.00 a share to $270.00 a share in one day. Those who were in on the initial price, and sold, multiplied their holding sevenfold.

What was most remarkable about this so-called New Economy was that most of the e-businesses that went public and sold shares that increased quickly in value had never shown a profit. One of the best known e-businesses, Amazon.com, had yet to show a profit by 2001, even though it had extensive sales. What people bought was promise. The stock market down-turn of 2000–1, however, ended the furor, as many of the companies went bankrupt, rendering their stock worthless. Many who were swept along in the buying frenzy, who did not have access to IPOs, and those who did not sell their shares for a quick profit, collectively lost billions of dollars.

How was it that so many people lost so much, that a few made enormous gains, and that the result was a more realistic look at e-business as business? Did the New Economy generate a new approach to ethics in business, were old rules still applicable, and was there any activity that at least with hindsight we can say was ethically questionable? A special section of *Fortune* in March of 2000[6] suggests that a number of ethically questionable practices were part of the reason for both the enthusiasm for and the demise of many dot-coms.

Creative use of general accepted accounting principles (GAAP)

The problem is in part that the rules that ought to govern accounting practices for Internet companies have not been developed. The Securities and Exchange Commission has appointed a Task Force to develop procedures, but as of 2000 it had not reached a recommendation. One questionable practice – because it is potentially misleading to possible investors – is the way revenue income is reported. As an example, Jeremy Kahn takes Priceline.com.[7] In 1999 it reported sales of $152.2 million, $134 million of which went directly from its customers to the hotels and airlines on which it booked rooms or flights. It reported the difference of $18 million as "gross profit." But that is usually reported as revenues, since all its other costs had to be deducted from that, which left the company with a loss of $102 million. The SEC allowed this, but the practice raised eyebrows in many financial quarters. Other companies increase their revenues substantially by including as income what was in fact "barter" or, for instance, the trading of advertising on the website for advertising in the print media. Yet many of these companies had never actually sold any advertising space on their sites and so what that advertising was worth was speculation. The net result, however, was to bolster income revenues, sometimes by as much as 50 percent for a startup Internet company.

These and other practices make the financial reports of dot-com companies look much better than they sometimes are. The financial reports in turn become the basis for publicity about the company and its stock and the basis on which the stock is promoted.

Questionable use of stock options and IPO tactics

"Family and friends" stock is usually stock given to family and friends by those involved in the development of a company before it goes public. The stock is made available to them at the initial offering price of a new company going public. They may in turn sell it if the price goes up, as many initial public offerings of stock did in 1999 and 2000, sometimes dramatically. Increases of 100 percent or more in one day were not uncommon. When such stock and stock options are given to members of customer firms, which in turn endorse and speak highly of the company when it goes public, there is certainly the appearance, if not necessarily the reality, of a conflict of interest.[8] Most large companies have a policy prohibiting employees from accepting gifts from vendors in order to prevent conflict of interest. Yet the practice is legal.

The "K-tel effect" is named after the company called K-tel. In 1998 the CEO, Philip Kives, started a publicity campaign, issuing statements about its having a new Internet strategy.[9] The hype caught on and speculators flocked to buy the stock, raising it well above its value. As it rose, Kives sold his shares in the company during the 30 days before the stock fell back to its previous value. Although selling one's shares in one's company stock is not illegal, hyping the stock and selling on the resulting rise without any sound basis for the increase certainly leaves those who buy the stock at a disadvantage. If executives sell their shares in their own company, they no longer have the incentive to increase the value of the stock over time for investors.

Self-interested boards of directors

The traditional role of a board of directors has been to oversee management so as to protect the interests of the shareholders. This assumes that the board will exercise a certain amount of oversight of management, and that it has some distance from management. By having small boards with few outside members some new dot-com companies have little effective oversight, and when the outside board members have little financial expertise and are hand-picked by the CEO, their work on the audit and compensations committees is not what a stock holder expects. The result has been little oversight and such practices as repricing the stock options held by a company's executives when the price of the stock falls below their striking price. Again, while not illegal, these practices in part undercut the incentive that stock options are supposed to provide, and dilute the value of the stock held by other investors.

The loss of objectivity by analysts

Analysts are supposed to give objective, unbiased assessments of the companies they study. Clients frequently depend on investment firms to provide analyses of stocks and recommendations about which stocks to buy, which to hold, and which to sell. When investment banks sell their consulting services to companies and then have their analysts report on those companies, the conflict of interest is apparent. But the practice is not made public or announced by the analyst. Not surprisingly, analysts tend to be more positive about Internet companies with which their banks or companies have a financial relationship. The situation is only exacerbated when the analysts own stock in the company on which they are reporting, for their desire to make the stock advance in price cannot be entirely divorced from the advice they give and the recommendations they make.

The upshot is that the law has not yet caught up with the supposed New Economy. During the period of the great dot-com bubble, the traditional restraints where considered to be inapplicable. The result was gross overvaluation of the price of initial public offerings. One wonders how a stock that has been evaluated by those who supposedly study it and know its value can be so mistaken that the stock, when offered publicly, increases 100 percent in value in a 24-hour period. One also wonders why the real evaluation then becomes evident to shareholders, who then sell the stock as it drops in value – often after the insiders have already sold theirs and made a killing.

Although not unique to startups and dot-coms, the use of stock options, a technique widely developed by high-tech companies, has raised serious concerns about fairness to shareholders.[10] Stock options have become an important part of executive pay and have been an attraction to workers in high-tech and dot-com companies who have been willing to work longer hours for less pay than they could get elsewhere. Stock options at one point had made one out of every ten workers at Microsoft a millionaire – at least on paper. But options represent a cost to shareholders. When employees exercise their stock options, the company issues new shares, which in turn dilutes the value of the shares of those who already own the stock. The portion of the company's assets that each share represents becomes less as the number of shares increases. The problem is that although the options really represent a cost, they do not have to be carried as such on the company's books. In order to keep its stock from being too diluted, resulting in paying smaller dividends per share, companies buy back their own stock. This constitutes a cost to the company, which it can subtract from its profits. But all this is represented in annual reports – in accordance with GAAP requirements – only by a footnote that indicates what earnings would be if option costs (as determined by a prescribed Black-Sholes model) were deducted from earnings. The ethical complaint is not that options are in themselves unethical, but that the reporting of them is far from transparent to shareholders. The least that fairness demands is not that companies stop offering options but that they report them in such a way that those interested in purchasing their stock get a true representation of the company's net worth, its assets and liabilities, without having to do so via small footnotes whose existence is not widely known or appreciated.

▲ TAXATION OF E-BUSINESS ▲

In the United States sales tax on both the state and the local level are an important source of revenue for the respective governments. Most goods are taxed at the time of purchase and the tax is paid by the customer buying the good or service. If instead of making a purchase directly in a store one makes it through a mail-order catalog, the state sales tax is levied only if one lives in a state in which the vendor has some physical facility. So those living in other states do not pay the sales tax. This is an accepted practice and is generally considered fair. A state only has the authority to tax the items that are bought and sold within its borders. Hence the analogy on which the law is based is that an in-state buyer purchasing from an in-state seller is covered in the same way they would be if the transaction were face to face. If the item is sent out of state, however, then the state does not have authority to tax those outside of its jurisdiction. Although this might seem unfair because those living outside the state can purchase the item tax free, and so more cheaply than those within the state, those in the state receive the benefits from the tax, while those outside do not.

Now make the same purchase on the Internet instead of from a mail-order catalog, and one often pays no tax. Is this fair? The issue of taxation and the Internet was initially put on hold in the United States until the status and importance of purchases on the Internet and the issues related thereto become clearer. The US Congress in 1998 passed the Internet Tax Freedom Act. It prohibited the taxing of Web purchases for a period of three years.

The issue has several facets. One is the fairness of taxing sales in other formats and not similar sales made on the Web. Is this fair to the non-Web retailers who in effect are forced to charge more for the same item as on the Web, and does it give the Web business an unfair advantage, even though those who purchase on the Web will have to pay shipping charges that will often be the equivalent of local and state sales taxes? Mail-order sales are taxed *and* the purchaser has to pay shipping. So Web-based businesses seem to be given an unfair advantage over mail-order businesses, which at least requires justification.

Second, the local communities and the states do not get the sales tax that they would if the sales were not on the Web. This may not be essential if Web sales are a small percentage of total sales. But if Web business sales become a major portion of total sales, then the local communities and states will have to find other sources of revenue to replace income from sales taxes. On the other hand, the cities and the state will not have to provide services to the vendors. In itself there is nothing unethical about not having a sales tax, since there are other means of funding the needs of cities and states.

Third, some states and cities worry that the federal government is entering into the sales tax business and may decide eventually to impose a national sales tax on Internet sales, while prohibiting comparable state and local taxes. This is a political rather than an ethical problem, and one that will find its resolution in politics.

A fourth difficulty is one of legal jurisdiction. States have the power only to tax those within their jurisdiction. Where are e-tailers located? They may not have facilities in any particular location and may even be based outside the country. Frequently they have the goods they sell shipped by other firms located throughout the United States or even throughout the world. The technical difficulty of figuring taxes in a variety of different locales in the US with different tax rates has been overcome by software using zip codes to calculate the appropriate amount and to report the sale and the tax due to the appropriate locale. Taxing only some and not other purchasers may raise the issue of fairness, but the difference in tax rates and policies among the many various jurisdictions is justified – to the extent that it is – by the different needs and resources of the localities and the differing services they provide.

Three major justifications can be given for the moratorium on Internet taxes. The first is that it prevented the "bit tax" or a tax on every e-mail or downloaded picture or piece of information. This was seen – arguably correctly so – as a means to protect the development of the Internet and keep it from the desire of many jurisdictions to tax all Internet use within their jurisdictions. Tax-free e-mail and Internet use have helped both to thrive, arguably to the benefit of the society as a whole.

The second justification was that e-business was just beginning and that making it tax free, at least for an initial period of time, would help bolster it and help it to grow and bloom. E-business seemed and still seems to be the wave of the future, and it would be better for society to help nurture it initially. This is not an infrequent or unknown public policy with respect to new industries, and localities often give tax breaks to attract a business that they think will help the community and eventually be taxed. This argument assumes that the moratorium is for a limited period, and that such protection from taxation is not a permanent practice. Any harm done to communities or states will be offset by the greater benefit to society overall through the development of e-business. The argument is at least plausible.

The third justification was that there was no consensus on how e-business should be taxed, and whether e-business was in fact completely comparable to other kinds of business or whether it required differential treatment and special taxes. The moratorium would give all levels of government a chance to study, discuss, plan, and collaborate before taking individual and possibly conflicting action or action that would kill e-business through over-onerous taxation before it even got started. The actions and decisions of other governments could be studied, and negotiations with them would also be possible. The three-year moratorium was thus justified as prudent public policy, which requires study and planning rather then precipitate action.

An extension was likewise justified because after three years all the questions had not been answered and debate among the federal government, the governments of other countries, and representatives of the states and local communities had not led to a consensus or provided a coherent plan on which to act. The vested interests of states and communities seeking income and of brick-and-mortar lobbyists seeking what they consider equal treatment have to be balanced against the benefits that society as a whole might receive from different approaches. What seems clear is that any "bit tax" would be counterproductive and serve to slow down the development of the Information Age.

Sales taxes are often held to be regressive in that they do not differentiate between the rich and the poor. The poor are taxed at the same rate as the rich. But because the poor have to spend all they earn to live, they pay more proportionately than the rich, who have a good deal to invest and save. To complicate matters, some argue that the better-off consumer is more likely to have a computer and Internet access than the poorer consumer. Consequently by exempting Internet purchases from taxes while taxing purchases made at the local mall or corner store, the poor are forced to bear a greater percentage of taxes than the better off. This obviously raises the question of what alternative kind of tax might be fairer and more equitable, if eventually revenue from sales taxes fails to meet the needs of communities and states.

Clearly the ethical issues are complex and there is no one best solution that is the obvious right choice. Taxes should be fair to all, businesses should operate on a level playing field whether they be e-business or brick and mortar and mail order, and communities and states need revenue if they are to perform the functions demanded, expected, and required of them. The issue of on-line taxation is raising many questions and will require imaginative solutions.

▲ THE INFORMATION TECHNOLOGY ▲ INDUSTRY

The information technology industry encompasses a large and diverse group of people with a great many specialties and degrees of expertise. It covers both hardware and software producers, as well as the many people working in Information Technology or Information Services in most of the businesses and institutions of any size. It includes those who simply enter data into a computer as well as those who design and produce hardware and software and manage computers, websites, and whole information systems. Some are engineers or software professionals, many are simply employees with a certain amount of skill in data input or routine programming. So it is difficult to generalize about the industry as a whole and the people who make it up.

As a result, it is often difficult to talk about and reasonably assign responsibility. This is one of the results and perhaps also one of the causes of the Myth of Amoral Computing and Information Technology. Although we can speak meaningfully about the responsibilities and obligations of doctors collectively as well as individually, and although we can do the same about lawyers, it is difficult to do the same with respect to those in information technology. There is no profession of computer technology, even if some would argue that there is a profession of computer engineering. One need not have a degree in computer engineering to be a programmer, although most of those who design computers probably are engineers.

The point is that if we talk about the responsibility of those in the information technology sector for the effects of their joint activity on society or for leadership in helping control or regulate or steer it in ways that benefit rather than harm society, it is difficult to identify the appropriate persons or groups. Doctors and lawyers are required to have a certain kind of education and pass certain examinations before they are allowed to practice their professions. The same is not true of those in information technology. This does not mean that those in information technology have no responsibility for what is done in their field or for its effects on society, but that it is more difficult to assign that responsibility and so more difficult for even the practitioners to know what responsibility to assume for themselves. One approach would be for those who consider themselves information professionals to take the lead in identifying themselves, their competence, and their responsibilities. Some of this is happening in computer engineering societies and in organizations such as Computer Professionals for Social Responsibility (CPSR). The function of such groups should be to develop guidelines of ethical practice for those in the industry, to promote and if possible enforce them, and to serve as watchdogs for anti-social aspects, developments, and trends as information technology develops. CPSR has been one of the groups that has taken the lead in attempts to protect individual privacy. There are many other issues as well.

Despite the difficulty of assigning responsibility globally, we can make some general observations, and can assign and impute responsibility in many specific kinds of cases.

One general observation is that those in the information industry are in the best position to defend the public interest against harm by those in their industry. They are the best informed about what is possible and what is being developed, and so in the best position to raise early warnings about developments in the field. They can lead discussions in the public fora, and educate the general population about issues. They can act as intermediaries between scientists, engineers, technicians, and the general public, translating technical discussions into understandable language, and clarifying ethical issues and implications. We see public debate on technical issues of human reproductive techniques, while we have little public debates on most information technology issues. Even proposed legislation gets little publicity or public comment.

It was those in the field who in February of 1997 uncovered the fact that Intel's Pentium III chip contained a "unique identifier" (a Processor Serial Number) that would identify the computer on visits to websites. Various groups united and called for a boycott of Intel, which was finally called off at the end of April, 2000. Microsoft's Office 97, which placed a unique identifier on all Office 97 documents, led to a similar outcry, so that Microsoft issued a patch that prevents the insertion of the identifier. In both instances consumer privacy was possibly threatened by innovations which were not transparent to customers or consumers.

A problem that both of these incidents demonstrates is that a good deal of what is done in both hardware and software is not made known to customers and the using public. The purpose of installing unique identifiers in these cases is not entirely clear, although both companies claim they were done in the interest of the users – a claim that was challenged in both cases. Intel and Microsoft were clearly responsible for the identifiers they placed in their products. They arguably were also responsible for informing customers about these innovations in their products. If they were indeed for the benefit of the consumer, then the consumers should have been informed. Not to inform them at least gives the impression that these identifiers were to be used not by the consumers but by others without the knowledge or consent of the consumer. Users have the right to know aspects of the products they buy that may cause them harm. Not to inform them sounds very much like deception. Although it might be argued that not all users want to know all the technicalities of the equipment or programs they buy, that does not mean that aspects of products that might affect privacy or safety should not be made known to users.

Another generalization is that the industry as such should keep the interests of the public in the foreground as it pursues development. The technological imperative tends to lead to the development of whatever is possible, regardless of its impact on the public. To say that the industry should circumscribe this imperative means that those in the industry should consider the effects the envisioned technology may have, where and how they might prevent the negative effects of such technology, and how they can bring to the public forum issues and trends that may adversely affect the common good.

A third generalization is that if the Information Age is to really become a reality and contribute to the general good, then it must be made as user-friendly as possible. Computers and the associated technology should become easier to use. The development of increasingly powerful chips and cheap memory has helped in this direction, since ease of use frequently requires complex programs. Intuitive voice commands for computer functions and for tasks one wishes to do are also a step in this direction. A model might be the basic telephone, which in its functioning has become a standard feature intuitively accessible to all users.

Responsibility and software

Those who produce and market software are ethically responsible for their products. This should be obvious, for all those who produce products commercially are responsible for what they produce, for their proper functioning, and for the harm that they might cause. Yet this seemingly obvious claim seems not to hold for those who produce software. Those in the industry have not accepted such responsibility, and the general public has not demanded it. Both are instances of the Myth of Amoral Computing and Information Technology.

Software bugs are an obvious and typical example of the failure to take responsibility for one's products. Software bugs (the name purportedly came from a moth that flew into a US Navy computer in 1945, causing a relay to jam) are mistakes in a software program that, under the appropriate conditions, cause it to fail, crash, or do something the program was not intended to do. In long and complicated programs bugs are said to be inevitable. That said, what responsibility do the producers of commercial programs have for the bugs in their programs? The first and obvious claim that users make is that programmers are responsible for finding and fixing the bugs in their programs, and that this should be done before the product is sold. This seems obvious to users, who consider the programs they buy to be comparable to other products they buy.

The state of the art in any field dictates what consumers can reasonably expect. Their expectation is that the products they buy will do what they are claimed to do, will function safely and work properly. They expect that products have been tested before being sold and any deficiencies corrected. They are reinforced in this belief by the law, which among other things holds producers of products strictly liable for any harm caused by their products. The exception, however, to these expectations and to strict liability is software.

Two observations seem obvious. First, software vendors should not ship software that contains known bugs. Yet it is common practice to do so. The problem is that in a complicated program fixing a bug may not be easy, and any fix may cause another bug. Many vendors therefore prefer to ship their product with the bugs in order to get it to market as soon as possible, and then either make available at a later date a patch to fix the bug, or wait and fix all the bugs found at once, resulting in a new and improved version of the program that those wishing for the update must buy. This common practice leads some users to delay buying the first version of any new program because it is typically a work-in-progress with many bugs that will eventually be fixed in later editions. Such an attitude reflects a reality that is very different from what customers expect with almost all other products. That customers more or less accept the shoddiness of initial computer programs does not justify the practice.

The second obvious observation is that software vendors should acknowledge bugs, take responsibility for them, and fix the flaws for free, willingly and at the least inconvenience to the consumer. It should not be up to registered users to have to search for patches that fix a product's defects, rather than the vendors contacting the registered purchaser and offering the patch freely and as soon as it is available. This sounds like good business as well as the ethically correct thing to do. But it is not common practice.

More often than one would like, a computer program that one installs causes the computer to crash. Sometimes the crash requires that the operating system be reinstalled and all the programs and special features thereof that one had on one's computer also be reinstalled. This is time consuming if one is able to do it oneself and costly if one needs outside help. Yet such damage and harm are not covered by any warranty. For software is not a product you buy but something you license the use of on terms that the manufacturer stipulates – which usually includes any disclaimer about what is called "consequent damage" resulting from the use of the program.

Admittedly, sometimes the crashes result from the incompatibility of the new program with programs existing on one's hard drive. But if the user shuts down all running applications, as one is usually instructed to do, and the programs are still incompatible, then that shows some defect either in the program code or some cause that is the responsibility of the supplier of the program.

Bugs, mistakes, and program failures are the fault of those who produce them, but the costs of the defects in terms of lost time, money, and aggravation are borne by the customer. This is unlike the situation with other products, and is on the face of it unfair.

Security holes are not bugs in the ordinary sense of the term, but are failures in a program that allow unauthorized access to one's computer, possibly to the operating system and to all of one's files, when one accesses the Internet. Such holes were common in Windows 95, and though less common have been found in more recent versions of Windows, as well as in Linux, Unix FTP servers, and MacOS. Hackers can break into a system and steal data, deface a website, or do other damage. Clearly it is the responsibility of the producers of operating systems and other programs that render computers vulnerable to attack from hackers to make sure the software they provide is secure. If later some hole is discovered, it is their responsibility to provide the appropriate plug and make this available quickly and easily. The temptation has been not to publicize such holes, since that is bad publicity. The result is that users are left vulnerable longer than they should be. Companies that use such systems are also responsible for keeping up to date on security holes and for plugging them immediately. Yet studies have shown that many large corporations are very slow about doing anything about such holes, leaving their computers and their customers' information vulnerable.

The problem of security holes is in part a systemic problem that can best be resolved not only by individual firms but also by the industry as a whole. There is presently no standard way to inform all users of these problems, no central depository of information about them, and no agreed-upon procedure for solving them. Some companies are better than others in responding, providing timely fixes, and informing users immediately.

Licenses

Part of the problem is the nature of the software. We have already seen that with respect to property, it is not really exactly like other products covered either by copyright or patents. Although consumers may think that when they purchase a program they are buying that program, they are in fact only buying a license to use the program.

The conditions for the sale are set by the seller and stated in the licensing agreement that is usually included in the package, if one buys the program in package form, or in an initial statement that appears on the screen before one uses the program. If in the package, the license is usually sealed in a shrink-wrapped enclosure, so in effect one buys the program without knowing the conditions of sale. By using the program one implicitly agrees to the conditions.

Sometimes the agreement is made explicit by hitting "I agree" after the conditions appear on one's screen before one is allowed to use the program.

Is such a transaction fair? Transactions are usually considered fair if they are entered into freely by both the seller and the buyer, and if both parties have access to the appropriate information concerning the sale. In the case of programs, the second condition is arguably not met. Although the program may be returned for a refund if one decides not to accept the stated conditions, one learns the conditions only after the sale. It might also be argued that most of the conditions are similar despite the program, and that users should by now be familiar with them. But this itself, even if it were accepted as constituting appropriate access to relevant information, raises another problem. The similarity is a result of the fact that access to all programs is contingent on conditions set by the seller, and the interests of all sellers are similar. Can the conditions themselves be evaluated from the point of view of fairness? The answer is surely yes.

Shrink-wrapped commercial software licenses (and their "click-on" counterparts) typically limit use of the program to one or two computers owned by the buyer, prohibit resale of the program or giving it to anyone else, and disclaim any responsibility for any damage, losses, or injuries caused by the use of the program or consequent upon its use. The seller in fact claims all the rights and none of the responsibilities that typically go with the sale of a product. When such licenses have been challenged in court, they have frequently been found not to be binding. Hence their legality has been at least questionable.

The situation, however, began to change in 1999 with the introduction of the Uniform Computer Information Transactions Act (UCITA), which was developed by the National Conference of Commissioners on Uniform State Laws. This is a model statute that can be adopted by each of the state legislatures. It has been attacked by many groups as making legally binding many of the conditions in software licenses that have been found to be non-binding by courts. If UCITA is adopted by a state legislature, then in that state the shrink-wrapped license becomes legally binding, even if some of the terms seem outrageous or unfair. The law effectively shields software vendors from liability for their program's defects, bugs, flaws, and the harm caused by them. UCITA was opposed by 26 State Attorneys General, the Consumers Union, and the Association of

Research Libraries, among other groups.[11] License provisions may restrict "fair use," defining what use buyers have, regardless of copyright law provisions. Licenses continue to be unavailable prior to purchase. By April of 2001 Maryland and Virginia had adopted UCITA as state law.

UCITA clearly defends the interests of the commercial software industry. If adopted as law, it is legally binding. But that does not mean that it cannot be criticized from an ethical point of view as being unfair to consumers and their interests.

Legal liability

We have already seen that with respect to copyright, software sometimes is treated by analogy to a book and sometimes by analogy to a machine. The courts have taken a similar analogous approach to legal liability with respect to software.

If a software program controls a machine or part of a machine or if it is embedded in a machine, then for purposes of liability it is considered a machine. Software failures in machines have resulted in injury and death, as well as in missile failure and the like.

The producer and supplier of computer programs that are embedded in machines or that run machines should be responsible for the harm they do. Such machines may either be potentially life threatening or not potentially life threatening. If the former, prudence and ethics dictate that special care should be taken to keep the programs as simple as possible, to rely on them as little as possible, to build as much safety into the whole as possible. When not seriously life threatening, then less stringent rules apply, although the liability that is associated with machine use still applies.

At the other extreme, some programs are clearly comparable to a book. In some cases they *are* a book, as when Encyclopedia Britannica put its encyclopedia on-line, and Encarta is available on a CD-ROM. In these cases, the one who issues the program and its contents is subject to the same liability rules as are booksellers. Courts have not held authors, publishers, or booksellers liable for faulty information in books. They argue it would be unreasonable to expect publishers and booksellers to read and verify the information in all the books they sell. Nor are professionals held strictly liable for the services they provide. There is no mass production of goods and no large body of consumers, such as justifies strict liability.

Warranties cover goods or products and an implied warranty

implies that the product is at least of average quality and fits the usual consumer purpose in buying that good. If the product is defective, it will be replaced. One can also sue for the harm the product caused and for certain kinds of injury. Warranties cover goods but not the information in books. Hence, if you buy a book that is missing 15 pages, you may return it for a good copy. But if the information it contains is not what you wanted or is in some ways mistaken, even if your following it causes you harm, that is not covered by warranty.

Negligence requires the showing of fault on the part of the producer or seller, such that harm results to the user of the product. More is recoverable from a manufacturer under negligence than under simple warranty – including payment for pain and suffering and possibly for economic loss.

Strict liability does not require that one show negligence or intent, simply that a defective product resulted in harm. It applies to products made for the mass market. The justification for strict liability includes the notion that this is a type of self-insurance, in that a manufacturer can pass the cost on to customers by a slight increase in the price of each item; that the manufacturer is in a better position to sustain the cost of the harm than the individual user is; that such liability provides an incentive for the manufacturer to take greater care in making sure the product is safe; and that the manufacturer is in the best position to correct any defects quickly and is more likely to do so if it is exposed to possible suits under strict liability. But strict liability does not apply to services or to information or books, and so would not apply to programs that are like books.

But what of programs that do not operate exactly as machines and are not just the electronic equivalent of books? Many programs not only provide information, but also do something with it in an application. Moreover, many application programs, as we have already noted, may not cause physical damage, but may cause a computer to seriously malfunction or crash and require time and money to restore the computer to working order. There may also be consequent damages than arise because one cannot fulfill an order on time or fulfill the terms of one's contract or otherwise meet some obligation.

An argument can be made that such harms suffered as a result of programs, although not bodily harm, are real harms comparable to some of the harms caused by defective products. If the program is mass marketed, then the arguments that justify strict liability for products would seem to justify strict liability for computer programs as well. So far the courts have not held this, and UCITA, if adopted, would preclude any claim for damage incurred as a result of a program that excludes such liability in its shrink-wrapped or "click on" license agreement. Nonetheless, there is a strong ethical argument in defense of extending strict liability to software programs that are not actually comparable to books.

This third group of programs are clearly neither books nor machines. Word processing programs are one such, and tax preparation programs are another. Should tax preparation programs be held to the same standards as professional accountants or tax preparers? The cost is of course much less, and the service is restricted to manipulation of the numbers entered. That is the responsibility of the person using the program. The program in this case might be held to be a tool, rather than something that acts as a professional, with professional responsibility. A program such as a word processing program or a spread sheet or a database do something. A word processor is often compared to a typewriter. Makers of typewriters are of course not responsible for what is written on them. And if they break, then the usual remedy, if there is one, depends on the warranty provided at purchase for a limited amount of time. Similarly, one can argue that such programs should be warrantied to work as advertised and be warrantied for a certain amount of time. During that time warrantees usually allow replacement of defective merchandise. The warrantee does not cover consequent damages. If you were counting on your typewriter to write up a contract and it didn't work when you needed it and you lost the contract, the warranty will not cover that harm. The same seems appropriate by analogy with word processing programs and with computers.

Computer programs that are customized are a different matter. If they are such as they can cause harm or death, then, if negligence can be shown, liability can include not only the cost of repairing the harm but also recompense for the pain and suffering.

Strict liability applies to mass produced products that potentially cause harm. Although there is a strong argument for applying strict liability to computer programs that are mass produced, the difficulty of demonstrating and evaluating the harm done by the product probably makes the implementation so difficult as to be impractical. That does not diminish the ethical requirement to try to prevent harm to the extent possible.

Finally, some programs, instead of substituting for a product, substitute for a service. We have already mentioned tax preparation and providing information. The remedy for poor service might be malpractice suits for doctors or lawyers. If the program is a substitute for a doctor or lawyer, the manufacturer is not liable for poor information (like a book, even a medical book) but usually for poor practice or negligence. Professionals who use expert systems or other programs might be held liable, but not the program.

The upshot is that the Myth of Amoral Computing and Information Technology and the technological imperative have diluted legal and to some extent moral responsibility with respect to those in the information industry. This need not have been the case and should not continue to be accepted. As children become adults they are expected to accept responsibility for their actions. As the computer and information industries mature, no less should be expected and demanded by society.

▲ NOTES ▲

1. See the DoubleClick home page on the Web.
2. Federal Trade Commission, July 10, 2000 (http://www.ftc- gov/opa/2000/07toysmart.html). The Federal Trade Commission blocked the sale, then settled with the company, allowing it to sell its database to a qualified buyer that would follow the same policy as Toysmart had stated to its customers. Other companies such as Boo.com and Epidemic.com are reported to have sold their customer databases at auction after they failed.
3. John Schwartz, "Giving Web a Memory Cost Its Users Privacy," *New York Times*, September 4, 2001, p. A1.
4. http://www.covisint.com/info/about.shtml.
5. Federal Trade Commission File No. 001 0127, released September 11, 2000.
6. *Fortune*, March 20, 2000, pp. 82–120.
7. Jeremy Kahn, "Presto Chango! Sales are Huge," *Fortune*, March 20, 2000, pp. 90–6.
8. Melanie Warner, "Wooing Potential Customers with Options," *Fortune*, July 10, 2000, pp. 139–46.
9. *Fortune*, March 20, 2000, pp. 110–16.
10. See Justin Fox, "The Amazing Stock Option Sleight of Hand," *Fortune*, June 25, 2001, pp. 86–92.
11. "UCITA Fact Sheet," at http://www.cpsr.org/program/UCITA/ucita-fact.htm.

chapter six

Ethical Issues on the Internet

▲ DITTO.COM AND VISUAL ▲ SEARCH ENGINES

The Internet is a vast treasure of information. It contains not only text material available on almost any topic one can think of, but also millions of visual images. Search engines have long been used to locate information, but only recently have search engines been developed that locate pictures. Pictures can be copyrighted, just as text can be, and in principle there is no difference between the protection given each by copyright. The copying of pictures falls under the same provision of fair use as does text. No one complained when search engines helped a user locate a text. However, an artist complained and brought a law suit against Ditto.com, a search engine for pictures, which not only leads one to the site on which the picture appears, but shows a thumbnail-size version of the picture so that viewers can decide whether it is the picture they are interested in.

This seems to be a service to those searching for pictures for any number of reasons. But Leslie Kelly, a photographer, claimed Ditto.com violated his copyright by reproducing his pictures for commercial purposes without his permission. It also makes it very easy for anyone to copy the thumbnail and use it on his or her own website without any consideration of copyright. Ditto.com claimed that reproducing the image in thumbnail size and linking the picture to the site on which it appeared was fair use. Simply describing a picture in text is a poor substitute for someone searching for a particular image, and simply referring viewers to a site that may contain hundreds or thousands of images in addition to the one sought lessens the utility of the search engine and does not serve the needs of those searching. But Kelly complained that Ditto.com does more than that: by clicking on the thumbnail one can obtain a fully downloadable image.

A federal court judge ruled in favor of Ditto.com. But the case was appealed by Kelly, and went to the Ninth Circuit Court of Appeals in California.

Prescinding from the legal discussion, is the practice by Ditto.com and similar image search engines ethically justifiable?

▲ THE INTERNET ▲

Use of the Internet has become so common and its use by and for business so ubiquitous that it is hard to believe the Internet itself as we know it did not come into being until 1982 and that the World Wide Web was not introduced until 1991.

The Internet is a global network of computer systems. No one owns it, it is not controlled by any government or business or organization, and it is not operated for profit. The Internet makes possible a large number of activities, including e-mail, on-line conferences, bulletin boards, chat rooms, information providers, and business activities. The World Wide Web (WWW) is a special system of Internet servers that support documents formatted in Hyperlink Text Markup Language (HTML).[1]

The fact that the Internet is not for profit and not controlled by any entity is essential to it as we know it, and reflects its history. It could have been different. The Internet grew out of the United States Department of Defense's Advanced Projects Agency Network (ARPANET).[2] It was originally oriented towards research and communication. Although sponsored by the United States government it was developed for the most part at universities and research institutions, and from the beginning was an open and collaborative enterprise. The software developed was free, and so could be improved by any of its users. In 1983 the Advanced Research Project Agency (ARPA) adopted the TCP/IP (Transmission Control Protocol and the Internet Protocol) to become the Internet. New networks began to be formed both in the United States and in other countries. Since the basic source code was open, and so non-proprietary, others were able to develop and build on it. In 1990 the ARPANET ceased to exist and by then the Internet was becoming more and more commercialized. Government funding and development was replaced by commercial interests. In 1993 the first Internet browser,

Mosaic, was introduced, making it much easier than it had been to access different Web pages or sites. In 1994 Netscape introduced its browser and a year later Microsoft introduced its Internet Explorer. There are well over 200,000,000 users of the Internet and the number is constantly growing.

The development and management of the World Wide Web is overseen by the World Wide Web Consortium, which was founded in 1994 to oversee and coordinate changes and improvements to the technology underlying it. It develops global standards. It has over 500 member organizations, both business and not-for-profit.

A brief look at the domain names, which identify sites, indicates the range of different kinds of groups that utilize the Internet: government (.gov), education (.edu), nonprofit organizations (.org), military (.mil), commercial business (.com), network organization (.net), and individual country designators (e.g., Canada (.ca)).

The fact that the Internet is global and that it is neither completely commercial nor government controlled means that the Internet and the cyberspace that it creates and in which it exists is public space, with freedom of access to those who have a computer and a service provider or way to access it. Anyone can start a Web page. For this reason some have said that the Internet is a kind of anarchy with no one in charge, and to that extent it makes users vulnerable in ways that they are not in organized society. Cyberspace is thus a realm that people enter that is in some ways unique, and although some of the ethical issues found there – such as fraud and theft – are familiar, others are new. While all this is so, we should not be misled by the words we use. What we call cyberspace is not a separate space, but is part of the world in which we live. The same moral or ethical rules apply as apply in all other aspects of society. Among the issues that we shall look at are the governance of the Internet and the role of business therein; security and encryption; issues of property as changed by the Internet; and freedom and censorship, as exemplified by pornography.

▲ GOVERNANCE OF THE INTERNET AND ▲ THE ROLE OF BUSINESS THEREIN

The Internet and its governance

The fact that the Internet is free in several senses, namely that the technology behind it is built on open and so non-proprietary software and that it is in principle accessible to all, is crucial. One can easily imagine a very different situation, if instead of government and university and research groups developing the Internet, it had been developed by a private business, which held proprietary rights to it and its use, and could charge for access, as well as for each use, and could license pages to those who paid enough and perhaps even only to those it chose to accommodate. Similarly, if it were completely government sponsored and funded it would be different from what it is today. It is only because it is in some ways free that it has developed and had the huge impact that it has on the everyday lives of so many people in so many parts of the world. That in itself constitutes a compelling argument for the necessity of keeping access free and open if it is to provide the full range of social benefits that its champions envisage and promise.

Nonetheless, the Internet does cost money to run, and a large portion of it has already been commercialized. Not only are many of the sites business sites but there are also pay sites that one cannot enter freely. Although access to the Internet is free, one needs a computer to access it, one needs either a modem or some way of connecting the computer to the Internet, and one needs an Internet Service Provider (ISP) to perform the actual connection. Businesses, schools and universities, and institutions usually provide access for their employees or members. Individuals can buy the access service through an ISP vendor, such as America on Line (AOL). Those in countries other than the United States have similar needs and providers. Though employees and students do not pay to use the Internet via the services provided by their organization, the organiz-ation must pay to maintain and run the server, for the connection and for the people the server requires; also it must pay the costs involved in backing up and archiving records of use, and the like. In these ways the Internet is not free, and the degree of access to it varies from society to society.

Although access is at least in theory unlimited and global, and the number of sites is extremely large and growing, anarchy does not prevail. One constraint is the discipline of the technology itself. Anarchy would prevail if each country or each server or each user could use any protocols they chose, leading to incompatibility and the chaos of confusion and inoperability. If all are to be able to access all sites anywhere in the world, the latter clearly must be compatible, use the same protocols, and speak the same or mutually understandable computer languages.

The danger of any particular government or any corporation controlling the Internet, deciding on content and access, is obvious, and has so far been avoided. For any business to control or to try to control the Internet would be clearly to act against the public interest, and so would be to act unethically.

Yet since there are costs associated with running the Internet those who pay them may wish to lessen them to the extent that they can. Governmental sites are underwritten by state funds and are part of the service that citizens pay for through their taxes. Educational institutions pay for their servers just as they do for their libraries and laboratories. But many sites and many servers seek to gain income through ads placed on their sites. AOL, Windows Explorer, Netscape – all make extensive use of ads on their sites, even though Windows Explorer and Netscape do not charge for their browser software itself. They can afford not to because of indirect income they receive from their widespread use, just as network TV programs, which are free, are paid for by commercials.

The dominance of business interests has raised a variety of concerns. Access to the Internet is sometimes provided free to schools, but the price is the presence of ads on the screen as children browse the Web. Schools can of course decline the free service and pay for their connections, but students will still encounter a multiplicity of ads as they use their search engines or access a variety of websites.

The World Wide Web Consortium has a large number of corporations as members, each of which pays a $50,000 annual membership fee. Governmental and not-for-profit organizations pay only $5,000. Individuals can have only associate membership. The consortium is run democratically, but one can worry about the dominance of business interests or of governmental interests or of any particular nation's influence. We have already seen one of the effects of commercialization in the form of the introduction of cookie technology. Before cookies the Web was a place one could browse anonymously. Since the introduction of cookies, surfing the Web has become a different kind of activity. As we noted, that need not have been the route the Web took, and it can still be reversed. But as the members of society discuss whether the Web should be controlled by business, by government, by the users (and so the people), or whether it should not be controlled at all, we should remember that control is exercised in many ways.

Businesses have an interest in keeping the Web free, for that is the only way it is available to the millions of people who use it. If there were a charge for use, it would obviously limit the number of users. But there are various ways of paying, and opening oneself to risk or providing personal information are just as real a cost as paying money. Nor are cookies the only danger. When a user surfs to a new site, a header is sent by the user's browser listing the URL of the site from which the user comes. This is used by some companies to collect a small referral fee from the previous site. But it also helps the new site know a little more about the surfer and his or her surfing habits, which it can and often does record and add to information about the individual, or at least about the computer's IP number, which we saw can often be correlated to information about one. It is also possible to see where one goes next.

The ethics of control and the justification thereof are issues that have not clearly been raised, but the ethical and social responsibility of businesses to contribute to keeping the Web free and to keep it from being completely commercialized is a topic that is ripe for discussion.

Just as clearly, if government controlled the Internet and tracked all users the way businesses did, only even more thoroughly and collated that information with all the other information it obtains on its citizens, it is easy to imagine a controlled society such as depicted in the novel *1984*. Big Brother would indeed be watching us all. The fear of that happening is a strong reason not to allow control of the Internet by government, although such control is being exercised in some countries. An open society should resist such moves, although some governmental control, as we shall see later, is appropriate.

The Web has been used to rally protests of all sorts and to mount boycotts of businesses as well as to promote an endless number of causes. Critics of business and of government have a ready outlet in the Web and they should not be suppressed, as might be threatened if the Internet were controlled by either business or government. The absence of any control of the Internet, however, could also lead to negative consequences, and as in other realms of social life, there are limits to what is acceptable and what a society can allow if it is to protect the freedom and interests of all. This calls for a mix of governmental intervention, business and free market operations, public access and voice, and the promotion and protection of the Internet as a social and public good, run for the common good of all.

Actual gatekeepers of the Internet are the search engine sites that categorize and list sites. Without them, people could not find a site, and it would be lost in the vast multitude available. To survive commercially, a site has to be carried by the search engines, and to be useful, non-business sites must also be able to be located. The gatekeepers thus become Yahoo, Google, Excite, Infoseek, and others. They can screen-out terrorist and other illegal sites, at least making them difficult to find, even though they cannot do anything about their existence. Users depend on the gatekeepers, on their accuracy, objectivity, and comprehensive or specialized coverage. They play a key role and are commercial enterprises, even though they do not charge for listing sites. But they must be trustworthy as well as efficient. In any listing the one who makes the list must decide what criteria to use in ordering the list.

Any choice, whether it be alphabetical, most heavily used, closest to the request, and so on, will give preference to those appearing first. If some company pays to have its name listed first or very early, that skews the objectivity of the listing, unless the search engine clearly indicates that this is its policy. Then a user knows that, when searching for any information or type of business, that is the criterion used. That gives the searchers some information; but in most cases it is not the most pertinent or desired information. Hence they may well prefer a search engine that uses other criteria. If search engines are to be trusted, then they should give the websites closest to what one requests in a search, not the site that pays the most. If the latter is the standard, then that should be clearly stated, lest the function between identifier and advertiser becomes blurred. Whatever the criteria used, they should be stated by the search engine so that users are not misled and do not work under erroneous but natural expectations. To accept payment to violate the stated criteria would be to act unethically. Fortunately, most of the larger and more popular search engines understand this and do not accept payment for placement in their lists, although they do use a variety of criteria and there are techniques by which companies can move closer to the head of the line.

Domain names

One aspect of Internet governance concerns the allocation of names and what is known as cybersquatting. In order to know what computer to contact the Internet relies on a four-place set of numbers (e.g., 201.123.89.12), known as an IP address for each computer that accesses the Internet. A particular hostname links that name and number, and although one can reach the party in question by entering either the number or the name, names are what most people use (e.g., www.ibm.com) and the way sites are usually accessed. In 1991 the National Science Foundation took over responsibility from the Department of Defense to oversee the allocation of domain names, and it contracted with Network Solutions, Inc. (NSI) to actually handle issuance of domain names (except for .mil and .gov names) and to maintain the database. Other countries handled their own high-level domains. In 1998 the Internet Corporation for Assigned Names and Numbers (ICANN), a not-for-profit corporation, was formed to gradually take over the tasks previously performed by NSI. The intent was to allow the Internet community to govern itself, rather than its being run by the US or any other government. ICANN is international and is authorized to work out the details, including granting authority to other organizations to accept registrations for domain names. ICANN includes commercial, non-commercial, and other interested groups. Especially significant are the facts that it is international, self-governing, representative of a variety of constituencies, and neither governmental nor for-profit. But the system will only work if it is fair and perceived as being fair, which means it must be publicly accountable for its decisions.

When new high-level domain names (such as .biz and .info) were proposed to and initially accepted by ICANN's Domain Name Supporting Organization (DNSO) there was a wave of protest that other proposed names were not chosen. A number of US businesses that had competed for the right to register other names claimed their applications were unfairly rejected and lobbied Congress for a change in the system.

The allocation of domain names to businesses has spawned a number of ethical issues and disputes about fairness. Anyone can apply for a domain name, which must be different from any other in use. For a small annual fee the applicant has a right to the exclusive use of that name for the year (or other period of time indicated), with the right to renew thereafter. One can register as many domain names as one is willing to pay for. Large companies usually use their company names as their domain names, such as microsoft.com and ibm.com.

Cybersquatting is the registering of a popular name, other than one's own, as an Internet address. Most people tend to assume that the better-known companies, movie and entertainment stars, politicians, sports figures, etc., would have a website identified by their name with an extension of .com or .net. Thus, these domain names are of importance to those companies and individuals. If someone else gets them first, then they have to persuade the original holder to sell them that name. If they want it badly enough, they may pay a great deal.

As a result cybersquatters have purchased domain names that they anticipate will be purchased from them at a premium by the company or celebrity who wants it badly enough. With new high-level domain names such as .biz becoming available, the temptation for some is to register a large number of possibly desirable names with the intent of selling them. There are in fact domain name brokerage sites that list domain names that people have registered and are offering for sale.

Cybersquatting has been likened to extortion. While not actually extortion, a strong case can be made that it is unethical to register for oneself a name that is an obvious domain name for a well-known corporation or celebrity with the intent of selling it to them for a handsome profit. The only point in doing so is to take advantage of the rules of domain name allocation for personal profit at the expense of the corporation or celebrity. In 1999 the United States passed legislation outlawing the practice,[3] and ICANN has similarly adopted resolutions to prohibit cybersquatting. Nonetheless, there are difficulties and borderline cases, even if one admits that cybersquatting is unethical.

The US law focused on registering a domain name similar to a trademark with "a bad faith intent to profit from that trademark." There is general agreement that if someone chooses a well-known trademark to register for the purpose of selling it later at a substantial profit, that goes against the intent of domain name registration and the usefulness of domain names to the general public. The law now sees this as an infringement of a trademark. But the courts have since held that trademark protection does not give a complete monopoly of all domain names in some way "the same" as the trademark. James Strickland, known as "Strick," registered the domain name "Strick.com" in 1995. In 1997 the Strick Corporation, which owns the trademark "Strick," sued for use of its trademark, but the court ruled that Strickland was not cybersquatting, did not seek to sell his domain name for a profit, and had a legitimate first claim to register that domain name.

Amazon.com has filed a variety of suits for infringement of its trademark by others in their domain names, including Amazon.NE.Kr by a Korean man, and Amazon.Com.Gr by Greece's biggest bookstore. A third case raises a different problem, namely the registration of Amazom.com by two competing booksellers. They take advantage of users' spelling and typing errors to get book buyers on the Web to their site.

Trademarks, moreover, are not the only issue. Is it ethical for a business to capture domain names that would be desirable to a competitor by registering them, thereby preventing use by a competitor of the obvious domain name for its site? Is it ethical for politicians to prevent opponents from registering their obvious domain name, and for individuals to register domain names that would be obvious choices for celebrities of all kinds? Is it ethical to register a name with one letter different from that of a competitor – business, political, or other – with the intent of getting those who type the error to your site?

Clearly the latter is unethical, because you are intentionally deceiving and taking advantage of those who type the error. You know they do not intend to visit your site and that they intend to visit the other one. You then take advantage of their mistake for your own purpose, be it to try to sell them your product or to provide disinformation about the competing site or in other ways turn them against their intended site. The same is also true of the other two cases. Domain names are not an area of competition. They are a service provided to the general public as well as to those who register them. To deprive anyone or any business of the obvious domain name that customers or interested parties would try to access their site is to undermine the efficiency of the system for either profit or personal advantage of whatever sort one has in mind. No one would seriously want to universalize such a practice, and the results overall are more negative than positive when all concerned are taken into account.

On the other hand, registering a domain name that clearly indicates one's opinion of a product, even if it includes the producer's trademark, is not deceptive and is simply an expression of free speech. Does a disgruntled employee or a customer who has had a bad experience with a company have a right to register a negative-sounding website on which he states his position? The right to freedom of speech protects such people's right to express themselves. Verizonreallysucks.com was registered by a hacker magazine,

2600. Verizon had earlier preempted Verizonsucks.com by registering it. Surely no one would be duped into thinking the site *2600*
registered was Verizon's official site. Brand names or company
names or trademarks do not prevent criticism of the company in
question.

What of the preemptive registering of negative domain names
with one's name or trade name? Is that ethical? Does it prevent free
expression? Unlike the registering of obvious domain names, which
we argued was unethical, the registering of negative sites is not the
same. There are no obvious domain names in the same sense, since
there are an indefinitely large number of ways to indicate a negative
reaction to a company or brand or person. Domain names that are
registered, however, should not be registered and then not used. To
do so is once again to undermine the system. So some companies
register negative domain names of their company to direct the user
to the company's home page. Although the user may not get a site
that they expected would be negative, they did not expect anything
in particular, unlike someone wishing to access a company's legitimate site. Moreover, by listing the site the company in effect
produces negative advertisements about itself, and if a large number
of these appear in search engines the result is probably more harmful
than any negative site that the company preempts. In sum, although
not unethical, the practice hardly seems likely to be widely adopted.

▲ SECURITY AND ENCRYPTION ▲

Encryption is a technique that attempts to hide the content of a text
from anyone except the intended recipient. It goes back at least as
early as Caesar's time, when messages to Roman armies were
encrypted by substituting each letter of the alphabet for another
letter. To read the message, one needs the key, which says which
letters substitute for which. This simple substitution cipher has been
made much more complicated. In World War II the United States
broke the Japanese code, and thus was able to read messages which
the Japanese sent in code, believing they were secure.

Encryption has a long tradition in war and a clear military use. It
has also been used by governments. But its widespread use by
business and individuals is of very recent vintage and is due to the
computer and the Internet. The computer made it possible to break
codes quickly, and necessitated a new kind of encryption which was

developed in 1972. The vulnerability of the Internet made encryption the method of choice for protecting sensitive and personal data and information transmitted to others.

The two weak links in the traditional encryption technique are the ease with which computers can test substitutions by brute force at tremendous speeds and so break them, and the need to send the recipient the key. If this is intercepted, the chosen cipher is given away. The first difficulty can be overcome by using the computer to produce longer and longer keys (streams of binary digits or bits) needed to set up and so break the code. In 1974 IBM produced an encryption chip with a 128-bit key. The National Security Agency (NSA), which was in charge of encryption, encouraged IBM to reduce the strength of the key to 56 bits, which it argued was strong enough for business purposes, but weak enough that the NSA could break it if it were misused by terrorists, thieves, spies, or others. In 1976 public key cryptography was developed, which overcame the second weakness of codes. The person originating the message has two keys. He makes the first one public, so any who wishes to send him a message can use it. This encrypts the message. But the message is encrypted in such a way that it requires a second key to decipher the message, which only he possesses. So there is no danger of the deciphering key being stolen en route to the person wishing to send a message, since the second key stays with the originator. The strength of the key still depends on its length.

The ethical dimension arose in the attempt to balance the security that individuals desired in sending e-mails or in releasing their credit card numbers or social security numbers over the Internet and the national security that the government wished to protect by being able to intercept and read messages sent by criminals and by those who threaten the country's security.

We have already seen the importance of trust in e-business and in the use of e-mail and the Internet. Unless customers trust vendors to deliver as promised and vendors trust customers to pay as promised, and both trust the Internet, transactions will not take place. Since e-mail is routed in a variety of ways and can be intercepted and read at many points along its journey, and is then archived by servers, anyone sending a personal e-mail would much prefer that it only be read by the intended recipient. Since an e-mail can be likened more to a postcard than a letter, the wish to provide it with an envelope is understandable. Those en route can still see that x sends a message to y, but cannot read it. Similarly, given the

reality of hackers and identity theft, who gain easy access to transmissions, people are reluctant to use their credit cards on the Internet
or provide their social security or similar sensitive personal information without some assurance of the integrity and security of the
transmission system.

The US government recognizes these legitimate desires on the
part of business and individuals. Nonetheless, it argues that unless it
is able to break encrypted transmissions, it is hamstrung in pursuing
criminals, money laundering, terrorist communications, and other
threats to American security. For a number of years, therefore, it not
only prohibited the export of strong encryption to certain governments, such as Libya and Iraq, but also controlled the export of
strong encryption, and pushed for the adoption in the United States
of encryption of a strength that it considered adequate for most
purposes of business but still able to be cracked. It also encouraged
the use of a two-key chip, provided that a copy of the key, divided
into two parts, was stored in two government appointed facilities,
such that they could be used by government agencies to read
encrypted material if proper legal permissions were obtained, similar
to those needed for a wiretap.

Although a plausible policy, opponents argued against it on three
grounds. The first was that it gave too much power to and placed
too much trust in government. Although any given administration
might abide by the law, one can never be sure that future members
of government will do likewise. Second, it put US companies that
sell encryption at a disadvantage *vis-à-vis* their foreign competitors,
and so it led to companies like Microsoft limiting the strength of the
encryption in the US to what it was allowed to sell abroad so that it
would not have to have many versions of Windows. Third, and most
important, the law was ineffective in achieving its end, because
terrorists or criminals or anyone else so desiring could simply obtain
stronger encryption from abroad.

In 1999 the United States changed its policy. In 2000 it recommended adoption of the Rijndael algorithm as the new Advanced
Data Encryption standard (with bit lengths of 128, 192, or 256) for
government and commercial use. It also allowed the export of a key
of any length without license, after an initial review by the Department of Commerce, to any country, except Iran, Iraq, Libya, Syria,
Sudan, North Korea, and Cuba.

Strong encryption makes it unlikely that business secrets or bank
transfers or sensitive data will be intercepted and misused by third

parties. It clearly has ethical uses, and that is its justification. Nonetheless, it can be used for unethical purposes and to cover up unethical as well as illegal activities, which will be harder for law enforcement agencies to track than would otherwise be the case. Once again we have the technological imperative driving development. There was no public debate about whether to develop cryptography in this way and whether it would be better to protect personal information privacy by alternative means, whether it would be wiser to secure transactions and bank transfers by other means, and so on. With the rise in the need to guard against terrorism, it is unclear whether a reasoned balancing of the need for national security and the need for protecting legitimate business transactions from interference, theft, or compromise, and the need of individuals to protect their personal information, will result in changes of governmental policy in the United States and worldwide. However that turns out, the fact that private individuals have to consider encryption in their routine and ordinary use of the Internet indicates the way the technological imperative and the Myth of Amoral Computing and Information Technology have skewed the public's sense of what is normal and acceptable.

Encryption, security, and business

Given the present situation, a variety of measures can and should be taken by a company to protect its files and documents in its information systems. This is especially true, from an ethical point of view, of information on customers, such as their credit card numbers. Measures include, among others, encryption, fire walls, authentication and authorization, intrusion detection, and virus protection. Breaches of security and violations of privacy can take place from within and from without a corporation, and a company must protect itself from both types of breaches.

Internal breaches are of many kinds, from someone in the company seeking, innocently or out of curiosity, advertently or inadvertently, something on another person's computer screen which is either private or secret and restricted to only certain people in the firm, to an employee directly engaged in sabotage or theft. The former may happen while someone is using the computer and someone else casually walks by, or from someone leaving something displayed on a screen while they are absent from their desk. All employees should be taught to protect both private information, such as employee records, and secret information about the firm from such simple and sometimes casual violations of privacy or secrecy.

Employees are usually given access to only certain kinds of information within the company's information system and access requires both identification and a password. Internally many companies do not pay very much attention to authentication procedures, and anyone knowing someone's name and password can gain access. Such a casual approach may be appropriate for much material in the firm. But it is not appropriate for material that should be kept private or secret. The reason is that access is too easily compromised. Security suggests changing passwords periodically, perhaps even frequently. But if employees have to keep track of many and of constantly changing different passwords for different kinds of access, it is not surprising that they keep them written down or filed in their computers. Attaching post-its with their passwords to their computer screens is not unusual, but it is an obvious breach of security. The protection of the privacy of records and of company secrets is a function and a responsibility of all who have access. Paradoxically, sometimes as security on the corporate level increases, it tends to decrease on the user level because it is too complex for the non-specialist. It is the obligation of the company to put proper systems in place and to train their employees. It is the obligation of employees to take the precautions necessary. The company should distinguish different levels of security needed for different kinds of information and protect the more sensitive material more carefully than the less sensitive.

Web security is a special problem, since so many users access it for so many different reasons. The receiving of information of a routine and generally available kind is different from interactions that involve sending sensitive data or files. Encryption and authentication systems are the most widely used approaches. But once again these tend to be double-edged swords. Encryption is often used to protect transmissions that leave the company. It is not normally used internally, although it might be, especially for transmitting sensitive material. A company may wish to have access to the e-mail and Web use of its employees. Yet if messages are encrypted, they can be kept private and unavailable for inspection, unless management requires that it have a key to all encryption codes used by employees.

For use on the Net, employees may go through anonymous servers that do not let their searches and contacts on the Net be identified or tracked. These systems supply each user with an anonymous address from which and to which mail and messages are sent. Mail thus arrives without a sender's name and address and cannot be retraced back. This prevents tracking from the outside. But it can also be used to prevent tracking from the inside. Whether such use is permitted by the employer depends on how strict the control management has over employee access and use. This should be decided and made known. Anonymous servers are also sometimes used by spammers to hide the identity of the source of the ads they are sending. Anonymous servers can be used with or without encryption.

Unfortunately, hacking is no longer the province of specialized computer nerds. Websites are now available that either list passwords or make available hacking programs for those wishing to gain access to passwords.

Security and privacy are sometimes at odds and sometimes coincide. Information system tools to guarantee both are constantly developing, which will tend to make protection of both better. But in the interim, the technology is developing so quickly that many people have difficulty keeping up, adding confusion to the threats that already exist to both security and privacy.

Anonymity, secrecy, and the Internet

Earlier we saw that truth is a necessary virtue and value that underpins the Information Age. Without truth and the trust that it engenders, transactions that can and should take place will not, misinformation will have equal place with information and lead to inefficiencies and counterproductive results. Business, which has been especially aggressive in capturing more and more information about Internet users, trades on a dual system of values, and there is an internal inconsistency in the way the Internet is developing. Business counts on the information it has about users being accurate, at least for the most part. If it is not, if customer A has an income of $20,000 a year rather than the reported $100,000, he or she is targeted in the wrong way. If customer B is a minor, pretending to be an adult, any promotion sent to B is likely to be misdirected, and so on. The information business seeks about customers and potential customers has to be reasonably accurate to be useful. But many businesses, while expecting and counting on truth from and about their customers, do not inform them of the practices they use to get such information, and deliberately or unintentionally deceive them about their practices through privacy and other statements that are overly technical, complicated, convoluted, long, incomplete, and difficult for many users to really know what the practice is and whether they should in fact be opting out. We have already seen that a policy that required one to opt in would be a better approximation to respecting one's right to informed consent. Moreover, the lines between information, advertising, and editorializing are much more blurred on the Internet than in newspapers or magazines, for instance, where ads are labeled as such. Disclosure by business of their practices on the Internet is often not transparent or else non-existent, once again undermining trust.

The way the Internet is developing means that a similar inconsistency is pervading other aspects. E-mail service providers allow users to choose their own names, and often provide the option of their also choosing one or more aliases. Aside from cyberspace, people typically have only one name. Actors may have a stage name, and a few authors publish under a pseudonym. But the notion of having and using an alias is associated with criminals and is somewhat suspect. Why would a person use an alias? Why would they carry on activities under an assumed name? What do they wish to hide? That these questions arise and the expectation is that people use their real names are explicable because there is enough free space in society in which one can act with anonymity, preserve one's privacy, and achieve one's legitimate ends without falsifying one's identity. If society were different, then the general attitude towards aliases and disguising one's identity would be different. If it were different, then the level of trust would diminish and people would constantly have to be on their guard against being duped or used in ways they do not want.

Now consider the Internet and e-mail, chat rooms, news groups and other discussion fora, and other ways of interacting and communicating on-line. The fact that e-mail providers offer alias options routinely and that many people use aliases says a great deal about the Internet. Business and professional people typically use their names in their e-mail addresses because they want to be identified and their addresses easily remembered. To use an alias in business or professional life would be confusing and dysfunctional. Truth, in this case not identifying oneself by another name, promotes the interests of business and of those in it.

Why is this not the case in other contexts on the Internet? The answer seems to be that the anonymity that people enjoy in their ordinary lives is not available on the Internet. This is not because such anonymity was not and is not possible, but because the Internet has been structured for and by business and other interests that have sought to capture unlimited information about Internet users.

Most people do not use their aliases, their pseudonyms, their fictitious identities to do anything illegal. They are as law abiding on the Internet as they are in other areas of their lives. The reasons are multiple, and different individuals may use aliases for different reasons. Some may use it to avoid or to identify spam; some to play games as they communicate in chat rooms or post to bulletin boards or websites; some to try out new personalities, avoid discrimination, be judged on the basis of what they say and not how they look; still others to preserve their privacy, or protect their personal information, or to feel more secure. There are undoubtedly many other reasons.

Whatever the reasons, the Internet, which is a source of information and should foster truth, is in fact encouraging dissimulation, falsehood, misrepresentation, and subterfuge. To some extent these are tactics of self-defense and ethically justifiable. Since they are widely used, people should know they are aliases and are not real names, that people may not be who they say or pretend to be, and so no real deception takes place. But any such defense, if successful, shows a deep and internal inconsistency between truth as fundamental to the Information Age and the actual structure and functioning of the Internet. The practices have in turn led not only to the widespread uses of aliases but also to electronic defenses of various kinds, from anonymizers to filters to authenticators – all commercially available, although sometimes also free.

Spamming

Although the Internet is not for profit and much of what it contains is available for free, every user of the Internet is perceived by business as a potential customer, whether or not they know it.

Unfortunately, most users fail to realize the extent to which their activities on the Internet are anything but private. If someone posts a message on a bulletin board or enters into a discussion with others on a list or news group, he or she should realize that the message or comment or conversation is open and available for viewing by anyone with access to that site. That is potentially everyone. What many people do not realize is that their messages or comments are archived and stored, and that there are programs and websites that retrieve this archived data, such as Deja News, which indexes over 15,000 bulletin boards and news groups and can sort an individual's entries by frequency and type.[4] The uses to which this information is put by marketers might surprise many users. Have you made a comment in favor of a democratic senator? You might be solicited for a donation by the Democratic Party. The websites you visit also provide information about your interests, which are put to commercial use. Have you recently inquired about the level of pollution? You might find yourself with many ads for antihistamine products.

Cookies technology, as we have seen, allows website owners to keep track of how often a given individual visits its site. The website places a cookie on the receiver's hard drive, so the site manager can know that you have visited before and can keep track of your visits and what you choose to view. This is defended as being in the user's interest, since it can save time and allows the user to be greeted with a personalized message and with ads of interest to the user. However, the site manager can combine that information with any registration information you have provided and with other information about the user, and then sell that information to interested marketers.

One result of such tracking is direct marketing, another is the equivalent of electronic junk mail, sometimes referred to as spam (a "Stupid Person's Advertisement"), and the sending of such junk mail is called "spamming".[5]

While some would claim that spamming is no more unethical than sending junk mail, there is an important difference because electronic junk mail takes time to read and delete, and many users pay for the time they are on the Net. While ordinary junk mail comes in the mail and can be easily tossed in the wastebasket, the receiver is not paying for that time the way the receiver of spam is. Regular junk mail costs the sender postage for each item sent. Electronic junk mail can be sent virtually simultaneously to thousands of recipients at no additional cost to the sender, although there is a cost to the service provider, who in turn will pass that cost on to its users. Hence the sender has little incentive to limit the number of mailings since the cost of the mailing is passed on to the recipient – clearly without the latter's consent. The cost to the user may be small from any one item but can grow as the spamming increases. The problem is especially acute for those who may receive a hundred or several hundred spam messages each day, not only taking their time and costing them money, but also jamming their mailboxes or overloading their capacity. Moreover, from an ethical point of view, many spammers can be faulted for using stolen e-mail addresses, false return addresses to hide their true origin, and misleading information on how one can be removed from a list which in fact does not work or is ignored. When messages are offensive or are sent simply to harass the receiver, clog the receiver's mailbox, and otherwise disrupt the receiver's legitimate use of e-mail and Internet access, the intent and the action are both unjustified.

In addition to all of the above, spam, if delivered in great bulk, can and does overload systems. In 1998 an overload of spam caused Pacific Bell's Internet e-mail server to crash. It took four days to restore the system. It is not difficult to imagine the cost to Pacific Bell and the inconvenience and even damage to those using the system. AOL estimates that 40 percent of its e-mail is spam.[6]

Ideally, such e-mails should be sent to those who request the information, and it should be easy for anyone who wishes to be removed from a list to do so. Sources should be accurate and clear.

The defect of the present system from an ethical point of view is that much is done without the user's knowledge or consent. The possible harm from unscrupulous website managers is enough to cause serious concern. But even legitimate managers, driven by the desire to make a profit or to advertise their products to likely users, use techniques of which users are not informed and about which many users would like to know more. Many people may be willing to trade information on their interests for advertisements and discount offers. Those who choose to can be identified or can identify themselves. Yet those who do not wish to be identified and tracked should be informed of when they are being tracked and should be given the option of choosing not to be so tracked. Two defenses are to use only an alias when using Usenet and other e-mailable public places, and then immediately deleting all the mail received at that e-mail name and address. The other is to use an e-mail filter that identifies and deletes or transfers to a special folder many kinds of e-mail. That either is necessary is once again an indication of a system that can and should be changed.

Chat rooms usually require only an e-mail address to register. So one under any name or alias will do. Then one chooses a nickname. Chat room advice given to children and used by many others is to never give one's real name. No one in such a room is ever sure who the other people in the room are. So the chat room is in fact anonymous, except insofar as one can be tracked there as one can be tracked anywhere else on the Internet without one's knowledge or consent. The dangers of chat rooms are many, the clearest being the dangers posed by a sexual predator who uses the chat room to arrange a physical meeting and contact either with a child or an adult. Would chat rooms be less useful if one had to use one's own verifiable name and address to enter, and, for children or teenagers, their verifiable age? They clearly do not have to be set up as most of them are. Yet no one is forced to enter them or to chat, and freedom of expression argues for as little constraint on Internet activities as possible, as long as they do not harm anyone. The anonymity that results from people using nicknames works two ways. On the one hand, it protects the vulnerable from potential harm, discrimination, spam, and the like, since they cannot be identified unless they reveal this information. On the other hand, it also protects the predator or spammer from being identified. Nonetheless, chat rooms, among others, raise the issues of anonymity, security, and responsibility on the Internet that deserve more analysis and discussion than they have received. Accepting the current system is once again to accept the Myth of Amoral Computing and Information Technology and to accede to the technological imperative.

Anonymity, security, and responsibility

The Internet as it has in fact developed has reversed the ordinary conventions about anonymity, although this need not have been the case. In ordinary space in a city of any size one moves about anonymously in the sense that one's identity is not known to the vast majority of others. One enters stores, makes purchases, drives one's car, and so on without the need to identify oneself and without anyone trying to do so. The general rule taught to children is "Don't speak to strangers." Although we may strike up conversations in a bus or subway or restaurant with someone sitting next to us, we usually converse with those with whom we are acquainted. And it is usually not far into a conversation with a stranger that people exchange their names. On the Internet, however, we have seen that our browsings are not anonymous. Our IP number is recorded, cookies are placed on our hard drive, we are tracked and often identified by name and information about us linked with other information about us already collected from other sources. We use our real names in sending regular mail, but aliases in e-mail, giving us a certain anonymity. We speak in chat rooms with strangers and identify ourselves by factitious names, as do they. The personal act of communication takes place in an impersonal setting, and our words are open to view by as many people as are allowed to view the chat room at one time, and to that extent public. What is anonymous in the physical world becomes identifiable in cyberspace and what is identifiable in the physical world is made anonymous, although to some extent public in cyberspace.

Noting this is not to say whether it is good or bad. But it is different, and it could be otherwise. Children's and teen sites would be safer if they were restricted by some authentication process to children and teens. In postings and in discussion groups many people do use their own names, and some discussion groups are not only monitored but also closed to anyone but members of certain organizations that run the list serve. Anonymity is not a necessary part of chats or conversations, and simply knowing someone's name doesn't make them really known to you any more than using their invented nickname. But in the former case the starting point is one of truth and of at least possible accountability for what one says, which is now absent.

Anonymity in the activities of ordinary life does not negate responsibility and accountability. We are responsible and accountable for what we do. And if we do anti-social acts in public we will be held accountable for them by those around us who may interfere or call in public authorities.

Anonymity on the Internet tends to diminish both responsibility and accountability. People anonymously spread rumors or slander or make innuendos about others – public figures, businesses, other individuals – through anonymous e-mail. In chat rooms and discussion groups adults can pretend to be children, children can pretend to be adults, people can pretend to have expertise they do not have or to be kinds of people they are not. There is no responsibility for what one says and no accountability. As a result it is difficult to talk about responsible discourse. The overall result is to reduce trust and reliability on the Internet. There are times and places for pretend and play, and the Internet can serve that function and provide appropriate sites for such interactions. Contacting and having interchanges with people from other countries and cultures can be mutually enriching. They are all the more enriching when built on trust and truth, reliability, accountability and security, rather than doubt, fear, caution, and possible mistrust. Yet the Internet is being structured in that way in large part because of the absence of the legitimate kind of anonymity we enjoy in modern society at large and are denied in cyberspace.

The above discussion should not be taken to mean that the Internet should be closed, or open only to certain individuals or groups, or made more restrictive. Open access is one of the great benefits of the Internet. But there is no reason why open access has to be accompanied by lack of responsibility and accountability. People should be free to express themselves, but freedom of speech does not mean irresponsible speech or anonymous speech with no accountability.

▲ INFORMATION AND PROPERTY ▲ ON THE INTERNET

We have already seen some of the issues related to property in the Information Age. The Internet, which provides such easy access to a wealth of material and which makes it extremely easy to locate, view, and copy, raises even more issues. Possibilities that did not exist before the Internet now pose questions that copyright law was not written to answer. The Legislature has attempted to catch up, and the courts have applied older law to the new issues. As examples we shall consider the US Digital Millennium Copyright Act, one of the few US Supreme Court decisions on digital information copyright, and a few of the problems that arise from the development of websites.

The Digital Millennium Copyright Act

The Internet is possible because of its use of digitized data. It is able to transmit these data as electronic signals in packets at enormous speeds. Anything that can be put in digital form – text, pictures, movies, music – can be so transmitted. In digital form the copy is as good as the original. There is no loss of quality as there is in reproductions or copies of photos and no deterioration as there is in videotapes.

The purpose of the Digital Millennium Copyright Act (DMCA), passed in 1998, was to bring US law into agreement with international treaties signed at a meeting of the World Intellectual Property Organization in 1996. But its provisions remain controversial. Its primary focus is on protecting software code that in turn is intended to protect copyrighted materials. It was opposed by scientists, librarians, and academics.[7] What makes it controversial is not the intent to protect copyrighted material, but the way that it does so. It prohibits the "circumvention" of any "technological protection measure" that a copyright holder uses to restrict access, including passwords or encryption. It also makes illegal the cracking of any protective code. It outlaws the development and sale of code-cracking programs (with certain exceptions, e.g., for testing programs). Critics claim that this indirectly extends copyright protection to whatever it is that the code writer wishes to protect, rather than to what copyright law itself was written to protect. All agree that if someone cracked the protective code on an electronic site or document and did in fact violate copyright law, the latter would be the legal offense. But, critics of the law argue, by making it illegal to attack code, the law undermines research into security and encryption.[8] The law, they claim, is overly broad and confuses copyright protection with electronic security measures. The US is the only country to have adopted this approach.

On the positive side, however, the law did enact what had previously been simply judicial interpretation with respect to Internet Service Providers (ISPs), including libraries and educational institutions. Under special provisions in the Act,[9] ISPs are not liable for copyright infringement if one of their users posts material in violation of copyright law, as long as the ISP acts in good faith and does not know that a violation has occurred. Hence universities are not legally responsible for what students or faculty post or for the infringements of copyright of which they may be guilty, as long as the universities are not informed of any infringement.

If the law is overly broad on the one hand, it does not clarify a great deal in the area of electronic copying, except to allow institutions, including libraries, to make up to three digital preservation copies of copyrighted work. The failure to address other issues raised by electronic publishing has led to the courts again bearing the burden of interpreting the law and applying it to areas not explicitly covered by legislation.

Tasini v. The New York Times

One of these issues is the question of the claims of authors when what appeared in print, for instance in a newspaper or magazine, is later digitized by the publisher and made available on the Internet.

Is this simply a change in the medium or does it constitute republication? A test case went to the Supreme Court, with a verdict that some found counter-intuitive. In *Tasini v. The New York Times*[10] the Court held that authors who write articles for newspapers and magazines, unless the authors also sell electronic rights to their writing, sell only the right to the publication of the work as part of the original collective work. What made the decision noteworthy was that the Court held that electronic publication of the original newspaper or journal, such that individual freelance articles could be accessed separately and not as part of the original format (e.g., of page of the newspaper, as would be the case in a microfilm copy of the newspaper), was a violation of the author's rights. As a result, the *New York Times* argued, electronic access to the historical record, that is, to all the freelance articles that appeared in the *New York Times* or any other newspaper or magazine for which the publication had not secured electronic rights, would no longer be available to the general public. What makes this counter-intuitive is that the Internet offered the possibility of direct and easy access to material that may be hard to come by in its original print form. Instead of having to find a library that might have a microfilm copy of a newspaper, one could access the articles easily and quickly in electronic form. Faced with the task of eliminating all freelance articles that appeared in the *New York Times* from 1980, when the new copyright law went into effect, the *Times* offered authors the option of having their articles remain in such databases as *Nexis*. Those articles for which the author does not give permission would have to be removed.

It is impossible to say whether the Court's interpretation of copyright is what the Legislature intended, because the Legislature never considered the possibility of electronic means of publication and access at a later date. The core of the author's argument hinges on the fact that although a print publication buys the right to publish a freelance article, the copyright is only on the collective work (e.g., the issue of the paper in which it appears). The author retains the rights to other uses, unless the author expressly transfers those rights. The author may therefore sell the article in other forms, as in an anthology of his or her work, while the newspaper or magazine may not. To license the articles as part of the newspaper to electronic databases is in effect to offer them for sale as separate entities. The newspaper makes the extra revenue and the authors are deprived of the reward for their labor.

The obvious solution after the *Tasini* decision is for print publications to purchase electronic publishing rights from their freelance authors at the time they purchase the right to publish their work, or for electronic publishers or the original publisher to pay freelance authors for the right to publish their work in the databases. These are the simplest alternatives until and unless Congress changes the law. The bone of contention is work already published. Arguably the public is served by having available such items as back issues of the *New York Times* available on-line and by being able to access and download not only those items written by the newspaper's reporters (whose work is owned by the newspaper as "work for hire") but also by those freelance writers whose work also appeared in the paper. If back issues were only available in microfilm in libraries, they would clearly be less accessible to the general public. But if the newspaper is paid for granting a company such as Nexis the right to make these available, shouldn't the author receive part of the compensation?

Given the rules, if libraries want to maintain the complete historical record of publication, then they will not be able to rely only on digital databases, which might henceforth be incomplete. They will have to continue storing hard copy and microfilm, which have to be accessed physically at the library.

Libraries are also struggling against interpretations of fair use that may make it illegal to have copyrighted material available on-line. This may even threaten inter-library loan. If a library makes books and journals available to readers, then those readers will tend not to buy those items, unless they expect to use them often or want to mark them up and otherwise damage their usefulness for other readers. The existence of libraries arguably cuts into book and magazine sales. Now have the library make an electronic version of the book or magazine and make that similarly available. Instead of having one borrower at a time read the item, it is now possible for any number of readers to access the item at the same time. Instead of making a photocopy, on-line readers can download the article or book and print it out in hard copy. Do these changes make a difference in principle in what the library does? Is loaning a book to 100 patrons one after the other different in principle from making it available to all 100 at the same time on-line? If the loan of physical books is allowed, why not the sharing of books or journals or parts thereof via fax or on-line? Conversely, if the latter are not allowed, why is the loaning of books and the inter-library loaning of books and journals allowed? An answer might be that on-line the items are available to anyone and everyone, possibly undercutting sales of the book or item, while inter-library loan is sufficiently difficult and time consuming that its effect on sales is minimal. But for works that are out of print this argument doesn't hold, since the item is no longer for sale. What should constitute fair use in such cases? Does the situation change if some company decides to digitize out-of-print material, paying a fee to the copyright holder? Must libraries then use that source for their patrons because to make available their own digitized version would be to compete unfairly and deprive both the company and the copyright holder of their revenue? The two separate but related issues are: what does the law say and what does ethics demand?

At the heart of all these controversies is the issue of fairness to authors, to publishers, and to the general public. The courts are interpreting copyright law as it has been written and as it exists. That is a different task from deciding whether the law as written is fair to all. It is up to legislators to decide what is fair for all and whether to change copyright law to reflect the changing reality of information and access to it. In the interim various alternatives are being tried. In 1996, for instance, the National Writers Union set up the Publication Rights Clearing House (PRC), which receives royalties from some on-line sites that sell magazine articles, books, and other texts. The PRC in turn sends authors an appropriate royalty for each of their items downloaded. This preserves the rights of authors, while making material available on-line. Unlike accessing material in a library, however, there is a charge – and often a relatively considerable one – for each item downloaded.

Web pages

It is now possible for anyone to create and have their own Web page. There are simple programs that a variety of companies and ISPs offer to enable one to create a Web page. The pages can, moreover, easily be multimedia, with text, pictures, background designs, music, as one desires. The ease with which the pages can be created and the ease of copying almost anything – from text to sound to graphics on the Internet – has raised the problem of rampant violation of copyright.

Copyright law, we have by now come to appreciate, is often intricate and one needs knowledge of a host of judicial decisions to know exactly what is allowed and what is not allowed, what is legal and what is not. The fact that many of the decisions that have been handed down have been split decisions by the higher courts and that higher courts have overturned lower courts is an indication that what is allowed is not intuitive. The average person – adult or child – surfing the Web and creating his or her own home page, often has the erroneous impression that everything on the Web is free for the taking, unless there is an explicit charge. Copyright symbols are not required to indicate that something is copyrighted. Some things may be copied freely, others may not. Knowing which is which, unless there is a clear indication one way or the other, is difficult to determine. So the rule of thumb advocated by universities and schools, as well as by most Web programs, is to assume everything is covered by copyright unless the contrary is explicitly stated.

This is in fact what most people assume in the world of print. But there it is not as easy to copy anything and simply paste it seamlessly into one's own creation. Moreover, on the Web it is so easy to copy that some people erroneously believe that it is legitimate to do so. This applies not only to graphics, but also to text. Some feel that statements made in an open chat room or posted to Usenet are public statements and in the public domain, which is not legally the case. What one receives in e-mail is, like what one receives in a letter, also covered by copyright.

Linking also raises ethical as well as legal issues. Most of the time linking seems to cause no problem. One can include links in one's page to other websites that contain information that the viewer might wish to pursue. But linking to an internal page that contains the data to which one wishes to lead a viewer should not lead directly to an internal (as opposed to a home) page, if doing so avoids the site's security payment system, or if it avoids the advertising on the site's home page that supports it. One should also not link to sites that state they do not grant permission for linking.

While accessing, reading, and even downloading information for one's own personal use are generally permissible on the Web, copying and posting without permission are not. Once again we encounter the paradox of the wealth of information and the ease of access and copying and the countervailing legal restrictions controlling free use. The weighing of intellectual property rights on the one hand, and the benefit to the general public from the free use of information on the other, is becoming more and more complicated. Technological protections that restrict copying are possible. Yet the more pressing task is the ethical one of determining how best to protect legitimate rights and still produce the most good for society – a task which thus far has not received much public attention.

▲ CENSORSHIP AND PORNOGRAPHY ▲

In addition to ownership the Internet also raises ethical questions with respect to content – violence, instructions on how to create bombs, and pornography, for instance. We shall take the issue of pornography as a surrogate for a discussion of questionable content.

It is estimated that there are over 1 million pornographic sites on the Internet. This includes websites, news groups on Usenet, bulletin boards, chat rooms, and FPT servers. Pornography is also transmitted by e-mail and shared with peer-to-peer data sharing technology. Some people have even claimed that the pornographic sites have been the most creative in developing the resources of the Web for commercial purposes. Some of them have been overly intrusive, advertising and appearing as pop-ups on sites and from sites that the user does not think are in any way related to pornography. Children using a search engine for "toys" will encounter listings for "sex toys" and under other unlikely listings (e.g., for girl, boy, dog, missionary, beaver) sex pages will appear because the site has been identified by the Web page under a large number of key words.

There are three issues: (1) pornography versus censorship, (2) pornography and children, and (3) child pornography. The first raises the issue of free speech, the second the possibility of controlling access, and the third the policing of what in many jurisdictions is illegal material.

Pornography is, of course, not an issue that is limited to the Internet. But the Internet has raised it to a high-profile issue because of the vast amount of material readily available and because of the problem of child access.

Pornography versus censorship

There is no legally significant definition of pornography. What people consider to be pornographic texts or pictures varies greatly. For some, any depictions of full nudity is pornographic, while for others it is only the depiction of explicit sexual acts, and still others fall on a spectrum in between. For some, context is important, and for others the intent to lead to sexual arousal is key. Pornography is in itself not illegal, and in the United States is covered by the freedom of expression guaranteed by the First Amendment to the Constitution. But that does not mean that all pornography is legal, and in fact some or much of it is not. That portion (and exactly how great a portion is disputed) that is obscene, is illegal.

The dominant legal definition of obscenity comes from a 1973 Supreme Court decision, *Miller v. California*.[11] To be considered obscene, material must pass a three-part test. A jury must decide: "(a) whether the average person, applying contemporary community standards, would find that the work, taken as a whole, appeals to prurient interests, (b) whether the work depicts or describes, in a patently offensive way, sexual conduct specifically defined by the applicable state law, and (c) whether the work, taken as a whole, lacks serious literary, artistic, political, or scientific value."

The difficulties with this approach, according to critics, are multiple. Who is the "average person"? Is each of us average, or are we to imagine some average aggregate of views? Either approach has obvious difficulties, since people's views vary considerably on sex and its depiction. Each of the states may legislate differently as to what is prohibited and what is not, and some states have no legislation concerning obscenity. What is legally allowed in one state and in one community may be considered obscene and illegal in another state or community. This seems to make obscenity relative. It also means that what someone may post on the Web in a jurisdiction in which it is legal to do so, may be accessed by someone else in another jurisdiction where it is considered obscene and so illegal, and where the poster will be legally guilty of distributing obscene material. The third test is not a community test but a determination about national views, yet it is very vague and open to interpretation and serious disagreement. Nonetheless, any material that passes the first two parts of the test and fails the third, as decided by a jury, is obscene and illegal. In addition, child pornography, or the presentation of children in sexual acts, is by definition obscene and illegal.

The problem is one of balancing freedom of speech and pornography.

Many people hold that all pornography as they define it is unethical. It has as its purpose sexual arousal, and to deliberately engage in such activity outside of marriage is unethical. Hence those who consume as well as those who produce and distribute pornography act unethically, although the latter two groups are worse than the former because they are also engaged in the action of corrupting others. Some feminists hold that all pornography is immoral because it makes women into sexual objects, shows them being degraded, and leads to their being treated badly by men in real life. Still others argue that it leads to bad consequences, sexual abuse, rape, a deterioration of sexual values, an engrossing of those who view it, and an acceptance of aberrant sexual practices. Those who defend it claim that it offers a harmless sexual release that might find other, negative outlets, that it is harmless to the user and, providing those depicted are not forced, does no harm to anyone, and hence overall produces more good than harm.

Whatever one's view of the morality of pornography itself, holding it to be unethical does not require that it be legally prohibited. Any attempt to do so comes up against the right of freedom of speech, which protects the right of each individual, within certain limits, to express him or herself in speech and in other media that are considered forms of expression. Freedom of speech may be curtailed. But it should only be done when other stronger rights are being infringed or when serious public harm is threatened, such as by yelling "Fire" in a crowded theater or inciting to violence by one's speech. The dispute between those who would censor and prohibit all pornography and those who would allow it hinges are their respective perceptions of the harm or lack thereof that results from allowing pornography. Taken as a whole, studies and empirical data as to the effects have so far all been inconclusive.

As a result, many communities have come to a *modus vivendi*. Pornography – as opposed to obscenity – is permitted as long as it is kept under control and available only to consenting adults. Pornography is not allowed on network TV, but it is available in some locations on special paid cable channels. It is not available in many bookshops or on many magazine racks, but it is available in or on some, often sold only to adults, and often with their graphic cover pictures obscured. The aim is not to prevent consenting adults from having access, but to prevent access by children and casual customers or viewers who would find exposure to the material offensive.

This *modus vivendi*, however, was shattered by the Internet. Although some argue that one still has to search out pornographic material, it is more readily available than it ever has been, it is available in greater number and types, it can be accessed inadvertently using search engines, and it is sometimes sent in the form of advertisements via e-mail or pop-ups or misleading come-ons to those who did not solicit it and do not wish to receive it. Moreover, since the Internet is not bound by geographic borders, images and text posted in any number of ways on the Internet in one state or in one country become available in other states and countries. What may be acceptable in one place may not be acceptable in another. This exacerbates the problem of acceptable content, of the definition of pornography, and even of the definition of obscenity, as well as making more difficult the enforcement of any obscenity laws.

The issue of pornography versus freedom of speech came to a head with the passage of the US Communications Decency Act of 1996, which criminalized not only obscenity but indecency (and so non-obscene pornography) on the Internet. The aim was to protect children from exposure to all forms of pornography.

Pornography and children

The Internet differs from TV insofar as TV is a passive medium in which the recipient has the choice of a channel but no choice as to what he or she sees on that channel. Moreover, network TV and basic cable channels are in general family viewable; that is, there is no explicit sex and no full-frontal nudity. There is, of course, violence and themes unsuitable for young children. But there are rating systems in place that warn parents, and most TVs offer parents a means of blocking certain channels from use by their children. Soft-core pornography is available on some pay channels in some locales. Hence pornography, if seen as a problem on TV, is one for which a social accommodation has been found. Newspapers that come into the home do not contain pornographic material, and other pornographic print material, if available, is usually available only to those over 18 years of age.

The Internet poses special problems because pornography is so easily available and control of access by age, e.g., through the use of credit cards, is only partially successful. A great deal is available free, and, as we have noted, is easily found through search engines; searches on seemingly innocuous topics can lead children inadvertently to pornographic sites. Thus, critics claim that pornography on the Internet must be regulated as it is on TV and in print. Opponents of such regulation do not claim that children should have access to pornography. There is general agreement that they should not. What they are argue is that adults should have access, if they so desire.

Pornography, as opposed to obscenity, is legal in general and covered by the right of freedom of speech and so should not be censored on the Internet. To make available to adults only what is acceptable for children is to restrict adults in such a way as to abridge their right to freedom of speech. Moreover, they argue, unlike TV, someone must actively pursue pornography on the Internet. It does not suddenly appear by clicking through channels, since there are no channels. One must request a particular site or click on particular links.

Defenders of pornography on the Internet further argue that there are adequate means to prevent access by children. There are programs such as SurfWatch, Cyber Patrol, ChildSafe, and Net Nanny. The latter tracks websites, news groups, and chat rooms to block pornography, hate literature, bomb instructions, and anything else a parent wishes to block. It provides a log so that parents can be aware of the sites their children are accessing. It allows different access settings for different members of the household, depending on their maturity level, and can be set to block transmission of personal information (such as name, address, phone number, credit card number) on the Internet. ChildSafe allows a parent to see what their children are doing from any place the parent has access to e-mail. Such tools are inexpensive and provide the protection parents want. So even if in searching for "toys" the child hits a program that leads to a pornographic site, Net Nanny will block access to that site. Moreover, many pornographic sites require proof of age before allowing admittance, and even those that are free usually warn of sexually explicit content and require that one click a statement agreeing to the terms, including a statement that one is at least 18 years of age. Children can, of course, lie about their age, click and gain entry. But that, critics claim, is a decision they make and it is the responsibility of parents to supervise their behavior. Nothing is forced on them.

Despite these safeguards, NetValue, an Internet research firm, reports that, in a survey it conducted in September 2000, children spent 64.9 percent more time on pornography sites than on game sites, and 27.5 percent (or about 3,000,000) children under age 17 visited a pornographic site, of which 21.2 percent were 14 or younger.[12] The conclusion drawn by opponents of pornography is that pornography on the Internet must be controlled by legislation. The conclusion drawn by defenders of free speech is that if parents are concerned they have to take responsibility for supervising their children by using the various filtering and blocking tools available. They should not rely on government to do that job for them at the expense of the rights of adults.

So far the courts have held that the Communications Decency Act of 1996, which criminalized indecency and so pornography on the Internet, is unconstitutional and violates the constitutionally guaranteed freedom of speech.

Schools and public libraries have also struggled with the issue, and there is disagreement within those communities about whether to block access to Internet sites, and so both engage in censorship and possibly block access to legitimate sites, or to rely on education and supervision. In 2000, 63 percent of teachers surveyed indicated they used some sort of filtering or blocking programs in their classrooms.[13] Proponents of the use of filters in libraries and in schools argue that the teacher or librarian can always override a filter if a child needs or wants access to a legitimate site, such as one dealing with breast cancer that a filter may block.

In April, 2001, the United States passed the Children's Internet Protection Act (CIPA), which required elementary schools, secondary schools, and libraries that receive Universal Service Discounts or funds available under the Library Services and Technology Act or Title III of the Elementary and Secondary Education Act to use blocking or filtering technology to prevent access to obscenity, child pornography, and visual depictions "harmful to minors." The local school board or library or other local authority is to decide what is inappropriate.[14] For the three years 1998–2000, 5,000 libraries received over $190 million from the named federal sources.

Several aspects of this law deserve mention. First, it mandates the blocking not only of obscene material for adults but also of material inappropriate for minors under the age of 17. Second, what is deemed inappropriate is left to the school board or other local authorities. Third, it does not mandate any specific tool to be used for blocking or filtering, but leaves this up to the local responsible parties. And fourth, it applies only to those schools and libraries that receive the designated federal funds. Its scope is much less broad than the Communications Decency Act.

Nonetheless the Act was challenged in court by the American Library Association (ALA) and the American Civil Liberties Union (ACLU). The ALA claimed that first, no filtering technology effectively protects children. Their use consequently gives a false sense of security. Second, decisions about what should and should not be made available to children and how that goal is to be accomplished are and should be made at the local level without the federal government mandating blocking technology. Third, the law restricts access to constitutionally protected information. And fourth, the law forces libraries – especially those in poorer and more geographically remote areas – to choose between needed funding and imposed censorship.

Neither the ALA nor other opponents of the CIPA are in favor of children accessing pornography. The issue is rather the use of federal legislation to censor material that is not otherwise illegal and to mandate the way that limiting access by children must be done. Whether a law can be drafted that both protects children from pornography on the Web and respects the right of adults to access legal pornographic material on the Web if they so choose remains to be seen.

The Internet is at the heart of the Information Age, and information is most useful when freely accessible to all. If this is so, then censorship of what appears should be held to the barest minimum compatible with the right of all to protections and security. While it goes too far to say that anything anyone wants to place on the Internet is acceptable, government interference has in some countries been clearly excessive in the realm of political speech, and any government interference runs the risk of overregulation. In an area such as obscenity, when the criterion for what constitutes it is local, national mandates about accessibility will tend to be towards the most stringent locales, rather than the most liberal. Nonetheless, that is not the end of the ethical aspect of the issue. Those who provide pornography (not obscenity) in most physical locations are restricted in various ways. The packaging should not be offensive to casual customers. Pornographic videos are usually kept in a controlled section of a video rental store, or stores carrying such material are restricted by zoning to certain sections of a city or town. Comparable restraints would be appropriate for pornography online. A site's home page should not contain any pornography, should clearly state that the site contains nudity and sexually explicit material, that some people may find the material offensive, and that the site is restricted to adults. Ideally, entry to such sites should be restricted to those who can prove they are adults. Adult verification systems presently exist, but minors can easily obtain verification. Nonetheless, this puts the burden on the minor, which means that there should be an education program, similar to the programs dealing with sex education, in which children are taught about the nature and dangers of pornography and how to avoid it.

Parents should take responsibility for installing the kind and level of filtering they think is appropriate and should supervise their children's use of the Internet. Just as some cities restrict pornography to certain areas, it is possible to set up a special domain for sites that carry sexually explicit material and to prohibit them form using .com or .net or .org or other domains that do not indicate the types of material they carry. Adult sites should also exercise restraint, and not use tactics to trick surfers to their home page unwittingly and unintentionally. To do so is deceptive and unethical. Search engines should discriminate between sites that are pornographic and carry explicit sexual material from sites that deal with issues of sex or toys or other terms and should clearly designate these or refuse to list pornographic sites under categories that are not clearly appropriate and that may mislead viewers. PICS (Platform for Internet Content Selection) is a rating system for the Internet sites comparable to "V-chip" technology used on individual TVs to filter programs containing designated levels of violence, pornography, or nudity, and might be developed to help limit unwanted access to pornography on-line.

There are a variety of ways that society has found to balance freedom of speech and pornography in the physical world and comparable approaches and ethical analyses can be fruitfully applied to pornography in cyberspace as well.

Child pornography

The third issue, child pornography, is less controversial than the other two. But it raises two problems: one of definition and the other of cross-border availability.

No one openly defends child pornography. The Supreme Court decisions defining obscenity identify child pornography as falling automatically within its scope, making it illegal and not subject to the three-part test specified for deciding on obscenity. The reasoning against child pornography is that it clearly exploits children, who are too young to give informed consent to the sexual acts that they are made to take part in. This violates their rights as well as causing them direct harm, making it so clearly and seriously unethical as to justify making it illegal.

Other arguments for its being illegal include the harm it causes the children who take part in it by exposing them to possibly thousands of viewers; that it degrades children in general; that it is connected with pedophiles who prey on children and circulate and trade a large number of the materials in question; and that it has no social value.

In the United States in 1999 the US Ninth Circuit Court of Appeals in San Francisco declared that the section of the Child Pornography Prevention Act of 1996 (CPPA) dealing with "virtual" child pornography was unconstitutional. The Act[15] defines child pornography as

> any visual depiction, including photograph, film, video, picture or computer or computer-generated image or picture, whether made or produced by electronic, mechanical, or other means, of sexually explicit conduct where (a) the production of such visual depiction involves the use of a minor engaged in sexually explicit conduct; (b) such visual depiction is, or appears to be, of a minor engaging in sexually explicit conduct; (c) such visual depiction has been created, adapted, or modified to appear that an identifiable minor is engaging in sexually explicit conduct; or (d) such visual depiction is advertised, promoted, presented, described, or distributed in such a manner that conveys the impression that the material is or contains a visual depiction of a minor engaging in sexually explicit conduct.

The Court held that including images that are computer generated or in other ways produced without using real children, the inclusion of adults who appear to be children, or depictions that convey the impression of a minor engaged in sexual conduct when no minor is actually involved, criminalizes material protected by the First Amendment and that the language is unconstitutionally vague and overly broad.[16]

The dissenting judge argued that the other two judges considered only harm to actual children who are subjects of child pornography as justifying banning it. The state, however, has other interests in attempting to eliminate child pornography and holds that there is serious harm produced to society by virtual images as well as by real images. Requiring that only photographs of actual children engaged in sexual activity be banned makes the task of law enforcement incredibly difficult, for it requires identifying the particular children to prove that they are not virtual images or the faces of one child superimposed on the body of another. This leaves a loophole in the law that child pornographers can, will, and do exploit. Moreover the dissent argued that Congressional history indicates that drawings and similar depictions are not included in the scope of the law. The decision, appealed to the Supreme Court, was affirmed.[17]

The situation gets even more complicated when we move beyond the boundaries of the United States. Most countries have some sort of law against child pornography. But the laws vary considerably. In the United States the law specifies anyone under 18 as included. In other countries the age is lower – 17 or 16. In some countries virtual child pornography is banned, in others it is not. In most the production and distribution of child pornography is illegal, but in some the possession of child pornography is not illegal. In some countries the Internet Service Provider (ISP) is held responsible for either preventing or eliminating child pornography reported to it on its sites, while in others the ISP is not held responsible. In most cases the law is similar whether or not the child pornography is on-line, but not in all. In some countries child nudity is considered pornographic while in others it is acceptable. Local standards differ dramatically in different cultures, and obviously more so than local standards within any given country.

In January, 2001, UNESCO convened an international Expert Meeting to deal with "Sexual Abuse of Children, Child Pornography and Paedophilia on the Internet." The aim was to devise approaches to eliminate the sexual abuse of children and of pedophilia on the Internet. Since child pornography rings and distributors operate worldwide, UNESCO correctly sees that law enforcement, crime detection, and extradition have to be developed on an international level of coordination and cooperation.

The need to control child pornography seems clear cut, yet the difficulty of doing so is an example of the legal issues raised by the global access available through the Internet. Whose laws apply to the Internet: the laws of the jurisdiction of the sender, or of the receiver, or of both? Different jurisdictions have different laws on freedom of speech and on control or absence of control concerning pornography.

Similarity of laws makes enforcement much easier. Whose laws should change should be decided in many cases by ethical arguments rather than by legal or business arguments alone. The lack of adequate international background institutions, such as law and law enforcement mechanisms, is blatant in this case, and points to the need for international standards and the coordination of police enforcement agencies, governments, non-governmental organizations, ISPs and others directly involved in the Internet, and the general public.

The Internet carries enormous promise and has great potential for the future development of business. But if this promise is to be realized, business must be careful not to ignore the ethical norms that apply in other areas of life and that apply here as well. The Internet is not the Wild West of nineteenth-century America, and to treat it as such will be to undermine its development.

▲ NOTES ▲

1. For definitions of technical terms used in computer technology, see the Webopedia (ww.webopedia.com).
2. For the history of the Internet see Michael Hauben, "History of APARNET" at http://www.dei.isep.ipp.pt/docs/arpa.html, and "History of the Internet" at http://www.securenet.net/members/shartley/history/arpanet.htm, among other histories available on-line.
3. The Anticybersquatting Consumer Prevention Act (Title III of PL 106–13) signed by President Clinton on November 29, 1999, which amended Section 43 of the Trademark Act of 1946 (15 USC 1125).
4. Matthew Hawn, "Easy Now to Keep Tabs on Users' Internet Postings," *New York Times*, January 6, 1997, p. C5.
5. Spam is used in several senses. Usually it refers to unwanted advertising, sent via e-mail or posted to a news group although irrelevant to the purpose of the group. See Elizabeth Gibbens, "Hey, Das Blinkenlights, Want to Get Spammed?" *New York Times*, June 2, 1997, p. C4; also http://spam.abuse.net/spam/whatisspam.html.
6. Roberta Furger, "Spam! How it Happens and How to Beat It," *PC World*, November 1999, pp. 147–54.
7. See "The Digital Millennium Copyright Act," at http:www.gseis.ucla.edu/iclp/dmcal.htm.
8. Edward Felton, a Princeton professor, withdrew a conference paper describing the weaknesses of an encryption system out of fear of violating the DMCA. See Lawrence Lessig, "Jail Time in the Digital Age," *New York Times*, July 30, 2001, p. A21.
9. The Online Copyright Infringement Liability Limitation. ALA Washington Office, "The Digital Millennium Copyright Act," at http://www.ala.org/washoff/osp.htm.
10. Decided June 25, 2001, *New York Times Co., Inc. v. Tasini*, 121 S.Ct. 2381, 533 US (2001). For text of the decision see http://a257.g.akamaitech.net/7/257/2422/28jun20011200/www.supremecourtus.gov/opinions/00pdf/00–201.pdf.

11. *Miller v. California*, 413 US 15 (1973).
12. Reported by National Coalition for the Protection of Children and Families, Current Statistics at http://www.nationalcoalition.org/stat.phtml?ID=53
13. National Coalition for the Protection of Children and Families, Current Statistics at http:www.nationalcoalition.org/stat.phtm?ID=53.
14. See American Library Association, "American Library Association files lawsuit challenging Children's Internet Protection Act," and Multnomah County Library Press Information Center, "Children's Internet Protection Act: Questions and Answers," at http://www.ala.org/cipa/coparpessrelease.html.
15. Chapter 110, 18 USC, section 2256.
16. See "Free Fakery: Ninth Circuit Declares Virtual Child Porn Ban Unconstitutional," About, Current Events: Law, http://law.about.com/library/weekly/aa122099a.htm
17. *Ashcroft v. The Free Speech Coalition* (No. 00–795), Apr. 16, 2002 [122 S.Ct. 1389].

chapter seven

Information Technology and Society: Business, the Digital Divide, and the Changing Nature of Work

▲ I LOVE YOU ▲

On May 3, 2000, a virus-worm called "I Love You" was unleashed across the world. It sent itself to everyone in the receiver's Microsoft Outlook address book, deleted or overwrote JPEG and MP3 files, and forced many systems to shut down. By May 4, computers in at least 20 countries had been infected. Worldwide, it caused over US$7 billion in software damage, time lost, and lost commerce. The virus-worm was not the first of its kind, but it was until then one of the most damaging.

On May 11, a week after it was launched, the virus was traced to Onel de Guzman, a student at the AMA Computer College outside of Manila. Since there was no Filipino law prohibiting such activity, de Guzman could not be prosecuted.[1] Were he to show up in other countries in which his action was illegal, he could be prosecuted. But since there was no Philippine law against what he did at the time, extradition to another legal jurisdiction was not possible.

While not illegal, was de Guzman's action unethical, and if so what can we learn from this case?

▲ THE INTERNATIONAL LEGAL ▲
COORDINATION PROBLEM

The case of the "I Love You" virus illustrates how an individual in one part of the world can dramatically influence large numbers of people around the globe, and it raises what I shall call the "international legal coordination" problem. This is the problem of coordinating national laws in such a way as to promote rather than impede the beneficial developments that are foreseeable in the global Information Age as far as global business is concerned. The problem itself, however, raises four related problems:

1 Why isn't ethics enough – why do we need law?
2 Whose law should be adopted or coordinated?
3 How can nations achieve the required coordination?
4 How can such legislation be enforced?

I shall use the "I Love You" case to discuss these four problems, and then extend the analysis by looking at three other cases.

The question of why ethics is not enough is a legitimate one, and the view that it is represents the position taken by many businesses and others. Those who argue for self-policing by business stress that if ethical standards are demanded by the public, out of self-interest business will establish and adhere to ethical standards. This is a version of the argument that the market is self-correcting, and that market forces will produce better results on the whole for society than legislation will, which often misfires and in the case of developing technology threatens to do more harm than good by overregulating a budding commercial resource.

There is no doubt that ethics is necessary, and that ethical people and ethical norms that cross borders are essential to the successful development of business in the Information Age. But there is ample precedent for the necessity of legislation as well. If we look back at the development of the Industrial Age, the worst offenses required legislation to change and mold business practices. Sweatshops, unhealthy working conditions, extremely long hours, child labor, environmental damage, to name the most obvious, were only ended through legislation. In most cases business interests argued against the legislation that finally prevailed. Self-regulation did not produce the needed changes, in part because there were always some who took advantage of the absence of law. The worst aspects of capitalist development were tamed by legislation. As we enter the Information Age, symbolized by the computer and the Internet, we do not have to go through a similar long period of Wild West development and exploitation allowed and protected by laws that serve vested interests instead of the good of all. We can and should learn from the past and one country can and should learn from others. The needed interplay of ethics and law in issues of globalization and information technology argues for national legislation and international legal coordination that prevent problems from emerging, rather than for an approach that simply reacts to harm after new deleterious practices have been adopted.

The "I Love You" virus shows the fragility of business and communications that rely more and more heavily on the Internet. A lone hacker in the Philippines caused billions of dollars of damage worldwide. We have already argued that trust is central to the Information Age and to the Internet, and trust is best achieved through ethical behavior on the part of all participants. But security against those who do not play by the rules is also essential. Hence the need for legislation.

The "I Love You" case is an easy one from an ethical point of view, since there is such widespread agreement that harming innocent computer users is seriously unethical and so is an action that should be make illegal. The problem in this case is not arguing that the action should be made illegal, but accomplishing it in a uniform and adequate manner on a global level.

Saying this, however, is easier than devising appropriate and properly balanced legislation. For those opposed to legislation are correct in their fears that legislation can impede the development of the Internet, of the Information Age, and of business in this Age. The legislation must be sufficient to capture uses of the Internet and of information technology that harm others without at the same time preventing the development of new and presently unforeseen possibilities. Clearly, launching viruses such as "I Love You" should be made illegal. Yet research on worms, viruses, and other innovative approaches to the Internet should not be outlawed. Harmful use should be distinguished from research and development, and laws should not be written so broadly as to inhibit such research and development.

The second issue is: whose law? The problem with the "I Love You" virus was that the Philippines had no law under which it could bring criminal charges against Onel de Guzman. The Philippines was not alone in this regard, and even in the United States no appropriate legislation appeared until 1986, when the Computer Fraud and Abuse Act was passed, by means of which it was possible to prosecute Robert Morris, who in 1988 unleashed the first Internet worm. In June, 2000, the Philippine President signed into law a bill covering electronic commerce and computer hacking. The great variety of different laws passed by different countries raises the possibility that what is legal in one country may not be prosecutable in another with different legislation. A uniform set of laws would be preferable to match the uniform access across borders that the Internet provides.

The question of whose law should be the standard cannot be answered in the abstract. But in the development of a standard, ethical considerations should have a prominent part, and business or vested-interest considerations should be considered along with the effect of different actions on the common good.

At this point someone might ask: but whose ethics or whose notion of justice? The reply is that although customs differ from society to society, basic ethical norms do not. No society could long exist that did not prohibit the arbitrary killing of its members by one another, or that did not have a notion of property and its proper protection. Worldwide there is a consensus on the importance and centrality of human rights. Most countries are signatories to the UN Declaration of Human Rights. Where there are differences in conceptions of justice, this usually stems from using different criteria in allotting benefits and burdens. The role of negotiation in international affairs and international business is to mediate such disputes. In a fair negotiation each party recognizes the other(s) as an equal; no party is forced to accept a solution that it feels is unjust; but all must be ready to relinquish some of what it thinks it deserves in order to arrive at a solution that all affected parties can accept as being preferable to the alternative of no interaction or deal. When applied to legal coordination, this means that nations apply their own accepted ethical norms but should consider the laws of other nations and the benefits that all derive from the coordination of laws.

How can appropriate international legal coordination be achieved? We have various models from which to choose in related areas. But in each case one can argue that ethics should play a larger role than is present in each of the models.

In 1994 the General Agreement on Tariffs and Trade (GATT),

which stipulates that contracting states should provide "most favored treatment" to other contracting states, added 21 agreements dealing with various aspects of trade. In 1995 GATT established the World Trade Organization (WTO) as a mechanism to settle disputes between member states. This is one model for international legal coordination, called harmonization. The aim is to promote and facilitate free trade among member nations for the benefit of all.

A second model is international treaties, such as those relating to human rights and to environmental protection. These have to be ratified by the contracting governments.

A third model simply has individual nations each pass their own laws, which they then mutually recognize as equivalent, insofar as they achieve substantially the same objectives.

There are three dangers in international legal coordination to be avoided. One is the temptation to agree to the least common denominator instead of maintaining at least minimal ethical standards; a second is to agree to a compromise middle position simply to get agreement; and the third is to arrive at either of these from the exclusive point of view of trade or vested interests without consideration of ethical norms.

On a large number of issues there is agreement among nations as to which practices are ethical and which are not. On these issues, agreement based on mutually recognized ethical principles and norms should be sought, and practices in a given country that violate such norms should be rejected in favor of practices that recognize and enforce them. In those cases on which ethical disagreements exist, compromise and negotiation may sound like a contradiction. But if any nation is to avoid imposing its ethical views on others, negotiation is ethical providing that as a result no country is forced to accept any condition that it believes is unethical. Negotiation thus involves each country, using its own ethical criteria, agreeing to a mutual practice that gives it less than it feels it is entitled to. Each freely giving this up in order to achieve more of what it wants is ethically acceptable.

Enforcement is the fourth problem. Although countries may agree to coordinate their laws, not all states enforce agreements or laws with equal vigilance. The WTO model allows one state to retaliate against another state that fails to abide by a WTO decision resolving a dispute. But retaliation is not a viable solution for many of the difficulties that arise from lack of legal coordination among nations with respect to the Internet.

Attempts are being made to develop appropriate legislation to control noxious worms and viruses through international conventions,[2] but as we have noted the task is not easy, in part because of the difficulty of defining a harmful worm or virus in such a way as not to prohibit beneficial uses of the same or similar programming techniques. This difficulty in fact makes clear the need for uniform legislation in all jurisdictions. For if the laws of one nation allow what those of other nations prohibit, the first nation becomes the location of choice from which to launch one's attack with impunity.

With respect to the "I Love You" case a problem is how to ensure that there are no safe havens from which one can launch noxious worms, viruses, and yet-to-be-devised ways of attacking computers and their contents. If there turn out to be some jurisdictions that refuse to pass or enforce appropriate legislation, then those countries should be considered Internet-rogue countries and treated accordingly. A principle of self-defense justifies blocking or denying to the extent possible all Internet access to and from the offending jurisdiction. Clearly, ethical exhortations are insufficient in such cases and official action is required. To some extent such action may be seen as violating freedom of speech or access. But these rights are not absolute and may be justly restricted by the right to prevent harm to oneself and others.

The fact that the Philippines attempted to prosecute de Guzman and moved quickly to fill the legal gap in its legislation indicates that there was no reluctance to do so. That many countries still do not have such legislation, however, poses a potential threat of possible attack from those jurisdictions. Enforcement, if it is to be effective, must be worldwide and consistent.

In addition to the "I Love You" case, the Internet and information technology have spawned a variety of other issues that raise the international coordination problem. Three such issues that we have already discussed to some extent are the control of pornography, especially child pornography on the Internet; the differences between American and European laws on information privacy; and the various notions of intellectual property, together with the correspondingly different terms of copyright and patent protection.

The need to control child pornography on the Internet is, like the "I Love You" case, clear cut from an ethical point of view, though complex from both a technological and legal perspective. Japan for a long time was the leading source of child pornography on the Internet,[3] with 70–80 percent of child pornography websites originating there. However, in May 1999 Japan passed legislation outlaw-ing child pornography (defined as 17 years old or younger). The action by Japan was significant. Yet there are other countries in which it is still not illegal. The international coordination problem stems from the fact that such child pornography websites are avail-able worldwide. Moreover, the applicable laws vary greatly from country to country. Although depicting small children engaging in sexual acts clearly constitutes child pornography, the age at which participants are considered adults varies. Child labor, for instance, is defined by the International Labor Organization as labor by those below the age of 14. In the United States and many other countries the age is higher. The situation is similar with respect to child pornography. Furthermore, in the United States and some other jurisdictions, it is illegal to possess child pornography, while in many places it is only illegal to sell or post such material. Even in countries that make it illegal to post such items on the Web, enforcement of a prohibition against accessing such sites is very difficult, if not imposs-ible, on any large scale. Some countries hold Internet service provid-ers and Web masters responsible for removing any child pornography appearing on sites they control. But the only way to adequately control the traffic in child pornography internationally is to stop it at its source. In 2001 19 countries, including Japan, Korea, Turkey, and Russia, staged coordinated raids on those who produce and distribute child pornography via the Internet.[4]

While the issue of child pornography seems clear cut, the issue of adult pornography on the Internet recapitulates on an international scale the difficulties of legal coordination and of jurisdiction that we saw on the national level in the United States. With the global access available through the Internet, whose laws apply to the Internet: the laws of the jurisdiction of the sender, of the receiver, or of both? Different jurisdictions have different laws on freedom of speech and on control or absence of control concerning adult pornography. As we have seen, the United States attempted to pass legislation (the Communications Decency Act) that would prevent access to such material by children, but it was declared unconstitutional. It was not that people supported children's access to pornography; rather, it was difficult to prevent such access without also preventing access by adults, which is held to violate their right to free speech.

In November, 2000, in an innovate ruling, a French court ordered US-based Yahoo to block anyone in France from an auction of Nazi memorabilia, citing a French anti-hate law. Rather than block Web users in France, Yahoo withdrew the Nazi memorabilia. But the issue of whether a country has the right to demand that an on-line provider in another country not make available certain products to those living in the first country is still debated. The onus should be on the country that wishes to block certain sites or that prohibits the import of certain products bought on the Internet. To allow any country to demand that providers in other countries limit access to the first country's inhabitants puts the burden on the provider. Nor is it clear, if the country threatens to impose a fine on the provider (France threatened Yahoo with a US$13,000-a-day fine), how it can collect it, if the provider has no assets in the country in question.

A European commission to study the matter of jurisdiction recommended that the laws in the country where the provider or website is located should apply. This seems to make the most sense. To require providers to consider every country that may access its site to determine what its laws are would be to hinder commerce and so harm consumers. The European Union is moving in the direction of the commission's recommendation. But that is only one group of nations. International legal coordination requires that all nations agree.

Similarity of laws makes enforcement much easier. The ethical argument for the greatest good comes out in favor of imposing the obligation on those who wish to restrict access to develop and utilize the technology necessary to prevent access by their users. It also comes out in favor of declaring the proper jurisdiction for legal action the jurisdiction in which the *provider* is located, rather than the one in which the user is located. Content, such as child pornography, that is widely agreed to be unethical should be addressed as we discussed above with respect to harmful viruses and worms. In deciding the appropriate laws for coordination, moral arguments rather than legal or business arguments alone should play an important role.

The second issue is the difference between the European and American approaches to the protection of personal information, especially on-line, which we noted in Chapter 2.

The 1998 European Union Directives require that companies must notify both employees and consumers about how information collected about them will be used:

- Companies can only use data for its intended purpose.
- Companies cannot transfer data on employees and consumers to countries with inadequate privacy protection laws.

- Consumers will have a right to access data collected about them.
- Consumers will have a right to have inaccurate data rectified.
- Consumers will have a right to know the origin of data about them (if this information is available).
- Consumers will have a right of recourse in the event of unlawful processing of data about them.
- Consumers will have a right to withhold permission to use their data (e.g., the right to opt out of direct marketing campaigns for free without providing a reason).
- Companies need the explicit permission of consumers to process sensitive information, including information on racial origin, political or religious beliefs, trade union membership, medical data, and sexual life.[5]

These provisions are not required by US law. There would be no international legal coordination problem if the European law applied only in European countries and US law applied only in the US. But what makes the European Union Directives noteworthy, apart from protecting personal information, is Article 25 which stipulates that personal data may only be transferred to a third country if that country "ensures an adequate level of protection," and that otherwise the member states "shall take measures necessary to prevent the transfer of data of the same type to the third country in question."[6]

The EU in effect makes its rules the mandatory ones for firms that wish to do business with it. As a result, data collected by US companies in Europe cannot legally be sent to the United States, just as data such as credit card information, collected by a European nation, cannot be sent to the United States, or Japan or China, or any other country without an adequate system of protection of personal information. Citibank, as a result, could join the German National Railway in the biggest credit card plan in Germany only after it instituted a series of safeguards comparable to those required by German law.[7] Some individual corporations such as American Express have made arrangements with European nations such that they can continue to do business in Europe, and do not transfer any records or data from their European subsidiaries to the American home corporation. United States negotiations with the European Union of behalf of American businesses in an attempt to find a general way to allow US corporations to do business in Europe without changing American law led to the development of what were called "safe harbor" conditions that a business could agree to that would allow it to do business in Europe. The provisions were in some ways comparable to the European restrictions, but in other ways weaker. The US government has been trying to convince EU officials that adequate privacy of personal information exists in the United States. But the US government's position represents the vested interests of business, not the interests of US consumers or the general public. So far the European Union has understandably failed to accept US assurances that the method of self-regulation by US business meets the requirements of protection mandated by the EU's Directives. The European community argues that human rights cannot be negotiated away, and that privacy is one such human right.

Should US law follow the European model in this case? Is the European argument that their law in fact protects the human right of privacy that is allowed to be flouted by US law correct? I have already argued that the answer to the question of what protection is appropriate for personal information does not hinge only on the right to privacy. The European Union properly named its Directive "On the Protection of Individuals With Regard to the Processing of Personal Data and on the Free Movement of Such Data".[8]

Based on the discussion in Chapter 2, the answer to the question of which country should change its laws – in this case, the US or the European Union – seems clear from an ethical point of view. Discussion of this issue has not been taken up by the general public. Yet it is in areas such as this that the ethical dimension should be brought to the fore and moral leadership and pressure exerted, rather than leaving the development of law up to representatives of business and advocates of their vested interests.

The third issue is the international coordination of intellectual property protection. Clearly, international trade in a great many areas from drugs to videotapes would be facilitated by internationally coordinated laws governing intellectual property, including copyright and patents. The World Intellectual Property Organization (WIPO), established in 1970, has been developing standards, but they are effective only if adopted by individual countries. And the division between developing and developed nations as to intellectual property rights continues. Even in developed countries the extension of copyright to life of the author plus 70 years and 95 years for works for hire is difficult to defend from an ethical point of view and the latest 20-year extension received little discussion in the United

States. Real negotiation between nations has only recently begun in an attempt to mediate between the positions of the developed and the developing nations with respect to drugs for AIDS and other diseases.

From our discussion of intellectual property in chapter 4 and what we have seen so far, we can arrive at certain conclusions about international legal coordination concerning intellectual property. Since there are different views about what is fair or just with respect to intellectual property rights, this is an obvious area for negotiation. The WIPO and the WTO have both been heavily criticized for working to the advantage of the developed countries and for lacking transparency in the process by which they arrive at their standards and decisions. To be ethically defensible, all those seriously affected should have a voice, their interests and views should be weighed fairly, and the process of arriving at standards and decisions should be clear to all.

While the argument for affordable life-saving drugs for poor countries carries a good deal of weight, a similar argument will not justify piracy of videotapes or computer programs. Ignoring intellectual property rights completely will in the long run be a poor policy for developing countries such as India, which is developing computer talent of its own by providing the benefits and incentives that recognition of intellectual property rights provides. Such talent can best be nurtured, become competitive in a world market, and look forward to developing its own software for world consumption if the incentives of intellectual property protection are recognized. Yet the current extremely long-term copyright protection afforded to software is not obviously necessary, nor does it make much sense, given the speed at which software develops. Arguably the whole area of intellectual property needs to be rethought, with competing claims considered, and different kinds of rights, different levels of protection, and different lengths of time given to different kinds of products. By lumping many diverse media under the copyright law it has been stretched well beyond the limits for which it was originally intended. The present one-size-fits-all approach of copyright and patent no longer matches the reality of intellectual property in the Information Age.

From these cases we can draw some generalizations about the international coordination problem. The first is that although national laws in many areas may legitimately differ and need not be coordinated, international commerce and the fruitful development of the Internet are facilitated and promoted by coordinating national laws. To the extent that international business is generally beneficial to all parties, coordination is a desirable aim. Second, where there are differences among the laws of different nations, such that one set promotes an ethically preferable alternative, coordination should take place by giving preference to that version. Third, since the deciding factor is ethical considerations, these should be explicitly raised in the various national and international fora, and should be seen as relevant. In this regard, public debate is essential, and a central concern for the common good should inform decisions about what the law should be. Finally, negotiation, with opposing sides being willing to take less than they feel they may deserve and demand, yet without being forced to accept what they feel is unjust, should be the aim.

▲ BUSINESS AND THE DIGITAL DIVIDE ▲

What has become known as the digital divide is the division of people into those that are computer literate and have access to the new technology of the Information Age, and those who are computer illiterate and/or do not have access. The divide does not necessarily take the form of the old divisions between rich and poor people within a country and between rich and poor countries, although it does overlap those divisions to some extent.

The divide is found within countries as well as between countries. In the United States computer literacy and access divides in some ways the older generation from the younger, and to some extent rich from poor. But neither divide is hard and fast. A larger proportion of younger Americans have great familiarity with computers and the Internet than older Americans, simply by virtue of the fact that the former have grown up with them while the latter have not. Families that can afford a computer often buy one for the children to learn on and for them to be able to access information on the Internet that will help them with their school work. Many grade schools and intermediate and high schools have computers available for their students, use them in class, or make them accessible. Libraries in many cities similarly make computers available for patrons and provide access to the Internet, e-mail, and other electronic services.

For many older people, computers appeared well after their school years, and early computers required mastering a good deal of code, posing a barrier to those who did not have a lot of time to spend learning the processes involved. Executives often never learned to type, since typing was done by secretaries, and executives had no need to know how to use a typewriter. With the advent of computers many shied away from them because of the keyboard, and because as executives they had others who could do the work required by computers. Even e-mail could be handled by one's assistant or secretary.

That divide is becoming somewhat less significant as computers and the use of the Internet have become easier and more intuitive. Even those who do not know how to type can get along quite well with traditional "hunt and peck" approaches to the keyboard. Many older people who use computers find that e-mail helps keep them in touch with family members and friends and the Internet gives them access not only to information but to on-line shopping.

The divide between rich and poor in the United States is also not as deep as one might expect because of the ready accessibility of computers in schools and public libraries.

The divide within the United States is replicated in other developed countries. The divide between the developed, and usually richer, countries and the less developed, and usually poorer countries, is much deeper. Within the less developed countries the divide between rich and poor is often very severe, with public accessibility and access to computers in schools very low. But there are a variety of indications that the prospects for reducing that divide in the future are good.

It has become almost a cliché to note that about half of the world's population has never used a telephone, much less a computer. Monthly access and telephone fees put Internet access out of the reach of the majority of people in African countries, if they have electricity to power the computer, which itself costs much more than most people in poor countries earn in a year. Although the Internet in theory could provide access to the world, and information to information-deprived people, little of this actually takes place. Governments of countries such as Saudi Arabia control all the Internet service providers, and in many countries all providers are state controlled. If only the elite have access to the Internet, and if independent access to other servers outside a country is available only through expensive long distance connections, the Internet poses little threat to repressive governments.

Given the various aspects of the digital divide, it can be argued that different portions of society have different ethical obligations. A liberal society has the obligation to see that the poor are not left behind digitally, by making access available in public schools and in public places, such as libraries, post offices, and government buildings where those without computers can get and send e-mail and access public as well as general and specialized information. But it is the obligations of businesses that we are most interested in here. What are they? Arguably they include the following, which may also be attractive to business as being good business practices.

A first task and obligation is to make computers and Internet use easy and intuitive, as the simple telephone is. With the advent of Windows and the use of icons to identify and initiate tasks, computers became easier and more intuitive than when a user had to master a host of commands that had to be entered. But as Windows has developed greater capabilities, it has tended to become more complex. Consider ordinary consumer appliances. They start with the push of a button and they end with a push of a button. All one needs to know to start a TV or a radio is how to push a button or turn a knob. Using either is easy and intuitive. The computer may start with the push of a button, but that is only the beginning of a complex set of actions required for any particular application. Consider also that to shut down a computer using Windows one must go the "Start" icon, which is counter-intuitive. Simply pushing the power button on a PC, as one would do with most machines, produces difficulty on attempted reentry. These are the simplest operations of a computer. Any actual use involves choosing and knowing how to manage the appropriate application. Surfing the Internet involves knowing how to access it and then knowing how to navigate it, which is easier and more intuitive than most applications, including word processing. But many of the screens provided by service providers are cluttered and not easy to decipher. Clearly, computer use is far from intuitive, and it is a pressing need of computer producers and engineers to make it as easy to use as possible. Only in this way can the computer divide be reduced.

Second, lack of literacy and in some countries the lack of knowledge of English are barriers to use. The computer is still tied to the written medium, with a keyboard as an integral part of it. While it may not seem much to require that those who use computers know how to read and write, and though some such requirement might help promote education in some societies, it does limit access. TVs, radios, and telephones are not so restricted. Moreover, literacy in which language and in which alphabet are also issues. Computers are multimedia and can and should be made less dependent on the written word. That barrier can and should be overcome to the extent possible by both speech activation and implementation of basic tasks and by the translation of content (keyboards, text, and voice) into native languages. Some progress along all these lines has been made, showing that these aims are not technologically impossible. Their possibility imposes the obligation on those able to bring it about to do so.

A third requirement for universal access to become a reality is the availability of computers at an affordable price. This might be achieved in a number of different ways. One is the production of dedicated machines at a very low price. The cost of computers has been constantly falling as their power has increased. But computers need not be universal machines for many users who need only rudimentary tasks performed. Dedicated machines that access the Internet and are as cheap as simple radios would overcome the cost barrier in poor countries and among poor users in any country. Another way of increasing access, which has been implemented to some extent in Brazil, is the recycling of used computers at little or no cost to those otherwise unable to afford them. Such computers are slower and have less memory than newer models, but are serviceable and adequate for basic use and for access to the Internet.

The fourth requirement is cheap access to the Internet via communication satellites requiring no infrastructure. Such access should be available from public places at no cost and might be provided by governments or by private businesses. But there is also room for imaginative free-enterprise initiatives that rely for their income not on user fees but on advertising, rather like network TV in the United States, or on private donations, as with support for Public Broadcasting TV and radio stations in the United States. Bangladesh can also serve as a model to emulate and adapt. The Grameen Bank is noted for making small loans to women in rural areas to buy cell phones and purchases access. They pay off their loans and earn a profit by making the phone available for cost plus a modest fee to anyone who wishes to use it. The "telephone lady" becomes the phone center of an entire village. Through her a village is in fact connected with the rest of the world. A similar system of providing loans for the purchase of a computer and Internet access could bring an entire village into the Information Age.

The obligation to develop easy, intuitive, and cheap access might in some cases be compared to the obligation of the pharmaceutical industry to develop orphan drugs, which are needed by many only in poor countries, but which are unprofitable to develop. In other words, the needs of those on the wrong side of the digital divide are of concern because, although not life threatening, being left behind will invariably adversely affect their quality of life. The obligation is shared by all those able to address the problem and the need.

The digital divide involves as well the separation of users and providers, and those who write software code and those who just use it. A comparable divide causes no problem in other areas and need not cause problems in the Information Age. Not everyone who uses a TV or a telephone needs to understand the internal operations of either, and the same is true of computers and computer programs. Yet the analogy is not completely accurate. Taking full advantage of the Internet, for instance, may involve having one's own Web page and contributing to discussion groups, posting messages or information, and so on. The amount of skill required to do these things has diminished, as programs have been devised to carry out these tasks. But some knowledge of how to use a variety of application programs is still required for many jobs and for full use of the computer.

The divide between producer and user, however, need not match that between rich and poor countries. The domination of the United States is lessening as programmers develop expertise in such countries as Russia and India, where even US companies are employing ever larger numbers of people. Just as manufacturing has tended to move to less developed countries, so has the manufacture and assembly of computers. For countries to compete in this area, however, education is necessary and those without universal basic education are being left behind.

Making information technology available cheaply and in readily accessible ways to countries that are just entering the Industrial Age, moreover, raises the ethical issue of undermining cultures, especially in less industrially developed countries. Although such action helps lessen the digital divide, some critics complain it undermines local cultures. What are the obligations of multinationals with respect to local cultures?

To the extent that a local culture does not violate ethical norms, multinationals are ethically required to respect it and to work with and not against it.[9] Although this requirement does not mean that multinationals must observe local cultural norms that are immoral, such as gender or race discrimination, it does mean, among other things, the use of appropriate technology. Concerning the claim that introducing computers and information technology into a culture unethically undermines that culture, two considerations must be borne in mind.

The first is that multinational corporations (MNCs) frequently find, rather than create, a market for those products that change the local culture. In China, for instance, millions of pirated copies of American movies, such as *The Grinch Who Stole Christmas*, are sold within a week of their opening in US movie houses. It is not the MNCs that create that demand or in this case that benefit from it. The introduction of TVs, cell phones, and the Internet into rural communities in poor countries will change those communities. This is all part of globalization. If the people of Moscow or Beijing like McDonald's and Coke, as they do, that is their choice. Nor is it all bad. The same is true of computers and information technology. MNCs are transferring knowledge and know-how as well as international standards. If they are sought by the host country and its people, MNCs cannot be ethically faulted for undermining the local culture.

Second, exactly what critics complain about when they charge multinationals with undermining local culture is often not clear. Multinationals should not be faulted if they indirectly help undermine a feudal society as it enters the stage of industrialization. There are better and worse ways of doing this, and the ethical obligation is to minimize the harm done to people. But to expect them not to impact local culture at all is to ask more than any company can legitimately be asked to do.

If an industrial society develops anywhere, it changes the agricultural culture from which it springs. It does not matter whether the system is capitalist or socialist, whether there is government control or free enterprise. An industrialized country is different from its agricultural antecedent. And the change produces a change in culture, broadly conceived.

Such cultural changes are part of development. The kind of technology that I have argued for in the poorest countries is technology that the people can afford, not the kind that exacerbates the division between the rich and the poor. In some ways that technology will help rather than undermine the culture, for it will make the broader culture available to all.

Like orphan drugs, however, once developed the question of who has the ethical responsibility to distribute it, remains. And here local governments and international organizations clearly have an important role to play. Not only is it the right thing to do, but it is also arguably the self-interested thing to do insofar as bringing all people into the Information Age arguably promotes the welfare of all, helps eliminate great disparities of access to information and development, and may help promote peace as countries and peoples no longer feel left out.

Although I have argued that the responsibility falls on those businesses able to develop the appropriate technologies, it falls as well on all those in the computing and information technology sector, especially those who are or aspire to be members of the computer and information technology profession. That profession is still in the process of development. Unlike doctors, lawyers, and some kinds of engineers, who have a professional code that includes ethical standards, there is as yet no identifiable computer or information technology profession, although there are many such professionals. As the profession develops, so will its responsibilities, including doing what it can to close the digital divide in ways that we have seen and in ways not yet imagined. Those in the center of development are the best placed to see what is possible and how to bring it about. The task is to keep vested interests and business interests from dominating to such an extent that the emphasis is entirely on what is profitable without concern for what is socially necessary and useful.

This responsibility may seem to go against what I have been calling the technological imperative, or the claim that whatever can be developed will be developed. But that imperative is fueled importantly by the profit motive, and the technology that will satisfy the needs of those on the wrong side of the digital divide may not be profitable to develop and market. The need to overcome that aspect of the technological imperative is as important as the need not to develop what may prove to be socially harmful.

▲ THE CHANGING NATURE OF WORK IN ▲ THE INFORMATION AGE

The computer has changed the workplace in some subtle and some not-so-subtle ways. The job of secretary has clearly changed, as computers have replaced typewriters, and secretaries no longer need shorthand or know how to operate dictating machines, but have to know word processing, database and spreadsheet programs, as well as a variety of other applications from e-mail to the employing firm's various on-line forms, regulations, and databases. The knowledge and skills required have changed, although they are still within the capabilities of someone with a high school education. These changes parallel the now ever-present computer in every office or on every desk, as even executives communicate by e-mail, and often directly enter or retrieve information that they previously relied on others to search out and provide. The ethical issues introduced by computers and information technology range from the responsibility for preventing carpal tunnel syndrome caused by continuous and repetitive data entry on a computer, to large issues such as the relocation of industries. We shall look at four sets of concerns raised by flex-time, teleworking, globalization, and expert systems.

Flex-time

The move from an agricultural society to an industrial society brought with it the new virtue of punctuality. The Industrial Age with its paradigm of the assembly line made each successive position in the line dependent on the successful completion of tasks in the previous positions in the line. Interdependence of this sort required that each person be present to do his or her task or the production line would be shut down. Workers dependent on each other in this way led to the regimentation of time, with people working in shifts of set hours.

Computerization, robotics, and the service economy characteristic of the Information Age have undermined the assembly line model. Although workers are still joined in their projects and activities, they are not serially related as before. They are neither physically nor temporally tied to one another as they were previously, since they are linked by their computers and the information systems and databases to which they contribute and from which they receive the information they need. Physical presence and proximity are no longer mandatory for many aspects of work. This leads to the need for different virtues and for different skills. The situation raises other ethical issues than those raised by the factory or workhouse and the dangers associated with machines. The tedium of repetitive work on the assembly line is now changed into the tedium of entering endless sets of data on a computer. The dangers of the assembly line are replaced by the danger of carpal tunnel syndrome, the pains that come from sitting in ergonomically incorrect chairs for hours on end, and the stress of entering data accurately at what often seems like ever increasing demands for speed.

The description so far raises the possibility of flex-time, of working at home, and of the possible end of tedious and repetitive work.

Flex-time results from the fact that without an assembly line it is no longer necessary for everyone to be in the same building at the same time, say from 8:00 a.m. to 5:00 p.m., or indeed any other set hours. Executives and other white collar workers have certain tasks that have to be done by certain times, but whether they are done from 7:00 a.m. to 4:00 p.m., or 8:00 a.m. to 5:00 p.m., or 9:00 a.m. to 6:00 p.m., or in the evening, often makes little difference. Central times of the day remain the hours during which people expect to be able to contact others in their own firms and in other firms. But even in these circumstances, e-mail, voice-mail, pagers, and mobile phones do not require that one be at one's desk to carry on business.

The introduction of flexible time schedules, or flex-time, makes it possible for some people to avoid the rush hours in their commutes to and from work; it enables mothers and fathers to see their children off to school in the morning or to be at home when the children arrive from school. It can make life easier for workers – easier than the regime demanded by the working hours of the Industrial Age. Not all firms have noticed that the regimentation of hours is no longer required. But many have, and it is certainly an advantage that many workers appreciate. Since this is so, at least considering it as a possibility and making some attempt to implement it as an option seems little to ask from employers.

Teleworking

The related possibility of working from home or teleworking is similarly something that many workers choose when it is available and is something that firms should consider. The International Telework Association and Council reported that there were 28 million teleworkers (21.2 percent of the adult workforce over 18 years of age) in the United States in 2001.[10] Teleworking has both its pros and its cons. On the one hand, people work from home, using their computers both to do their assigned jobs and to keep in touch with the other members of the firm, whether they too are at home or in the office. Obviously, to work at home one needs the discipline to set and keep one's regular hours, whatever they may be, to put in those hours in work without the distractions of taking care of children, preparing meals, or attending to household chores. Direct, physical supervision by one's boss is gone, as are both the support and camaraderie of one's workmates. There is no opportunity for office gossip around the water cooler or coffee machine. One works in isolation from fellow workers except for the contents of the computer screen in front of one. The need for trustworthy employees who put in the time for which they are paid is essential. Supervision moves from physical contact to evaluation of quantity and quality of work produced and submitted by computer, or to sales made, or to whatever other criterion of productivity is appropriate. Meetings, when they are necessary, are conducted sometimes face to face in a physical setting, but often they are conducted via conference telephone calls, or via Internet connections, or on the Internet in real-time interactions.

One can work in whatever clothes one pleases if one works in one's own home. Appearance is not an issue. However, as the US Occupational Safety and Health Administration (OSHA) at one point noted, safety is. What liability, if any, does a company have for a worker injured at home while working for the company? Since the company cannot control the possible hazards existent in workers' homes, should they be liable for accidents? OSHA's attempt to impose work-safe conditions on those who work from home met with such opposition that it had to desist.[11] But the issue of safety and liability remains unresolved.

If employees work at home, do they need space in the company's facilities? Many work partially at home and partially in the office. This means that they need their desk or space or computer when they are in the office but not when they are working from home. The question of how much space goes unused for how long is a cost consideration. On the other hand, those who work from home are not usually reimbursed for the space they use there or for the wear and tear on their own furniture, even though in some cases they can claim a tax deduction for a home office.

Those who work from home often feel the lack of social contact that the office provides. They are physically and psychologically isolated from their colleagues, have no opportunity for small talk, or office gossip, or even for informally discussing work and what is going on in one's company and in one's industry. The absence of physical contact takes a toll on some, while others adjust easily. But the sense of being part of a firm cannot help but be somewhat diminished.

A short step from teleworking is to move to outsourcing, whether using contract employees, consultants, or temporary help. If people do not have to be physically in an office and can do their work and communicate via computers and other electronic means, why does a firm have to have such employees at all? If they perform a specific set of tasks, why not hire them to do those tasks as independent contractors, consultants, or temporary employees rather than as full-time employees? By contracting work a firm can hire someone without paying them fringe benefits – health insurance, vacation time, 401(k), or other pension-type contributions, and so on. To make up for this the company has to hire out the work at a higher rate than workers would normally receive as employees, but it avoids overhead costs, fringe benefit costs, and makes no commitment to keep the people on for any length of time, meaning they can be fired – or rather, not rehired – without paying severance or other benefits.

Some contract workers find their work opportunities through advertising or through networking, sometimes through contracting with their former employer to perform tasks that the company needs done but doesn't want to hire a full-time employee to do. Some contractors and temporary workers are employed by agencies that handle all the paperwork for both the contacting company and the worker, and collect a fee for so doing. The agency locates the work and negotiates rates both with the contracting company and the person doing the work. Independent contractors usually offer some specialized skill that the hiring company needs and does not have in-house. The same is true of consultants, who are paid for their advice or some specific service.

The net result as these types of arrangements increase is that work is no longer defined in terms of having a job with a firm for varying periods of time, sometimes for all of one's working life. The bond between employer and employee is ruptured, and with it trust and commitment. Independent agencies replace dependence on an employer. One chooses when to work and from where, and negotiates for one's compensation, depending on how much in demand one's talents are. The security of a permanent position is traded for the freedom to work as one wishes. Although the result is one that some embrace, it is one that others dread. For them, the lack of security, the uncertainty of not knowing whether one will get an assignment, and the need for a steady income outweigh the supposed benefits.

The ethical issues concern conditions of employment. These are different for teleworkers employed full-time by a firm and those hired as contractors or consultants. The former have good grounds for expecting and receiving remuneration and access to working conditions comparable to those who work full-time in-house, even though to some extent they provide their own working conditions. The conditions of those who are not full-time employees, and whose number is growing, raise other ethical issues that are only slowly emerging.

A by-product of such changing work is that office space will no longer be required for those who telework. Nor will companies have to be located in large cities or in the center of certain districts. Whether this will lead to the end of the inner business districts of cities as we have come to know them remains to be seem. After the September 11, 2001 destruction of the World Trade Center in New York, many companies decided to leave the New York financial district and relocated in suburban cities and in other states. That tragedy served as an impetus for doing what changing working conditions already had made possible for some time. The issue of plant closings has led to the recognition that when a company closes a plant it has the ethical – and often the legal – obligation to give adequate warning to workers and the community, and to provide certain benefits to both. Whether the same is true of the closing of large offices is not yet clear, but deserves some moral consideration.

The Information Age has seen more people becoming self-employed and contracting their work. Even those who remain in traditional jobs are often asked to justify their positions in the light of what they contribute to the company's bottom line. Companies no longer have the tradition, even informally, of anything approaching life-time employment. Companies now consider downsizing part of the operation of an efficient company. With the absence of commitment of a company to its employees, employees have responded with a similar lack of commitment to the company. Employment advisers counsel employees that they can no longer count on companies to chart their futures and the promotion sequence as they once did. Each employee is now seen as in charge of charting his or her own future, both within a company and as on the lookout for other opportunities elsewhere.

The nature of white collar and service work has begun to change importantly and perceptibly in the Information Age. In addition to trustworthiness, independence and a certain amount of self-sufficiency are becoming important virtues that society should attempt to inculcate in students and those entering the workforce. Traditional jobs are disappearing and new ones with different expectations and different ways of operating are developing. Affordable healthcare and retirement in addition to Social Security become issues that both business and society must face. If employers no longer provide health and accident insurance, it must be possible for workers to obtain this at affordable cost through some other means.

The issue of tedium is one that can be eliminated in the Information Age, even though thus far sometimes the tedium of the assembly line has been replaced by the tedium of data processing. Computers and robots have the capability of doing the routine work, both on the assembly line and with respect to data input. Repetitive tasks are the easiest for robots and computers to handle. Yet heavy reliance on robots and computers, although it frees people from the tedium of those tasks, also often displaces the people who performed those jobs. The tasks that are left require either more initiative, imagination, expertise, or knowledge (and so typically, more education), or less of all of these, such as the menial physical jobs of scrubbing floors, emptying wastepaper baskets, washing windows, collecting garbage, and so on. The divide between the menial and the information oriented thus may grow rather than diminish, as the intermediate, low-skill, routine jobs are taken over by robots and computers. This is a problem that comes about as a result of the changing nature of work. But it is not one for which business can be blamed. Rather, it raises a social problem of keeping the gap between the groups performing each kind of task from becoming too large so as to cause social unrest, and of helping those in the undergroup to have adequate remuneration to support themselves in dignity and to preserve their self-respect.

Globalization

Globalization in its current predominant meaning is a fairly recent development. The term is used in a variety of different ways to cover different phenomena. The aspect that concerns us here is that made possible by the globalization of communications, especially the Internet, which makes it almost as easy to communicate with a fellow employee on another continent as with one a room away in one's own building. This ease of communication across borders greatly facilitates transnational crossings and allows multinational corporations not only to operate in many countries, but functionally to divide their activities among different countries, producing one part of a product here, another part there, assembling them elsewhere and marketing them throughout the world, while coordinating all the operations from a home base.

The possibility of coordinating the far-flung and disparate activities of a company through the Internet and related communication technologies has had an impact on both less developed and developed countries.

In the Industrial Age jobs attracted people to factories and cities and fostered immigration to countries where the new kind of work was available. Many unemployed in Europe, for instance, migrated to the United States. As a result labor became scarcer in Europe and wages increased, while wages in the United States decreased.[12] In the Information Age, instead of people moving, jobs are moving. Since work is no longer tied to a physical location and can be done anywhere, multinational corporations can hire workers anywhere in the world. In some case, such as India, we have already seen that computer programmers and specialists are hired by US multinationals, both to write code and to serve as customer-service technical people, handling telephone calls and working at hours that correspond to those of users in the United States. Much production has been moved from the United States – which is now predominantly a service economy – to less developed countries. This includes not only textiles and automotive production, but also the production of computer components and other information technology tools and their assemblage.

Since teleworking does not require one to be on-site, not only can workers work from home, but home can be in any part of the world. One result is that some independent contractors, such as programmers, find themselves in competition with their peers in less developed countries, where the needed wages to live reasonably well are much lower than in the United States. While this is a benefit for the worker from the less developed country it is a liability for the US worker. An anticipated result will likely be that the worker from abroad gets somewhat more than he or she would from a local company, while the US worker will be expected to work for somewhat less. From a global perspective this seems fair. From the perspective of the US worker it often appears unfair, since they are worse off as a result of the developing system. As yet unemployment in the United States has been kept within single digits and the negative impact has been offset by new job creation in the developing information industry. Nonetheless, the social system needs to be changed to provide a safety net of healthcare or insurance and supplemental aid for those who do not make enough to live at a decent level, lest the conditions of work revert to a previous period of gross worker exploitation. Nor does unionization seem to be a solution in the present circumstances, because the teleworkforce covers so many different skills, is so widespread geographically, and involves competing against peers who gain by the arrangement.

As in other areas affected by computers and information technology, we are still in the early stages of the changing nature of work. Yet, as a society, the public as well as business should be alert to the changes and should consider their moral implications.

Expert systems

Even the realm of the expert is being affected by the computer and the Information Age. Expert systems are programs devised to mimic the intuitions and expertise of those most skilled in their professions in such a way that their knowledge can be used by others. A typical example is a doctor who is especially good at diagnosing cancer in his patients. He is usually a cancer specialist, and known among his peers as standing out from the others in the accuracy of his diagnoses. How does he do it? He is usually not aware himself of how he does it. So the job of a programmer or knowledge engineer who will develop an expert system in cancer diagnosis is to follow the expert around for several months. As the doctor makes his diagnosis it is the job of the programmer or an assistant to ask the doctor why he made that diagnosis: what did he observe, why is that important, what did he guess, how did he follow up his observations and guesses in this case? What did he ask, and what did the reply lead him to suspect? How did he further narrow down possibilities? After forced analysis of his thought processes, the questions he asks, what questions the answers lead to, and so on, the programmer's task is to beak down the expert's diagnostic technique into sequential steps. Usually this results in a tree-like structure, where certain observations lead down certain paths, and certain answers lead further along a multi-layered sequence leading to a final diagnosis. The system thus constructed is then tested to see if it reaches the same results as the expert in new cases. If it doesn't, it is refined until it does.

Once the program is developed, then other doctors, non-specialists, as well as less skilled specialists, who think that their patient might have cancer, or who do not know how to diagnose the symptoms of the patient, can follow the program step by step to perform the diagnosis, make the observations, ask the appropriate sequence of questions as prescribed by each successive answer to arrive at a conclusion similar to the one the expert would. The use of expert systems has proven remarkably effective. When a specialist is not available, the programs allow general practitioners to diagnose diseases with much greater accuracy than before the introduction of expert systems. This is especially true in the early diagnosis of less common diseases or symptoms with which the attending physician may be unfamiliar.

No expert system is perfect, nor do they claim to be. There are many ways for the system to fail. An expert will recognize certain circumstantial features which make the given case different from others, but which did not arise during the period in which the program was developed. The designer or writer of the program may have missed something in developing the program, or perhaps neither the expert nor the programmer thought to ask or record some pertinent observation or inference. The possibility of misunderstanding, of failure to model all circumstances and possibilities, of the expert's being unable to articulate what he does of which he is not aware, and so on, all mean that complete reliance should not be placed on any expert program.

Nonetheless, suppose that an expert system allows a general practitioner to diagnose a disease with 80 percent accuracy, while without the system the accuracy would fall to 50–60 percent. Surely the doctor has an obligation to use the techniques most likely to help the patient, even though the program does not yield correct results in all cases.

The obligation of those producing the expert systems is to make them as complete and accurate as possible, not to exaggerate what the system is capable of, and to keep it up to date as expert knowledge increases. The obligation of those using the system is not to suspend their own judgment by relying completely on the system. It is, after all, a system, and must be used appropriately, in the appropriate cases and to the appropriate extent. The attending physician still is responsible for the care or lack of care that he gives his patient, and that responsibility cannot be passed onto the expert system or its creators, except to the extent that they are culpably mistaken or deceptive.

The key point of expert systems, however, is in the generalization of their nature and their use. Their widespread use changes the nature of the work of those who use them, as well as of those who produce them. Any field in which there is expertise is amenable to expert programs. Why make do with the simple talents of the ordinary practitioner in any field, when that talent can be enhanced by the use of expert programs? There seems to be no reason not to adopt such programs wholesale.

As we generalize and extend the use of expert systems, robots, and computers to all areas of business and work, what is being challenged is the ordinary view of the nature of work. Is work a series of tasks to be performed, or is it more than and different from simply the tasks required to produce products and earn a living? Consider the possibility of all production being done by computers operating machines and by robots. Some people would have to supervise the computers and machines, and perhaps make and program them, if these functions could not also be taken over by computers and robots. What would people do? Is the ideal to have all work done by computer so that everyone has the luxury of leisure to be spent doing whatever one wants or doing nothing at all?

The acquisition of more and more leisure time free from the demands of work is sometimes presented as an ideal towards which to strive. It is an ideal based on a view of work as forced labor, unsatisfying in itself, unfulfilling and degrading drudgery. Some work is of this type and should be eliminated to the extent possible. But there is another view of work which sees it not as forced labor or perhaps punishment for sin, but as a means of self-expression and development. If computers and robots can indeed take over most of the tasks of physical labor and even some aspects of intellectual labor, the ideal on this view would be to find self-fulfillment in one's meaningful activities.

If human beings are naturally active and not passive, then they are not fulfilled by simply being entertained or relaxing or doing nothing. They find meaning in their activity. And some of what is considered work today consists of creative activity of a variety of sorts. People do not only work for money, although they need a certain amount to live as they wish. But many who are wealthy enjoy the work they do, even though they do not need to do any. And many who are forced to work to live, also enjoy what they do. The tragedy is that so many do not. The Information Age opens up the possibility of transforming work so that it is meaningful and fulfilling. The ideal of unending leisure is a false one. The emerging challenge is to develop a new approach to work and to rethink its proper place in human life.

Moreover, the implications of the changing nature of work cut deeper than rethinking the place of work in life. Expertise is not limited to the fields of medicine, the professions, the trades, and productive labor. Consider the tasks performed by ordinary citizens. Serving on a jury is one. Are there expert jurors – ones who are knowledgeable, attentive, intelligent, impartial, and have all the other qualities citizens typically believe jurors should have? If so, then should juries use expert systems? At the extreme, if possible, should cases be decided by expert systems, should judges be replaced by expert systems, and should cases be tried by expert systems? We do not have systems capable yet of doing these things. But we do have what can be considered experts in each area. Would we want to require juries, judges, and lawyers to make use of expert systems in their areas? Jurors might make better decisions if they had a program to guide their thinking. Judges' decisions and sentences would be more uniform if informed by expert systems. And lawyers might serve their clients better if helped by expert systems. Yet deciding cases by computer, or even requiring – perhaps even allowing – decisions to be made with the help of computers involves a completely different set of assumptions about the legal system and the judgment of peers than we presently have.

At the extreme, we might have expert ethics programs in which those expert in the ethical analysis of cases have their thought processes programmed so that they can help lead ordinary people through the intricacies of moral reasoning. The assumption, of course, is that there is expertise in moral reasoning, and that those who have it are identifiable. Such might be true of people of outstanding virtue, such as Mother Teresa, or noted moral theologians, or noted professors of philosophical ethics. Of course, whoever decided to use such systems would remain responsible for his or her actions, and following the guidance of an expert system would not provide an excuse from blame for any wrongdoing on one's part. Nonetheless, if we wish to be moral, should we try to get the best guidance available?

These questions challenge our ordinary view of moral reasoning and responsibility. The next step on this chain of reasoning is to see that computers and the Information Age are raising in a new and pressing form the meaning not only of work but of what it is to be human.

▲ THE MEANING OF BEING HUMAN ▲

Norbert Weiner, in a ground-breaking book in 1954, raised the question of computers and what he called "the human use of human beings."[13] His thesis, which remains valid today, was that computers and information technology should be used not to enslave or dominate human beings but to free them to be able to act as human beings, and in ways commensurable with their dignity.

Joseph Weizenbaum raised a similar argument in 1976,[14] when he warned against the dangers both of considering human beings only as machines – computers, with less ability than could be developed in machines – and of failing to control technology so that rather than serve human interests it dominated or dictated those interests.

He pointed out indirect consequences of computers and one aspect of the changing view of human beings. The Copernican revolution jolted humans, as they no longer saw themselves as the center of the universe. Darwin shook their self-image by showing they descended from apes. Freud undercut their responsibility by showing how much people were influenced by forces beyond their control – early upbringing, unconscious and subconscious forces. The computer is having a similar impact as people: after having modeled the computer on man, many now model man on the computer. Man is an intelligent animal or an animal with reason. If reason is his highest attribute, and if computers can be built that are even more intelligent than humans, so much the worse for humans.

The tragedy is one of alienation, using Feuerbach and Marx's analysis. Humans make computers, and become alienated from them if they let the computers take over, and let them dominate them. They do so to the extent that they let computers make decisions for them and limit what they attempt to do to what the computer can do. This limits science to what can be studied by computer techniques. We saw some of this in the difference between the development of theory in physics in the Soviet Union and in the United States during the Cold War period. The Soviet scientists, having much less access to computers, developed theory to a greater extent than did American physicists.

Humans must keep control and decide what to do or not do. The argument of the technological imperative is that if it can be done, it will be done. Better we do it rather than someone else. That imperative says there are no limits to be set on what we do with computers. But there should be. We cannot turn ethics over to computers or have them decide or dictate what is proper for human beings.

The changing nature of work forces us to ask about the nature of human beings, the kinds of activities worthy of them, and the relation of human beings and computers or computerized robots. Science fiction presents us with various scenarios. In most of them either we see human beings only insofar as they guide space ships and pursue adventures, with little attention to what the masses do; or we see societies divided between the poor, uneducated masses left to eke out a living as best they can, on the one hand, and the information-wise, computer-competent leaders or masters, on the other; or we see a society in which a few control the information and technology of the new world and use it to dominate the masses. We are at present faced with none of these. But we are faced with having to make choices about work and how we structure it, about the proper use of information and technology, about the possibility of using information technology to spread development and democracy, and about the hard questions of those uses of information and information technology that we as a human race should not pursue and that we as individuals, governments, or groups should prevent others from pursuing.

Computers and information technology have been touted as a boon for direct democracy, with voters voting directly on proposed bills and public policy without the need for legislators as intermediaries. That model is oversimplified and unlikely to work in any of the proposed versions. Ordinary voters cannot be expected to have informed opinions on all the issues of government at every level or to have the time to study carefully and vote on myriads of proposals. Representative democracy seems to have a firm place in democratically run societies, even if occasional plebiscites and other instances of direct participation may be useful and preferable to existing alternatives.

Computers and information technology can be used in non-democratic ways to spread propaganda and control information as

well as disperse it. In countries where the government controls all
the Internet service providers, it effectively controls what the population has access to, much as it does when it controls the newspapers,
TV and radio programming, and other media outlets.

The sense of what it is to be human, of the importance of freedom
and responsibility that we find in many conceptions of what the best
in humanity offers, must be kept in mind as information technology
develops and is applied further.

▲ THE WEB AND THE INTERNATIONAL ▲ LACK OF ADEQUATE BACKGROUND INSTITUTIONS

The need for adequate background institutions goes well beyond the
issue of international legal coordination. Productive free-market
economies have for the most part developed together with democracy. This is no coincidence. For both markets and democracy
process information better and more efficiently than can or does any
centralized command economy or any other type of controlled
economy or any type of authoritarian government.

In Britain, Germany, the United States, and other developed
countries we have seen that legislation was necessary to end child
labor, to eliminate sweatshops, to introduce a minimum wage, to
improve working conditions, to protect the environment, to guarantee consumers their rights, and so on. Vested interests of course
remain, and big business has a great deal of influence on the form of
legislation. But in each of the cited instances legislation was passed
over the opposition of business interests. This was only possible
because of the existence of democratic governments that were and
are at least to some extent responsive to the people.

Central to responsive democracy are an opposition party and the
plethora of groups that make up civil society: trade unions, environmental and consumer groups, a free press and media with investigative reporters, and government representatives who are held
accountable by the people in regular elections.

We have seen in South Korea, Japan, and other countries – both
democratic and authoritarian – how the people forced leaders from
power when their large-scale corruption became public. We have
seen the power of the people in overthrowing the socialist regimes of
Eastern Europe and the USSR. Although authoritarian regimes can

institute development and bring countries to a certain level of productivity, they typically – as is evident in the case of the USSR – can go only so far.[15]

To unleash the potential of the Information Age requires the freedom to experiment and take risks and to try new approaches that are not allowed under strict authoritarian control. To some extent China is allowing a limited free market in certain areas, while keeping political power in the hands of the leadership. Whether it will be able to sustain the uneasy relation between free markets and lack of political freedom in the form of democracy still remains to be seen. History tends to indicate that the two do not fit well together, although usually a strong government, such as those in China and Singapore, can foster business better than a weak one, such as those in Russia or in many of the African nations. Moreover, authoritarian governments tend to support corruption at the top more than do democratic governments that are responsive to the people.

Authoritarian regimes in less developed countries typically serve the elite and the leaders of the country. They do not have to consider the benefit of the general population, and frequently do not. They have little incentive to do so, and are not accountable to the people. Tradition supports acquiescence on the part of people, and the absence of a free press keeps dissent from becoming organized.

By contrast, free markets and democracy have tended to develop together.[16] Free markets, among other things, establish many sources of economic power, which seek a voice in the government and a hand in running the country. If the market is truly free and not kept under the control of a small number of families or oligarches, it allows entry and new entrepreneurs. India in recent years provides an example of the rise of computer-based software and programming industries that presage a wave of the future. Modern technology, the Internet, cell phones, have all made it possible for people anywhere not only to become informed about what is happening elsewhere, but also to enter areas that do not require large plants and capital investments to begin and in which to compete. Multinationals and globalization can help spread democracy as well as free markets to the benefit of the people of developing countries.

Ultimately, however, the people must change their country. Freedom cannot be given to people or brought to them. They must seize it. Responsive governments cannot be dictated from without or imposed on countries. They must be formed from within. Changing conditions of labor will not result only from outsiders making changes but require that the conditions be changed internally – usually by their being demanded by the people and brought about by a responsive democratic government.

Nonetheless, multinational corporations and the governments of developed countries can and should be held morally accountable for their actions. They have a positive role to play, as do NGOs and the governments of developed countries. Developing countries are not condemned to repeat the long process of the development of capitalism. They can and should learn from the history of the development of capitalism in the West that laws and democratic processes, specifically political freedom, are necessary for free markets. The transfer of information and know-how can shorten their birth pangs, and in this regard multinational corporations can and to some extent are playing an important role.

Just background institutions are also needed if human society is to advance on all levels. We have already discussed the need for international legal coordination and the importance of international organizations such as the WTO and GATT. The issue of what global regulation of the Internet, the Web and its uses is appropriate and needed has still to be discussed. But just as appropriate background institutions – including appropriate laws – were necessary to tame industrial capitalism's negative tendencies, so appropriate background institutions will be required to tame the Internet and information technology's negative tendencies.

▲ CONCLUSION ▲

During the course of this book we have repeatedly seen the central role of professionals in the development and implementation of information technology, and the concomitant responsibility that goes with this central role. Are there uses to which computers should not be put? We have only touched on a few involving expert systems. Any application or use that will degrade or enslave or harm human beings should not be developed. The unanswered question is whether those in the industry are willing to take on the responsibility to police their peers.

A difficulty that information technology poses from a social point of view, and one that we have seen illustrated in a variety of ways throughout the previous chapters, is that so much takes place behind the scenes and out of sight of ordinary users. This invisibility is clear in the case of who is tracking and gathering information surreptitiously on Web users without their knowledge. It is also clear in the cases of computer chips carrying identifiers and hardware containing programs that operate in the background without the users' knowledge.

Invisibility is a relative term, however. What is invisible to the ordinary user is often clearly visible to those who have access to the design of computer chips or to the source code for programs and applications. In these cases society becomes dependent on the professionals for information about what is happening and for what is possible. It is too much to expect that those in the information technology area decide what is good and what is not good for society. But it is not too much to expect those in the area to inform the general public of developments that affect the public's interests, so that unethical activities can be uncovered or prevented or outlawed, and so that ethical dimensions of information technology can be intelligently discussed.

This book started with the Myth of Amoral Computing and Information Technology. That theme has been a constant one, and successive chapters have argued that there are ethical dimensions to these that have been largely ignored and should be brought to the light of informed public discussion. The danger of pursuing the technological imperative uncritically is one that follows from the myth, and hopefully can be avoided or mitigated by discussion. The need for continuing discussion by society at large is a third theme, and in this regard the role of those in the information industry is essential, as we have seen. This book has been an attempt to bring some of the issues into the public forum. The fourth theme has been that we as a society, as computer and information technology users and developers, should not simply accept the technological status quo as unchangeable. At the heart of any discussion of ethical issues in business and technology should be the conviction that business and technology are to serve human beings, not the other way round. What is good for business in the area of computing and information technology, as in all other areas, is not necessarily what is best for human beings. Society has not yet reached a point of no return where technology and business cannot be controlled. The task of those interested in ethics in business and in the business of information technology is to ensure that new developments and innovative practices benefit rather than harm human beings – both individually and society in general.

▲ NOTES ▲

1. Kim Zetter, "Viruses: The Next Generation," *PC World*, December 2000, p. 202, details the sequence of events from May 3, 2000 to August 21, when charges were dropped. See also ZD Net News (Reuters, June 14, 2000) at http://www.zdnet.com/zdnn/stories/news/0,4586,2587617,00.html?/chkpt=zdhpnews0.

2. See Stein Schjolberg, "The Legal Framework – Unauthorized Access to Computer Systems: Penal Legislation in 37 Countries" (first updated February 22, 2001), available at http://www.mossbyrett.of.no/info/legal.html; and "An International Policy Framework for Internet Law Enforcement and Security: An Internet Alliance White Paper," at http://www.internetalliance.org/policy/leswp.html.

3. Stephanie Strom, "Japan's Legislators Tighten the Ban on Under-Age Sex," *New York Times*, May 12, 1999, p. A6.

4. Warren Hoge, "19 Countries Join in Raids on Internet Pornography," *New York Times*, November 29, 2001, p. A9.

5. See "The European Union Privacy Directive," Lumeria, Inc., at http://www.lumeria.com/paper1/5.shtml.

6. Directive 95/46/EC of the European Parliament and of the Council of 24 October 1995 on the protection of individuals with regard to the processing of personal data and on the free movement of such data, available on-line at http://europa.eu.int/smartapi/cgi/sga_doc?smartapi!celexapi!prod!CELEXnumdoc&lg=EN&numdoc=31995L0046&model=guichett

7. Simon Davis, "Europe to US: No Privacy, No Trade," Wired Archive, 6.05 – May 1998: http://www:wired.com/wired/archive/6.05.

8. Directives 94/EC and 95/EC of the European Parliament and of the Council.

9. For the argument defending this claim, see Richard T. De George, *Competing with Integrity in International Business* (New York: Oxford University Press, 1993), pp. 52–3.

10. ITAC Telework News, Issue 1.3 (October 23, 2001), available at http://www.telecommute.org/newsletter/newsletter1.3.shtml.

11. For OSHA's current policy covering home-based worksites, see http://www.osha-slc.gov/OshDoc/Directive_data/CPL_2-0_125.html#purpose.

12. For an analysis of the effect of immigration on wages, see Bruce R. Scott, "The Great Divide in the Global Village," *Foreign Affairs*, January–February 2001, v.80, 1, pp. 160–77.

13. Norbert Wiener, *The Human Use of Human Beings: Cybernetics and Society*, 2nd. revd. edn. (Boston: Houghton, 1954).

14. Joseph Weizenbaum, *Computer Power and Human Reason* (San Francisco: W. H. Freeman, 1976).

15. For a more detailed account of the development of capitalism in post-

Soviet Russia, see Richard T. De George, "International Business Ethics and Incipient Capitalism: A Double Standard," in *Ethical Issues in Business*, ed. T. Donaldson and P. Werhane (Englewood Cliffs, NJ: Prentice-Hall, 1999), pp. 418–31, and my "'Sullivan-Type' Principles for US Multinationals in Emerging Economies," *Journal of International Economic Law*, vol. 18, no. 4, winter, 1997, pp. 1193–210.

16. Amartya Sen, in his *Development as Freedom* (New York: Alfred A. Knopf, 1999), defends the thesis that from an economic point of view capitalism in a democratic society is the most productive form of social system.

I n d e x